THE PRENTICE HALL EDITING WORKBOOK

Julie Lumpkins
Columbia State Community College

PEARSON

Prentice
Hall

Upper Saddle River, New Jersey 07458

© 2005 by PEARSON EDUCATION, INC.
Upper Saddle River, New Jersey 07458

ISBN 0-13-189352-1

Printed in the United States of America

Table of Contents

Preface

Welcome to *The Prentice Hall Editing Workbook*! This book was created to help students gain awareness of common grammatical problems while offering them the tools with which to resolve these errors. Perhaps this book best serves students of all writing levels because it offers practical paragraph exercises. While many workbooks allow students to practice good grammar skills through sentence-level exercises, *The Prentice Hall Editing Workbook* allows students to work on paragraph corrections more common in today's writing of e-mail, memos, letters, and the like.

For my sweet Hannah

Chapter 1: Nouns

What is a noun?

A noun names a person, place, thing, or idea: *veterinarian, restaurant, couch, justice*.

Types of nouns	Definitions	Examples
Proper	names specific persons, places, or things *(hint: first letter is always capitalized)*	*Brad Pitt, Wisconsin, Cadillac*
Common	names general people, places, groups, or things *(hint: no capitalization is needed)*	*manager, cities, lawyers, cars*
Concrete	things that can be experienced through the senses: sight, taste, hearing, smell, and touch	*garden, recording, lasagna, thunder*
Abstract	names a thought, idea, or quality *(hint: things not obtainable through the senses)*	*happiness, freedom, sadness, honesty*
Collective	names a group	*family, jury*
Noncount	names things that are uncountable	*salt, dirt*
Count	names countable items *(singular or plural)*	*hours, rivers*

Compound nouns, made up of more than one word, may be *proper* or *common*.

Person: Hillary Rodham Clinton

Place: San Antonio

Thing: Pike's Peak

Compound nouns may be hyphenated, one word, or two or more words.

Hyphenated: father-in-law

One word: driveway

Two words: parking garage

Tips for identifying nouns:

- Words that have a plural ending (*s, ies, es*) indicate nouns.
  The cars are locked.
  The families indicated they were hungry.
  The wishes of many children were answered.

- Demonstrative and possessive adjectives (*my, our, his, her, their, these, several)* indicate a noun is to follow.
  My house has been remodeled.
  His car is parked in the driveway.
  Several people from work felt ill today.

- Articles *(a, an, the)* may often indicate nouns. Articles modify nouns and help indicate that a noun will follow.
  The dog ran across the street.
  A pizza tastes better when hot.
  An apple is a healthy snack.

- Suffixes *(ment, ism, ness, ion, er, al, ure, ity, or, ance, ence, tion, sion)* may indicate nouns.
  The inventor of the telephone was Alexander Graham Bell.
  The pressure of success is overwhelming at times.
  The reunion was a wonderful event.

- Nouns serve as subjects of sentences, but nouns are also objects of prepositions, direct objects, and indirect objects.
  Object of the preposition: The number of students varies at our campus.
  Direct object: The girl read the book.
  Indirect object: The woman offered the man some advice.

Exercise 1.1

Underline the nouns in the following paragraph and above each noun write **P** for person, **PL** for place, **T** for thing, or **I** for idea.

Anthropologists are individuals who travel to little-known corners of the world to study exotic peoples or who dig deep into the earth to uncover the fossil remains or the tools and pots of people who lived long ago. These views indicate how anthropology differs from other disciplines concerned with humans. Anthropology is broader in scope, both geographically and historically. Anthropology is concerned with all varieties of people throughout the world. Anthropologists are also concerned with people who have lived in all periods. An anthropologist has not always been global and comprehensive. Traditionally, anthropologists have concentrated on non-Western cultures and left the study of Western civilization and similar complex societies to other disciplines. In recent years, this division of labor among the disciplines has begun to disappear. Now anthropologists work in other complex societies. (*Anthropology: A Brief Introduction, Fifth Edition by Carol R. Ember and Melvin Ember, pages 1-2.*)

Exercise 1.2

Underline the nouns in the following paragraph and above each noun write **P** for proper or **C** for common. Circle any letters that should be capitalized.

Ludwig van Beethoven was born in 1770 into a family of musicians. Both his grandfather and his father were professional musicians in the German town of bonn. Beethoven's grandfather was highly respected, but his father became something of a problem at the court because he was an alcoholic. As a teenager, beethoven was put in charge of the family finances and started a job at the court. In 1790, an important visitor passed through bonn. Joseph Haydn met the young beethoven and agreed to mentor him when he returned from london to vienna. In 1792, beethoven moved to vienna to study with the great master. He was much younger than haydn. In 1802, beethoven discovered the tragic truth that was to haunt him. He was going deaf. His disease progressed gradually. It took some years for him to become totally deaf, and there were periods when normal hearing returned. But by 1817, beethoven could not hear a single note, and his conversations were carried on by means of an ear trumpet and a notebook slung around his neck. beethoven could still hear music inside his head. *(Understanding Music, Fourth Edition by Jeremy Yudkin, pages 198-199.)*

Exercise 1.3

Fill in the blanks provided with common or proper nouns as requested in the following paragraph. Make sure to capitalize proper nouns.

_____ is one of my favorite cities to visit in the United States. In the
(proper noun)

past, I have enjoyed visiting a _____ and the _____. During
(common noun)   (common noun)

my most recent visit to _____, I traveled with my _____. One
(proper noun)   (common noun)

highlight of the trip was when I visited _____. While I was there, I
(proper noun)

purchased _____, _____, and _____ to bring
(common noun)   (common noun)   (common noun)

back as souvenirs. Next time I go to _____ with _____ I will visit a
(proper noun)   (proper noun)

_____ and the _____. Traveling with my_____ to
(common noun)   (proper noun)   (common noun)

_____ is one of my favorite memories.
(proper noun)

4

Exercise 1.4

Fill in the blanks provided with nouns (person, place, thing, or idea) as requested in the following paragraph. Remember to capitalize all proper nouns.

Recently, I went to the _____ to visit _____. While I
                                   (place)   (person)

was there, I saw the _____ and had the opportunity to talk with _____.
                   (thing)   (person)

My friend, who traveled with me, agreed that _____ can always be
                                                 (idea)

found in _____. Next time I visit, I hope to spend more time at the
            (place)

_____ with _____. Perhaps, I will never forget the
    (place)   (person)

_____ that I discovered while visiting. When I return in the future, I will
(idea)

bring my _____ with me. _____ says she would like
          (person)   (person)

to travel with me next time I go.

Exercise 1.5

Underline all of the nouns in the following paragraph. Above each abstract noun write an **A** for abstract.

My mother always said that "honesty is the best policy." As a child, I remember a few

occasions when I lied to my teacher or to my parents, but I quickly learned that

dishonesty is not so easily forgotten. One day, when I was a teenager, I lied to my

parents about attending a party. I told my mother that I was studying at a friend's house,

but actually I was at a party on the other side of town. On the way to the party, I

accidentally rear-ended a vehicle in front of me. I had to call my father to explain what

had happened. It was the first time I lied to my parents and I was caught. While my

parents felt sadness and disappointment, they respected me for eventually telling the truth. Now that I have children of my own, I tell them that "honesty requires integrity." I

will always remember that "honesty is the best policy."

How do nouns become plural?

Forming plural nouns takes practice. It is not easy to remember all of the spelling rules in making nouns plural; it is best to consult a dictionary for correct spellings. These few simple rules below outline most plural endings for nouns.

Most nouns become plural by simply adding *s* to the singular form of the word.

Singular	Plural
dog	dogs
cake	cakes

Nouns that end in *y* preceded by a consonant usually require the *y* to change to *i* before adding *es*.

Singular	Plural
lady	ladies
story	stories

Nouns that end in *y* preceded by a vowel usually require that *s* be added to form the plural.

Singular	Plural
play	plays
day	days

Some nouns that end in *f* or *fe* require the *f* to change to *v* before adding a plural ending.

Singular	Plural
wife	wives
life	lives

Some nouns that end in *f* or *fe* do not require the *f* to change to *v* before adding a plural ending.

Singular	Plural
roof	roof
chief	chiefs

Nouns that end in *o* preceded by a vowel require *s* to form the plural noun.

Singular	Plural
radio	radios
cameo	cameos

Some nouns that end in *o* preceded by a consonant form a plural by adding *es* to the singular form. Other nouns ending in *o* preceded by a consonant form the plural by adding *s*. *(Note: in a few rare occasions, some words ending in o become plural by adding either s or es. Example: tornados or tornadoes. Either spelling is correct).*

Singular	Plural
tomato	tomatoes
cello	cellos

Nouns that end in *sh, ch, z, x,* and *s* become plural by the addition of *es* to the singular word.

Singular	Plural
fox	foxes
bush	bushes

A small number of nouns become plural when the suffix *en* is added.

Singular	Plural
ox	oxen
child	children

Some nouns become plural with a change in the root word rather than by adding *s*.

Singular	Plural
woman	women
goose	geese

Some nouns are special exceptions to any rule.

Singular	Plural
alumna	alumnae
cherub	cherubim

Some compound nouns become plural with the addition of *s* to the main word.

Singular	Plural
brother-in-law	brothers-in-law
matron of honor	matrons of honor

A few nouns remain the same for both singular and plural spellings.

Singular	Plural
deer	deer
fish	fish

(**Tip:** remember that noncount nouns only exist in singular form.)

Exercise 1.6

Above each underlined noun in the following paragraph write **S** for singular or **P** for plural.

Should teachers go on strike? This question often leads to heated exchanges between supporters and opponents of strikes. Strikes may undermine teachers' images. Strikes may alienate middle- and upper-class citizens who traditionally have been among public education's strongest supporters. Becoming disgusted with strikes could lead these citizens to oppose needed <u>funding</u> for the <u>schools</u>. <u>Supporters</u> of <u>strikes</u> might include

<u>teachers</u>, <u>politicians</u>, <u>governors-elect</u>, <u>citizens</u> and community <u>leaders</u>. <u>Supporters</u> point

to <u>obligations</u> many state <u>legislatures</u> have placed on <u>teachers</u> to raise learners'

achievement <u>levels</u> in the <u>absence</u> of new <u>commitments</u> of state <u>revenues</u> to help them get

the <u>job</u> done. <u>Proponents</u> of <u>strikes</u> contend that <u>people</u> may talk a good <u>line</u> about the

<u>need</u> to improve <u>schools</u>, but little real <u>action</u> is likely without <u>pressure</u> that can be

exerted by a <u>strike</u>.

(Teaching Today: An Introduction to Education, Seventh Edition by David G. Armstrong,

Kenneth T. Henson, and Tom V. Savage, page 40).

Exercise 1.7

Underline the correct noun (either singular or plural) in the following paragraph.

When (student, students) create an oral presentation, they often think first about how they

feel nervous. Preparing a (speech, speeches) takes lots of time and patience, not to

mention confidence. Public speaking is the number one fear of most top (executive,

executives) in the work force. Most company (president, presidents) are more fearful of

public speaking than of heights or even death. Most college speech (professor,

professors) would agree that public speaking is one of the most valuable (class, classes)

that (student, students) take during their college experience. In most public speaking

(course, courses) students present at least four (speech, speeches) per semester.

Sometimes visual aids may help a speaker feel more confident in front of a large

audience. Visual aids may include the use of computer generated slides, (poster board,

poster boards), or flip charts to name a few. Most students who practice making speeches by using visual aids find that public speaking is easier to successfully accomplish after they graduate.

Exercise 1.8

Underline the correct noun (either singular or plural) in the following paragraph.

Studies have shown that (child/children) who study dance at an early age have better coordination as (adult/adults). A (dancer/dancers) who studies dance or gymnastic strengthens lower muscles in the body. Dancing and gymnastics also help (parent/parents) teach responsibility and discipline. Perhaps the most beneficial part of early dance study is the opportunity for families to interact with one another. A dance (class/classes) allows parents to meet and form friendships. Most (class/classes) are relatively inexpensive for a (child/children). Dance (costume/costumes) are additional items that are not included in most dance instruction fees. An average (costume/costumes) ranges from $30 to $50 depending on material. However, most dance (instructor/instructors) have their (student/students) wear dance outfits at least several times for different performances. Overall, money for dance classes is well spent.

What are subjects?

Sentences consist of two components: a subject and a predicate. A subject refers to how a noun may be used in a sentence. The subject of a sentence may be a noun or pronoun (*see Chapter 2 for more about pronouns*). Most sentences contain a simple subject, a word that indicates the topic of a sentence.

Example: The *dog* ran.

The complete subject refers to the simple subject plus any modifiers that describe the noun.

Example: *The brown dog* ran.

(Note: Adjectives and adverbs are modifiers. Articles, such as *a, an,* and *the,* are modifiers as well.)

Exercise 1.9

Underline the simple subject in each sentence in the following paragraph.

Many people are now aware of industrial pollution. The dumping of industrial wastes into the ground or into rivers, and the spewing of chemicals into the air through smokestacks are examples of pollution. People don't often realize how much humans have altered the environment by the ways they collect and produce food. Irrigation is one consideration. Water can be channeled from rivers. Rainwater can be caught in terraces carved out of hillsides. Ancient water can be pumped up from vast underground reservoirs called aquifers. Much of the water evaporates, leaving behind minerals and salts. The ground becomes salty with more irrigation. Eventually, the soil becomes too salty to grow crops effectively. Too many people raising too many animals can also have serious effects on the environment. People can easily imagine how the possibility of profit might inspire people to try to raise more animals than the land will support. For example, 300 years ago the Great America Desert was a vast grassland. The grassland supported large herds of buffalo, which became exterminated by overhunting. However, not all environmental problems are associated with food production. Food production has been greatly reduced by mankind. (*Anthropology: A Brief Introduction, Fifth Edition by Carol R. Ember and Melvin Ember, page 252*).

Exercise 1.10

Underline the complete subject in each sentence in the following paragraph.

Texan-style line dancing became popular across the United States in the early 1990s. While line dancing has been around for several decades before the 90s, a new salsa style of dancing has since evolved. This quaint new dancing style originates from a mixture of pop and country music. The fancy footwork is just as challenging as traditional country line dancing, but the steps have been freshened up a bit to resemble more of a Latin feel. The growing popularity of this dancing style is due in large part to the fresh new sounds of Latino artists, such as Marc Anthony, Jennifer Lopez, and Enrique Iglesias. Many night clubs and karaoke stages now feature the Latino, top pop sound. Growing interest in Latino music and dancing has not only revolutionized dancing, but has shed some much needed attention to diverse, ethnic performers.

What is a pronoun?

A pronoun may take the place of a noun. A pronoun or a noun is replaced by an antecedent.

Mary is a doctor. **She** is a doctor.

(The pronoun *she* replaces the noun *Mary*.)

Types of pronouns	Definition	Examples
Personal	names people, places, things, or ideas (*hint: there are three cases of personal pronouns—subjective, objective, possessive*)	*We* took *her* to the park. *He* is shorter than Sue. *I* saw *him* take food to *them*.
Relative	introduces some noun and adjective clauses	The person *who* was tardy was responsible for the group. The movie *that* I watched was incredible.
Demonstrative	refers to people, things, or ideas without specifically naming them	Whose chairs are *these*? *This* is the one I ordered.
Interrogative	creates and introduces a question	To *whom* does this belong? *What* is the time of arrival? *Whose* clothes are these?
Reflexive	reflects the verb's action back to the subject of the sentence	My husband locked *himself* out of the house. They treated *themselves* to dinner and a movie.
Indefinite	refers to nonspecific people, places, or things	*Either* of the doctors may submit his or her time sheet. *Everyone* is a winner at the carnival.
Reciprocal	refers to individual parts of plural antecedents	We look like *one another*. We cook for *each other*.

Personal Pronouns

Personal pronouns name people, places, or things. There are three cases of personal pronouns: subjective, objective, and possessive. The pronoun varies depends if the writer is talking about himself or herself, about other people, or about anything else. (*See chart below with first, second, and third person outlined.*)

	Subjective		**Objective**		**Possessive**	
	Singular	*Plural*	*Singular*	*Plural*	*Singular*	*Plural*
First Person	I	we	me	us	my, mine	our, ours
Second Person	you	you	you	you	your yours	your yours
Third Person	he, she, it who	they	him, her, it whom	them whom	his, her hers, its whose	their theirs whose

Exercise 2.1

Underline the personal pronouns in the following paragraph.

Sociologists are men and women who are endlessly fascinated by human social life and who actively strive to understand why people behave as they do. The topics they study vary from the routines of everyday life to the great transformations that remake our world. Some disciplines are best defined by their subject matter: botanists study plants; political scientists study governments. But sociology is quite different. It is the study of human relationships. The sociological perspective does not focus on individuals in isolation, but focuses on the impact of social forces on human behavior. The sociological perspective—the way they view social life—has several important qualities: it employs the scientific method; it encourages people to debunk or be skeptical of many conventional explanations of social life; it directs our attention to social diversity with a special emphasis on race and gender, and it displays a strong global orientation.

(*Sociology, Third Edition by Linda L. Lindsey and Stephen Beach, pages 3-5*).

Exercise 2.2

Underline the personal pronouns in the following paragraph. Above each pronoun write **S** for singular pronouns and **P** for plural pronouns.

When we awoke today, we learned that school was closed because eight inches of snow had fallen. My mother told us that more snow was on the way. My sister was glad that school was cancelled since she had a scheduled math exam. It was difficult for her to prepare for the exam since math is not her best subject. You should see my father trying to tutor her in math. They work on math problems together for hours. My mother said that school would probably be closed for the rest of the week. You should have seen how excited my sister was to hear the news. She jumped up and down and my father started to laugh. My mom and dad decided to take the day off from work. They both agreed that it was the perfect day to play in the snow. After breakfast, we bundled up in our warmest clothes and played outside for several hours.

Relative Pronouns

Relative pronouns introduce some noun and adjective clauses. Relative pronouns include: *who, which,* and *that.*

Exercise 2.3

Underline the pronouns in the following paragraph. Draw two lines under each relative pronoun.

The Tim McGraw concert that I attended last night was exciting. I received free tickets from my sister who works for a talent scout. When my sister called to tell me about the tickets, I couldn't believe it. Since I am a country music fan, I have seen Tim McGraw perform several times. The song that I love most is from his recent album. He sang my favorite song for his encore performance. The album that I think will be his best is due in stores in a few months. The performer who I believe is one of the hottest country acts today is also very kind. I met him backstage before the show, and he gave me an autograph. The autograph, which I carry in my purse, will be something I will treasure for many years. The person who I appreciate most is my sister for giving me the free ticket.

Demonstrative Pronouns

Demonstrative pronouns refer to people, things, or ideas without specifically naming them. Demonstrative pronouns include: *this, that, these,* and *those.*

Exercise 2.4

Underline the pronouns in the following paragraph and write a **D** above each demonstrative pronoun.

My brother and I recently visited the zoo. It was the first time we had spent the entire day at any zoo. When we arrived he exclaimed, "Look at that!" When I looked, my brother was pointing to a group of elephants near the zoo's entrance. Those were some of the biggest elephants I had ever seen in my life. These were special elephants donated from the South African area. The smallest elephant, a four foot tall baby, already weighed over 150 pounds. This was the smallest, but the cutest animal out of the group. We were able to see a live bird show as well. The parrots were my favorite. This is a worthwhile show to view. The trainer told us these were the most colorful animals in the zoo. I plan to visit the zoo again next year.

Interrogative Pronouns

Interrogative pronouns create and introduce a question. Interrogative pronouns include: *who, whose, whom, which,* and *what.*

Exercise 2.5

Fill in the blanks with an interrogative pronoun in the following paragraph. Remember to capitalize the interrogative pronoun if it begins a sentence.

_____ was considered one of the greatest English Baroque poets? Perhaps John

Donne (1572-1631) was just as important to the seventeenth century as William

Shakespeare was to the sixteenth century. _____ are some of Donne's greatest

poetic achievements? His most famous poem *Death, Be Not Proud*, is an affirmation of

the triumph that salvation wins over death. To _____ were his poems addressed?

For the most part, Donne wrote love poems to a woman some speculate was the niece of

his most famous patron. _____ poems were most popular? His metaphysical

poems, poems that are characterized by jarring associations and comparisons, are his

most popular. Later in his writing career, he wrote a series of religious, devotional

sonnets that are still widely read and studied in many religions today. _____

will John Donne always be remembered most for accomplishing? Perhaps his largest

writing contribution was that he applied his complex imagery to both sacred and secular

themes.

(*Adventures in the Human Spirit, Fourth Edition by Philip E. Bishop, page 287*).

Reflexive Pronouns

Reflexive pronouns reflect the verb's action back to the subject of the sentence.

	Antecedent	**Reflexive Pronoun**
Singular	I you he she it	myself yourself himself herself itself
Plural	we you they	ourselves yourselves themselves

Exercise 2.6

Fill in the blanks with reflexive pronouns in the following paragraph.

Stan and Jeff recently celebrated the first anniversary of their company's success. They

should be proud of _____. Their computer web design company has

become the largest business in the northeastern part of the United States. Stan

_____ was never a firm believer that the company would be so successful, but Jeff

knew the company would be a hit. The computer business_____ is a large,

growing industry. Stan and Jeff _____ were once college roommates

that both majored in computers. They _____ saw a need for a web

enhanced design company to handle major corporations' internet advertisement needs.

Stan _____admits that a large part of his success is due to Jeff. Jeff even said

in a recent magazine interview, "I _____ am grateful for the opportunity to

work with Stan. You should never doubt _____ if you have a dream."

Stan and Jeff's dream has proven to be not only worthwhile, but lucrative as well.

18

Reciprocal and Indefinite Pronouns

Reciprocal pronouns refer to individual parts of plural antecedents and indefinite pronouns refer to nonspecific people, places, or things.

Exercise 2.7

Underline the pronouns in the following paragraph. Write **R** above reciprocal pronouns and **I** above any indefinite pronouns.

My grandparents recently celebrated their fiftieth wedding anniversary. They love and respect each other. Everyone is always saying my grandparents make a wonderful couple. My grandfather says the secret to a good relationship is to always love one another. He credits the longevity of their relationship to good communication. Anyone would agree that my grandparents have good communication between them. They listen to one another and support each other in their hopes and dreams. At their fiftieth anniversary party, they danced to their song. Everyone agreed that the party was a wonderful event. It gave our family the opportunity to visit with one another.

Pronoun Agreement

A pronoun must match the noun or pronoun it refers to, called the antecedent. If a pronoun is singular or plural, it must agree with a singular or plural noun or pronoun. A pronoun and its antecedent must also agree in gender. If a noun is masculine, then the pronoun must be masculine as well. Some nouns may be both masculine and feminine. In this case, pronouns that reflect both genders (*his* or *her*) should be used. If a noun is neither masculine nor feminine, it is considered neutral and requires the neutral pronoun *it*.

Exercise 2.8

Pronouns are italicized in the following paragraph. Underline each pronoun's antecedent.

By 1799, ten years after revolution erupted, the French found *their* republic of virtue inhabited by citizens full of greed and prejudice. Having beheaded a king, the French were now ready to entrust *their* hard-won liberties to the military hero Napoleon

Bonaparte. Napoleon personified *his* principles of revolution. Napoleon satisfied *his* middle-class supporters by revising France's legal system and modernizing *its* government, thus erasing the vestiges of absolute monarchy and aristocratic privilege. He satisfied *his* own dreams of a French empire by crowning *himself* emperor in 1804 and embarking on a military campaign that devoured virtually all of Western Europe. With each conquest, Napoleon proclaimed *his* revolutionary values of liberty and republicanism, infecting Europe with liberal ideas. Napoleon proved a skillful propagandist for *his* own reign, disguising *his* power and cleverly manipulating the symbolism of the Revolution.

(*Adventures in the Human Spirit, Fourth Edition by Phillip E. Bishop, pages 324-325.*)

Agreement with Indefinite Pronouns

Perhaps the most misused pronouns in terms of pronoun/antecedent agreement are indefinite pronouns. While these pronouns are often used with plural antecedents, they should always be singular.

Singular Indefinite Pronouns		
another	anybody	anything
each	either	everybody
everyone	everything	much
neither	nobody	none
no one	nothing	one
somebody	someone	something

Example: *Everyone* needs to wash *their* hands. (**Incorrect**)

Everyone needs to wash *his* or *her* hands. (**Correct**)

There are a few indefinite pronouns that are always plural.

Plural Indefinite Pronouns		
both	few	many
others	several	

Example: *Both* of the runners *was* exhausted. (**Incorrect**)

Both of the runners *were* exhausted. (**Correct**)

Some indefinite pronouns require either a singular or plural verb. Usage depends on what the writer intends to say.

Singular or Plural Indefinite Pronouns		
any	all	more
most	none	some

Example: *All were* present. (**Correct**)

All was present. (**Correct**)

Collective nouns may be singular or plural, depending on whether the noun is being described as a unit or as individual members.

Commonly Used Collective Nouns		
class	college	committee
faculty	family	group
jury	orchestra	team

Example: The *faculty* decided *its* decision. (**Correct**)

(*The faculty acts as one unit, thus a singular pronoun its is needed.*)

Tip: It may be difficult to identify pronouns as the subjects of sentences since students sometimes mistake a prepositional phrase as a subject. Knowing how to identify prepositional phrases may make locating a subject and a singular or plural antecedent easier. Most students find it helpful to cross out the prepositional phrase as shown below.

Neither of the women brought *her* coat. (Notice in this sentence that *of the women* is a prepositional phrase. If you mark out the preposition phrase, the following remains:

Neither brought *her* coat.

It is easier to recognize that the pronoun *neither* needs a singular antecedent.

21

Exercise 2.9

Underline the correct verbs that agree with the pronouns in the following paragraph.

Numerous museums have fine collections of period and contemporary garments, particularly the Metropolitan Museum in New York, the Smithsonian Institution in Washington, D.C., and the Los Angeles County Museum of Art. Also, many (maintain, maintains) excellent libraries of fashion books and periodicals. Both garments and sketches (is, are) available for viewing by special request. Everybody (believe, believes) the Musee des Arts de la Mode in Paris is most impressive. Museums are important for up and coming designers to visit. Many (exhibit, exhibits) vast collections of costumes and periodicals. Some (feature, features) a permanent show for visitors to see. No one (know, knows) the importance of fashion on the world of architecture, history, and interior design. Many (is, are) directly related to the fashion industry. Few in the fashion industry (determine, determines) the fashion designs year to year. These designers are the top in the industry. (*Inside Fashion Design, Fifth Edition by Sharon Lee Tate, page 127.*)

Exercise 2.10

Write an appropriate pronoun in each blank and underline its antecedent. Make sure each pronoun agrees in number and gender with its antecedent.

One of my nephews has _____ own car. He received the car as a prize on a game show last week. Each of the game show winners accepted _____ prize before leaving California. My cousins also attended the taping of the show. Neither of them was present when _____ name was called. They were eating lunch nearby. One of the audience members had _____ lunch inside the building to ensure he would hear his name called. Each of the contestants wanted _____ turn at winning the grand prize. Luckily, my nephew was the winner. Everyone at the game show was

excited for my nephew. He chose the car he wanted to drive home. Each of the cars had

_____ special features. However, my nephew had always wanted a Ford, so he chose

a Mustang convertible.

Pronouns: Subjective and Objective Cases

Pronouns may be used as subjects or as objects. Whenever a pronoun is the subject of a
sentence, the subjective form should be used.

Subjective Case	
Singular	**Plural**
I	we
you	you
he, she, it	they

Notice in the following sentences how pronouns are used as subjects.

I walked through the park.   *We* went on vacation.
You need to call the doctor.   *You* guys are on time.
He went to concert.   *They* felt tired.

Whenever a pronoun is the object of a sentence, the objective case should be used. Use
the objective case when the pronoun is used as a direct object, an indirect object, or the
object of the preposition.

Objective Case	
Singular	**Plural**
me	us
you	you
him, her, it	them

Notice in the following sentences how pronouns are used as objects.

Nicole game *me* the car keys.   The movie was for *us.*
Steve saw *you* at the game.   The party was a surprise for *you.*
The girls gave *her* a birthday cake.   Robert saw *them* at the concert.

Exercise 2.11

Underline the correct pronouns in the following paragraph.

When (I, me) was younger, my family and (I, me) always watched the Olympic games on television. My father believed that Olympic winners were true heroes to be admired. (We, Us) watched the games, and we ranked the winners on notebook paper. My mother made popcorn for (we, us). My sister and (I, me) were allowed to stay up later than usual to watch all of the nighttime events. My favorite was the swim competition, but my sister's favorite was the gymnastics competition. My parents loved all of the games. We watched (they, them) discuss the importance of good sportsmanship and the commonality between the different nations. My parents disagreed on the outcome of the medals. Mom laughed at Dad, and she claimed that (he, him) was too easy of a judge. Dad always said that Mom would be too difficult if (she, her) was to actually judge. Looking back, some of my favorite memories of watching television were seeing the Olympics every four years.

Exercise 2.12

Fill in the blanks with either subjective case or objective case pronouns as requested in the following paragraph.

My first day of college was not what _____ imagined it would be. When _____ went
                                      (subjective)   (subjective)

to register for classes, all of _____ were full. I asked my advisor about other classes I
                                (objective)

could take. _____ told _____ to join a class waiting list in case other students did
            (subjective) (objective)

not attend the first day. Many students will not attend the first day and professors then

allow _____ spots to be filled. I was placed on a class waiting list and then _____
      (subjective)   (subjective)

showed up on the first day. My professors allowed _____ to add _____ classes, so
                                                   (objective)   (subjective)

24

my advisor's advice worked. _____ was lucky to get the classes needed to graduate. Not
(subjective)

all students that try to add classes late are as lucky as _____.
(objective)

Exercise 2.13

Fill in the blanks with either subjective or objective pronouns as needed.

What exactly does a designer do? No two designers will answer this question in the same

way because _____ do so many different jobs. As a rule, _____ work for a

wholesale apparel house or manufacturer. _____ might not realize, but a designer

works well over 40 hours a week. The head of the company, or chief operating office,

directs the overall operations that allow the company to function. _____ supervises the

sales personnel as well as the functions considered to be the business side of the

operation. In addition, depending on the size of the company, _____ may work closely

with the designer in choosing fabrics and finalizing the styles selected for the line. Steve

Maddox, a famous designer, has worked in the industry for many years. _____ clothing

line has been popular for several decades. Many that have worked with _____, believe

_____ is truly today's hottest designer. (*Inside Fashion Design, Fifth Edition by Sharon*

Lee Tate, page 57).

When should the pronouns *who* and *whom* be used?

Knowing when to use *who* or *whom* is difficult for many writers. *Who* and *whoever*
should be used in the subjective form, while *whom* and *whomever* should be used in the
objective form.

Example: Sam is the man *who* earned the new job.

(*Who* is correct in this example since *who* is the subject of the verb *earned*.)

Example: Christy, *whom* I walked with, forgot her umbrella.

(*Whom* is correct in this example since the pronoun is the object of the preposition *with*.)

(**Tip:** In order to distinguish when to use *whoever* or *whomever*, it will help if all the words in the sentence that come before *whoever* or *whomever* are disregarded. Substitute *he* or *him* for *whoever* or *whomever*. If *he* makes sense, then *whoever* should be used. If *him* makes sense, then *whomever* should be used.)

Example: Pass the bread to *whoever* wants a piece.
(By eliminating *Pass the bread to* and substituting *he*, it becomes apparent that *whoever* is correct. Since *He wants a piece* makes sense, *whoever* is needed.)

Example: Give the toys to *whomever* you please.
(By eliminating *Give the toys to* and substituting *him*, it becomes apparent that *whomever* is correct. Since *You please him* makes sense, *whomever* is needed.)

Exercise 2.14

Underline the correct pronouns in the following paragraph.

Recently, four downtown business owners were rewarded for their financial support to the local humane association. Joseph Smith is the one (who, whom) is responsible for donating the most time and money. Raising over $15,000, Mr. Smith credited his office assistant. She helped in raising money and making phone calls to solicit volunteer help. Mr. Smith's employees held an interoffice contest in which a silent auction was held. (Whoever, Whomever) was the highest bidder received the auctioned items. The auction raised over $5,000 total. Mr. Smith felt his business associate, Mr. Thompson, was a big help as well. Mr. Thompson was the person (who, whom) organized volunteer help in the community. (Whoever, Whomever) could help after work hours was encouraged to join the animal humane cause. When Mr. Smith received his award, he exclaimed, "This award will also go to (whoever, whomever) helped along the way." The event was such a success.

Exercise 2.15

Underline the correct pronouns in the following paragraph.

Miss Tennessee was the contestant (who, whom) the judges selected as the new Miss
America. When her name was called, she cried tears of joy. The new Miss America
thanked (whoever, whomever) had chosen her for this important role. To (who, whom)
will she grant her first interview as the new Miss America? She will speak on the *Today
Show* to (whoever, whomever) will fill in for the vacationing Katie Couric. This Miss
America will make history as the youngest contestant to wear the crown. (Who/Whom)
was the youngest contestant to date to wear the crown? Miss Alabama, who became
Miss America in 1957, was the youngest to wear the crown at age 19. The new Miss
America becomes the youngest to earn the crown as she just turned 19 two days ago. She
credits her grandmother for her success.

Chapter 3: Verbs/Verb Tense

What is a verb?

Verbs express action, occurrence, or indicate a state of being: *walk, eat, is, become, smell, taste, look.*

Types of verbs	Definitions	Examples
Action (Main) Verbs	show action, either physical or mental	*walk, ski, jump, work*
Linking Verbs	express no action, links a subject to a word or words that rename or describe the subject	*be, is, seems, was, were*
Auxiliary Verbs	combine with action verbs to convey information about tense, mood, or voice	*can, could, may, might, should, would, must*
Transitive Verbs	come before a direct object to complete the verb's message	*sent her, watched them, saw him, called him*
Intransitive Verbs	does not require a direct object to complete the verb's message	*She walked, He drove, They worked, He called*

Exercise 3.1

Underline the verbs in the following paragraph.

Richard Wagner (1813-1883) was a flamboyant, artistic egoist whose life had enough passion, betrayal, triumph and failure to be an opera itself. He blamed his initial musical failures on opera's commercialism and finally convinced a mad Bavarian king to finance his operas at the lavish Festival House at Bayreuth. Throughout his career, he engaged in titanic love affairs with the wives of patrons and musical colleagues. Wagner's musical ideas exceeded even the extravagance of his life. He envisioned opera as the synthesis of all the arts—myth, music, poetry, drama, and pictorial design. Wagner believed that he had to control everything about his operas: the text, music, design, and production. He rejected the trivial plots of conventional opera and turned instead to Germanic myth and legend. (*Adventures in the Human Spirit, Fourth Edition by Philip E. Bishop, page 361-362*).

Exercise 3.2

Fill in the blanks with verbs in the following paragraph.

We _____ to the ball game to watch my youngest brother who is the pitcher

this year. After we arrived at the ball field, my mother _____ to our neighbors

who were seated in the bleachers. They _____ my mother about their recent

vacation. They _____to Myrtle Beach and _____ in a condo on

the beach. They agreed this was the best vacation they had taken in years. While at the

beach, they _____ and _____ every morning. In the afternoons,

they _____ along the beach and _____by the pool. In the evening,

they _____ to several concerts on the shore and even _____ at a party.

Overall, they _____ this was the most stress-free vacation ever.

Linking verbs express no action, link a subject to a word, rename or describe the subject. Examples include: *is, seems, were, was, seem.*

Example: We *were* exhausted at the airport.

Stan *seems* intelligent.

Exercise 3.3

Underline all verbs in the following paragraph. Draw two lines under each linking verb.

Recently, there has been a growing popularity with reality television shows. Reality

shows seem to air on every major network. In the 1970s, television family sitcoms were

popular. Shows like *All in the Family* and *The Jeffersons* were favorites in many

American households. In the 1980s, television dramas were the new favorites among

avid television viewers. *Dallas* and *Dynasty* received the highest ratings week after week. Viewers tuned in to discover what shady, but powerful characters like J.R. Ewing or Alexis Colby were doing in their plush homes and high-rise offices. While television dramas remained popular throughout the decade, the 1990s brought about a new revolution in television. The coined phrase "water cooler show" described hits like *Seinfeld* and *Friends*. These sitcoms seemed to generate talk around every office water cooler in the nation. Finally in 2000, the overabundance of reality shows hit the scene. Shows like *The Bachelor* and *Survivor* have become the newest reality sensation.

Exercise 3.4

Fill in the blanks with linking verbs in the following paragraph.

Today the topic of film and literature _____ more lively than ever before, both inside and outside of classrooms. There _____ many reasons: From the cultural questioning of artistic hierarchies and canons to the increased mixing of different media in both literary and film practices, film and literature clash against and invigorate each other in more and more complicated fashions. Film and literature _____ two disciplines that work well with one another. One of the consequences of this renewed interest _____ that the intersections of film and literature need to be viewed from an unprecedented variety of angles. Novels, dramatic literature, short stories, and poetry _____ all intertwined with film. It _____ that film is directly connected with any form of literature. Film _____ once only thought of as a mere form of entertainment. Today, film _____ to encompass more than entertainment. Film _____ an important part of American lifestyle. (*Film and Literature: An Introduction and Reader by Timothy Corrigan, pages 1-2.*)

Auxiliary Verbs

Auxiliary verbs, also known as helping verbs, combine with action verbs to convey information about tense, mood, or voice.

Example: I *am running* for office.

Notice that *am* is an auxiliary verb that has been combined with *running* to create a verb phrase.

The three most commonly used auxiliary verbs include *be, do,* and *have.* See the section on *irregular verbs* at the end of this chapter.

Other **modals** include: *can, could, will, shall, should, would, may, might,* and *must.*

Tip: Sometimes the auxiliary verb may be separated from the main verb in a sentence. Words such as *always, usually, never,* and *not* may separate the auxiliary and main verb, but should not be considered part of the verb phrase.

Example: We *will* always *vacation* here.

Shawn *has* never *returned* the book to the library.

Exercise 3.5

Underline the auxiliary verbs in the following paragraph.

In the 1880s and 90s, several important artists intensified the impressionists' break with

tradition. These artists will always remain known as post-impressionists because their

works extended impressionist techniques in different directions. The most important

post-impressionists, Georges Seurat, Paul Cezanne, Paul Gauguin, and Vincent van

Gogh, shall never lose their popularity. Georges Seurat was the closest in technique to

Monet's pure impressionism, depicting scenes of urban life and applying unmixed colors

directly to the canvas. Seurat's most famous picture, *Sunday Afternoon on the Island of*

LaGrande Jatte, may serve as the best example of the pointillist style. The scene should

be seen as a typical scene of Parisian modernity. Had an impressionist painted this scene,

we might have expected the casual manner of Renoir. Instead, Seurat creates a subtle pattern of parallel lines and interlocking shapes. The pattern is created in the repeated shapes of the umbrellas, the ladies' bustles and bodices, and the gentlemen's hats and canes. Each figure should be treated with scientific dispassion and precision, flattened and contained by Seurat's formulas. (*Adventures in the Human Spirit, Fourth Edition by Philip E. Bishop, page 375*).

Exercise 3.6

Underline the auxiliary verbs in the following paragraph.

I will always remember my years in college. It may have been the most exciting time of my life. I was fortunate to attend a smaller university. I became involved in many student activities, and I met many friends. I never thought I would enjoy college. Actually, I was determined not to give university life a chance. I remember being angry at my parents for sending me to school, forcing me to leave my high school friends behind. I have never regretted attending college. I hate to admit that my parents were correct. Some of my closest friends I met while I attended college. The key to making new friends in a new area is to become involved. I still try to make friends any time I move to a new community. Perhaps my favorite part of college is the memories. I will always remember the friendships and the opportunities given to me. I appreciate my parents' support while I attended college. I hope to help my children in the same way someday when they attend a university or college of their choice.

Transitive verbs are followed by direct objects to complete the verb's message. **Intransitive verbs** do not require a direct object to complete the verb's message.

Example: We *sent* her a teddy bear for her birthday. (**transitive verb**)

    We *danced*. (**intransitive verb**)

Underline the verbs in the following paragraph. Write a **T** above any transitive verbs and an **I** above any intransitive verbs.

Exercise 3.7

We swam. Since it was over 95 degrees, we stayed all day. We applied sunscreen on our faces several times. Even though the sky appeared overcast, we were afraid of becoming sunburned. After lunch, we relaxed. We floated. Since it was so hot outside, the wave pool was crowded. We visited the putt-putt golf course at the entrance of the water park. We played. I won two games and my brother won one. We also rode an inner tube down the lazy river. I floated. My brother swam. Our parents just relaxed by the poolside. Perhaps the highlight of the entire day was the late evening fireworks show. We watched fireworks for about an hour. The fireworks were beautiful and the show was choreographed to music. On the ride home, we were so exhausted from the day's events that there was complete silence in the car. My brother and I slept.

Principle Parts of Verbs

Different tenses of verbs help to express time. There are two tenses, *present* and *past*. However, verbs have four principle parts: *present*, *past*, *part participle*, and *present participle*. Most verbs in the English language are *regular*, which means that the *past* and the *past participle* are formed by adding *d* or *ed* to *present* tense form of the verb. The *past participle* form of the verb requires the aid of a helping verb (*have, has,* or *had*). The *present participle* form of the verb requires an *ing* ending. See the example chart below.

Present	Past	Past Participle	Present Participle
walk	walked	has, had, have walked	walking
call	called	has, had, have called	calling
pretend	pretended	has, had, have pretended	pretending
enjoy	enjoyed	has, had, have enjoyed	enjoying

Exercise 3.8

Underline the correct verb choice in the following paragraph.

Michael (enjoy, enjoyed) the concert last night. His favorite band (perform, performed) for three hours. The press has (call, called) the show an exciting performance for all ages. Michael and Christy (receive, received) free tickets from a radio contest. They correctly (answer, answered) a trivia question about the band. After the concert, they (introduce, introduced) themselves to the lead singer backstage. The band (ask, asked) Michael and Christy to join them for an autograph session. Christy (call, called) her mother to tell her the exciting news. Michael and Christy (vow, vowed) to remain members of the band's fan club for life. The band (agree, agreed) that Michael and Christy were devoted fans. Michael's friends were (amaze, amazed) at how lucky he was to spend time with the hottest band on the charts. Michael and Christy (contact, contacted) the radio station to thank them for the free tickets. They (explain, explained) to the station manager that the concert had been the highlight of their entire summer.

Irregular Verbs

While most verbs in the English language are referred to as *regular*, over two hundred verbs are *irregular*. A *regular* verb forms the past tense and part participle with the addition of *ed* or *d*. An *irregular* verb does not become plural with the addition of *ed* or *d*; instead an *irregular* verb requires a different spelling from the root word.

Present Tense	Past Tense	Past Participle (*has, have*)
awake	awoke, awaked	awaked, awoken
become	became	become
begin	began	begun
bite	bit	bitten
blow	blew	blown
break	broke	broken
bring	brought	brought
build	built	built
burn	burned, burnt	burned, burnt
burst	burst	burst

buy	bought	bought
catch	caught	caught
choose	chose	chosen
come	came	come
cost	cost	cost
creep	crept	crept
deal	dealt	dealt
dive	dived, dove	dived
draw	drew	drawn
drink	drank	drunk
drive	drove	driven
eat	ate	eaten
fall	fell	fallen
feed	fed	fed
fight	fought	fought
find	found	found
fling	flung	flung
fly	flew	flown
freeze	froze	frozen
get	got	gotten
give	gave	given
go	went	gone
grow	grew	grown
hear	heard	heard
hide	hid	hidden
hurt	hurt	hurt
keep	kept	kept
know	knew	known
lay	laid	laid
lead	led	led
lend	lent	lent
lie	lay	lain
lose	lost	lost
make	made	made
meet	met	met
mistake	mistook	mistaken
pay	paid	paid
prove	proved	proved, proven
quit	quit	quit
read	read	read
ring	rang	rung
rise	rose	risen
run	ran	run
say	said	said
see	saw	seen
seek	sought	sought

sell	sold	sold
send	sent	sent
shake	shook	shaken
shoot	shot	shot
shrink	shrank, shrunk	shrunk, shrunken
sing	sang	sung
sit	sat	sat
sleep	slept	slept
slide	slid	slid
speak	spoke	spoken
speed	sped, speeded	sped, speeded
spring	sprang	sprung
stand	stood	stood
steal	stole	stolen
sting	stung	stung
strike	struck	struck
swear	swore	sworn
swim	swam	swum
take	took	taken
teach	taught	taught
tear	tore	torn
throw	threw	thrown
wake	woke, waked	waken, waked, woke
wear	wore	worn
weep	wept	wept
win	won	won
wring	wrung	wrung
write	wrote	written

Exercise 3.9

Underline the correct form of each irregular verb.

The senior class president was (chose, chosen) last Friday. Elections were held for one

week and over two hundred classmates voted. The presidential winner (send, sent) each

classmate a thank you note and his running mate publicly thanked everyone that had

voted for him. Jack will be (swore, sworn) in as the new class president on Monday. He

had (got, gotten) the idea to run for office from his brother, a former senior class

president. They (spend, spent) many hours making campaign signs together. Jack (know, knew) that becoming class president would not be easy since his running mate

was the class valedictorian. However, Jack (feel, felt) that running for office was

important whether he (win, won) or not. During the final debate before final voting, Jack

(went, gone) to the podium and (freeze, froze) in front of everyone. He was nervous.

After a few minutes, he laughed and said he needed to start over. The crowd cheered

because he was honest about his nervousness. Since finding out that he is the new class

president, Jack has already (began, begun) to make significant changes.

Common Irregular Verb Forms: Be, Do, and Have

Three of the most commonly used irregular verbs are *be*, *do*, and *have*. See the chart
below for verb tenses.

Be, Do, and Have

	Be	Do	have
Present Tense	be	do	have
Past Tense	was, were	did	had
Past Participle	been	done	had
-s form	is	does	has
Present Participle	being	doing	having

Exercise 3.10

Underline the correct form of each irregular verb.

We (was, were) traveling to Georgia last summer when we took a detour. We (had, has)

been to Georgia before, but we (had, has) never taken back roads. We (does, did) get lost

a few times, but luckily we stopped to ask for directions. When we travel, we (do, does)

read maps, but on this trip a map (was, were) no help. On our detour, we traveled to a

flea market where we (was, were) able to purchase souvenirs. The flea market (is, were)

an ideal place to shop since most vendors will let patrons bargain shop. We (has, had) shopped for three hours when we became hungry. Some local townspeople told us about

a restaurant. We (do, did) go to the restaurant and discovered wonderful cuisine. We

hope to visit next year. It was amazing how a simple detour allowed us to explore new

territory.

Chapter 4: Subject-Verb Agreement

A subject and verb must agree in number: *singular* or *plural*. A *singular* subject requires a *singular* verb; while a *plural* subject requires a *plural* verb. As a general rule, nouns that end is *s* are *plural*, but verbs that end in *s* are *singular*.

Singular: The *doctor calls* his patients every afternoon.

Notice that *doctor* is a singular subject that requires the singular verb *calls*.

Plural: The *doctors call* their patients every afternoon.

Notice that *doctors* is a plural subject that requires the plural verb *call*.

Exercise 4.1

Write **S** for singular if the underlined words are singular and **P** for plural if the underlined words are plural in the following paragraph.

<u>Sculpture</u> is the shaping of material into a three-dimensional <u>work</u> of art. Like painting,

it <u>is</u> one of the most ancient arts. Sculpture can take virtually any <u>shape</u> and can be

crafted in virtually any <u>material</u>. This art form <u>ranges</u> from the exquisitely proportioned

stone of ancient Greek statuary to the playfully modern <u>combinations</u> of Alexander

Calder. A full-round sculpture is shaped so that the work <u>stands</u> freely and can be seen

from all sides. Full-round <u>statues</u> of human figures may be on any scale, from small

<u>figurines</u> to colossal statues. Relief sculpture is attached to a wall or panel and is

commonly used to decorate a <u>building</u>, as in the reliefs on Lorenzo Ghiberti's <u>panels</u> for

the east doors on the Florence Baptistery and the sculptural <u>decoration</u> on the Gothic

cathedral at Chartres, France. (*Adventures in the Human Spirit, Fourth Edition by Philip*

E. Bishop, page 17)

Tip: When using first and second person singular pronouns *I* and *you*, the verb form is the same as using the plural pronoun *we*. However, using third person singular pronouns *he*, *she*, or *it* require a different verb form than the third person plural pronoun *they*.

See the table below using the verb *walk* as an example.

	Singular	**Plural**
First Person	I walk	we walk
Second Person	you walk	you walk
Third Person	he, she, it walks	they walk

Exercise 4.2

Underline the subject in each sentence; then circle the verb that agrees in number with the subject.

Sara (enjoy, enjoys) cooking classes at the local community center. She (take, takes) the class every Saturday with her mother. In the class, they (learn, learns) to make muffins, knead dough, and sauté vegetables. They (cook, cooks) desserts together as well. For part of their weekly assignments, Sara and her mother (create, creates) new gourmet dishes. Last week, the duo created a fresh baked apple cobbler. Sometimes Sara and her mother (make, makes) appetizers. Sara (plan, plans) the appetizer and her mother actually (create, creates) the dish. Sara and her mother (enjoy, enjoys) spending time together planning and creating their culinary masterpieces. Sara (love, loves) the opportunity to learn cooking tips from her mother. Her mother (appreciate, appreciates) the time she (spend, spends) with her daughter in the kitchen.

Subject/Verb Agreement Tips:

Compound Subjects: When two or more subjects are joined with the conjunction *and* a plural verb is usually required.

Jack and Jessica *were* late for the ballgame.

Hannah and Hallie *are* sisters.

Tip: Some compound subjects are considered a single unit which require a singular verb.

Steak and eggs *is* my favorite dish.

Peanut butter and jelly *is* a wonderful treat.

Tip: If compound subjects are joined by other conjunctions besides *and* (such as *or, nor* for example) then the verb may be singular or plural depending if the subject is singular or plural.

The judge or the attorney *is* responsible for calling the juror. (Both subjects are singular.)

The judges or the attorneys *are* responsible for calling the juror. (Both subjects are plural.)

If one subject is singular and the other compound subject is plural, then the verb should agree with the subject closest to the verb.

Either the judges or the attorney *is* responsible for calling the juror. (*Attorney* is closest to the verb *is*.)

Either the judge or the attorneys *are* responsible for calling the juror. (*Attorneys* is closest to the verb *are*.)

Neither the umpire nor the coach is responsible for the team's loss. (*Neither* is the subject of the sentence.)

Exercise 4.3

Underline the compound subject in each sentence; then circle the correct verb for each subject in the following paragraph.

Nashville and Memphis (is, are) two fun cities to visit. Logan and Michael (travel, travels) to Nashville every fall and to Memphis every summer. Logan or Michael (has, have) visited more than three times in the past two years. Either Logan or Michael (drive, drives) each year. Nashville and Memphis (offer, offers) visitors a lot to do. Neither Logan nor Michael (feel, feels) like there is enough time while visiting. Last year, Cynthia and her brother (was, were) traveling with Logan and Michael. The zoo and the museum (was, were) two places they all visited. Cynthia and her brother (has, have) only traveled to Memphis once, and they have never been to Nashville. Many restaurants and museums in Nashville and Memphis (offer, offers) discount coupons during the summer for all visitors. Logan and Michael (participate, participates) in the coupon program every year. Perhaps this is why their annual trip is so inexpensive.

Tip: Sometimes a subject may follow a verb, as in the case of questions or expletives (*there* and *here*). To make sure that the verb and subject agree, ask what the subject is doing.

Example: Are there any returned books?

Is David late for work?

Exercise 4.4

Underline the correct verbs for the subjects in the following paragraph.

"(Is, Are) there any questions in regards to the information covered in chapter four?" asked our teacher. "(Is, Are) we being tested on just the first four chapters or over all of the chapters in section one?" asked Katie. "There (is, are) four sections that students will be responsible for knowing," our teacher exclaimed. "(Do, Does) everyone have a copy of the study questions?" remarked Miss Stephens. The study guide and the chapters (contain, contains) lots of important information for the exam. "(Has, Have) everyone received all of the class lecture notes?" Miss Stephens asked. The class notes and chapter supplements (make, makes) a difference in the success of passing the exam. "Finally, (do, does) anyone have questions in regards to the test?" asked Miss Stephens. There (was, were) no questions, so Miss Stephens dismissed class early.

Tip: Remember that collective nouns may be either singular or plural depending on the usage.

The jury has reached a verdict. (*Jury* is counted as one unit).

The jury have reached a verdict. (*Jury* is considered as separate individuals).

Examples of collective nouns with verbs:

The board see(s)	The class meet(s)	The faculty listen(s)
The committee receive(s)	The family attend(s)	The group ride(s)
The jury understand(s)	The orchestra play(s)	The panel discuss(es)
The public acknowledge(s)	The team encourage(s)	The society prepare(s)

Exercise 4.5

Underline the collective nouns in the following paragraph.

The class of 2004 recently celebrated their graduation ceremony. The high school faculty was present to help with the celebration. When the ceremony first began, the audience was sitting quietly while the graduates entered the gymnasium. The audience saw the graduates; cheers were heard from all over the gymnasium. The crowd waved to the graduates while taking photos. The high school orchestra set the mood by playing three classical selections. The faculty commented on how lovely the ceremony was overall. The class of 2004 has made plans. The class president is attending a local college. Other classmates are entering the military. The local college has accepted many of the graduates for the fall semester. Overall, the group of graduates was one of the brightest to attend high school in quite some time. The faculty said they would be sad to see so many bright faces leave. The class agreed that leaving their friends behind would be difficult.

Passive and Active Voice/Verb Tense

Tip: When the past participle form of a verb is combined with the form of the verb *be*, it becomes known as *passive voice*. When the action of a verb is expressed on its subject, then *passive voice* occurs.

The presentation *was given.* (*passive voice*)

When an action is performed by a subject then *active voice* occurs.

The girl *jumped* over the rope. (*active voice*)

Exercise 4.6

In the following paragraph, fill in the blanks with the passive forms of the verbs in parentheses.

Yesterday was Sarah's birthday. She (*give*) _____ the day off from work.

She (*celebrate*) _____ with her family at a restaurant when she realized her

keys were locked in her car. She (*expect*) _____ the locksmith to come

to the restaurant parking lot within minutes, but it took over two hours for him to come.

She (*wait*) _____ on the locksmith while her friends ate birthday cake

without her. She (*angry*) _____ at herself for forgetting her keys in the first

place. She (*wear*) _____ to a frazzle in the parking lot knowing her

keys were locked in the car. When the locksmith arrived, the door (*open*)

_____ immediately, and Sarah entered the restaurant once again. Even

though she felt angry, she (*enjoy*) _____ her company. They (*laugh*)

_____ at Sarah for locking her keys in the car. They (*agree*)

_____ that locking the keys in the car is an easy thing to do. Next

year, Sarah vowed not to drive to her own party and she, too, (*laugh*)

_____ at herself before the night was over.

Problems with Verbs

Some of the most common verb problems occur with the verbs: *lie* and *lay*, *sit* and *set*, and *rise* and *raise*.

Verb	Definition	Tense Present/Past/Past Participle	Example
lie	to rest	lie lay has/have lain	I lie down in the afternoon. Mark lay on the cot last night. He has lain on the beach all day.
lay	to put	lay laid has/have laid	Lay the tablecloth down please. She laid the receipts on the table. He has laid the paper in the box.
sit	to rest	sit sat has/have sat	We sit and wait for Sue to arrive. Belle sat in the kitchen. He has sat under the tree today.
set	to put or place	set set has/have set	Please set the dish on the table. He set the baby in the swing. She has set the buffet table.
rise	to go up	rise rose has/have risen	The sun rises in the east. The gentlemen rose when the ladies entered. The sun has risen early this morning.
raise	to move upward	raise raised has/have raised	Please raise the window. She raised her hand to answer the question. They have raised the pay scale.

Exercise 4.7

Fill in the blanks in the following paragraph with the correct verb tense (*lie, lay, sit, set, rise, raise*).

Jill _____ early in the morning since her job begins at 8:00 a.m. She has

_____ late out of bed several times. Usually, her boss is very understanding about

her occasional tardiness. Every night before bed, Jill and her sister _____ their

alarm clock for 6:00 a.m. to allow extra time. Jill has _____ in bed after her

alarm has rung hoping to sleep a little later. Her sister makes sure that Jill _____ out

of bed in enough time to eat breakfast and catch the bus. Once Jill gets on the bus, she

45

_____ in the front since her stop is one of the first on the route. Doug, the bus driver,

lets Jill _____her briefcase and lunch in the aisle of the bus since there is not much

room for storage. As a thank-you gesture, Jill _____ a fresh danish on the

dashboard of the bus every morning for Doug. Doug _____ the danish in his lunch

box and enjoys the pastry on his morning break.

What are verbals?

Verbals originate from verbs but function as nouns, pronouns, adverb or adjectives.
Verbals include gerunds, participles, and infinitives.

Types of Verbals	Definition	Example
gerund	a verbal that ends with *ing* that functions as a noun	*Walking* is great exercise. (gerund used as a subject) Jacob loves *skiing*. (gerund used as an object)
participle	a verbal that is used as an adjective, either alone or as part of a phrase (a participle can also function as an adverb or as part of a phrase)	*Laughing loudly,* the girls entered the theater. The teacher, *impressed by the student,* cancelled the exam.
infinitive	a verbal form that is preceded by the word *to* (infinitives may serve as subjects, objects, or complements)	*To cry* would be a waste of time. (infinitive used as a subject) His dream was *to buy a home.* (infinitive used as a complement) Kadi likes *to attend the theater.* (infinitive used as an object)

Tip: Gerunds may serve as subjects or objects of sentences. If used as a subject, gerunds
are usually found at the beginning of a sentence, while as an object, gerunds may be
found at the end of a sentence.

Exercise 4.8

Underline the gerunds in the following paragraph. Above each gerund, write **S** if the gerund serves as the subject of the sentence and **O** if the gerund serves as the object of the sentence.

Eating a balanced diet is important for people of all ages. Parents need to practice eating healthy foods. Since children learn from their parents or guardians, eating healthy foods should be an important part of a child's routine. Children enjoy watching their parents create healthy habits. Establishing good habits requires patience and repetition. Avoiding junk food after school and at night is one way to practice healthy habits. Children need to be involved in establishing a good exercise routine and a good eating regime. Involving children in good health requires time. Exercising can be a fun activity that parents and their children share. The hardest decision for parents to make is deciding how to channel their child's energy into a productive activity. Creating new fun memories is most important. Exercising should be an activity that the family may enjoy year round. Establishing an activity that works well with the entire family may take some time, but will be well worth the effort.

Tip: A gerund may be an appositive (a noun or pronoun that follows another noun or pronoun to identify it).

Example: The woman's hobby, *cooking*, is her favorite activity.

Exercise 4.9

Underline the participles in the following paragraph.

Impressed by the recent theater performance, Katelyn bought season passes for the performance series. Katelyn attended the most recent performance, having heard the show was a Broadway success. The series, interesting to most of the season ticket holders, promises to be the best yet. Katelyn has seen many Broadway musicals, having been involved in college theater productions. The most recent production that Katelyn saw was *Oklahoma*. Impressed by the musical talent of the actors, Katelyn has decided to try out for the next local production in her town. Having heard the musicians perform has inspired Katelyn to pursue singing as a hobby. The inspiration, coming when it did, has helped Katelyn to have more confidence. Singing as she works, Katelyn dreams of her big day on stage.

Exercise 4.10

Underline the infinitives in the following paragraph.

Tara loves to play croquette, a game that requires players to hit a wooden ball with a mallet through a type of obstacle course. The primary objective of croquette is to entertain. To build a player's skills is one of the biggest challenges of the game. Most croquette players agree that the purpose of practicing is to play a stronger game. Tara loves to play the game with her family. When she was eleven, she started playing at the amateur level. Finally at age 13, she played the game to win. To gain self-confidence is a great feeling, and Tara practices five times a week to gain confidence in her skills. The person to beat is the person who is able to play with control and with grace. When she first started playing, Tara's biggest mistake was to play the game without mental preparation. To maintain skill is Tara's main responsibility. Tara's family supports her desire to play competitively.

What is an adjective?

An adjective is a word that describes a pronoun or noun: *red, thin, large, beautiful*. Adjectives may also describe other adjectives.

Types of Adjectives	Definitions	Examples
adjectives with articles	most used group of adjectives that are preceded by an article: *a, an, the*	an ***unusual*** circumstance, a ***sweet*** treat, the ***guarded*** treasure
proper adjectives	formed from proper nouns	an ***English*** tea, a ***Greek*** wedding, a ***French*** cuff
descriptive adjectives	adjectives that describe shape, color, and manner	a ***red*** car, a ***square*** table, a ***strange*** feeling
positive, comparative, superlative adjectives	used for comparisons, either regular or irregular	*happy, happier, happiest gorgeous, more gorgeous, most gorgeous*
predicate adjectives	follows a linking verb and modifies a subject	Samuel felt *tired* after driving all day.
personal adjectives	are similar to possessive pronouns	*my, our, your, his, her, its, their*
definite relative adjectives	the words *whose* and *which*	Was that the man *whose* daughter got married over the weekend? Jill arrived at ten, at *which* time the lecture was just beginning.
indefinite relative adjectives	introduce noun clauses	Some examples: *whose, which, what, each, every, either, neither, any, some, both, all, much, little, less, first, second, third*
interrogative adjectives	used in the form of questions	*Whose* paper is on the table? *What* taxi did she take? *Which* direction is the pool?
demonstrative adjectives	the words *this, that, these, those* and *such,* also words like *latter, former, very,* and *same* when used with the word *the*	*That* necklace was stolen from the ship. The *former* mayor was appointed to the committee. The *very* person I came to see was out of town.

Tip: Some pronouns may act as adjectives in a sentence.
The girls require *less*. (*less* is a pronoun)
The girls require *less* effort. (*less* is an adjective)

Exercise 5.1

Underline the adjectives in the following paragraph. Write a **P** above any proper adjectives.

The invention of modern dance—the expressive and often spontaneous dance form based on a rejection of ballet's classical rules—is often credited to American Isadora Duncan. Duncan earned her first dancing job after she exclaimed, "I have discovered the art of which has been lost for two thousand years." She was known for her "free dances," in a flowing white costume, moving lyrically on her scandalously bare feet to the strains of Beethoven and Wagner. The American scene also fostered a budding genius in symphonic music. Composer Charles Ives captured the aural flavor of American popular life. Ives's musical techniques had none of the abstract rigor of composer Schoenberg's methods, but did explore broad dissonances. The creative architecture of Frank Lloyd Wright fit into the same flavor of American popular life. Influenced by his boyhood summers on a Wisconsin farm, Wright believed that a building should reflect its natural surroundings and mediate between its occupants and their natural environment. Wright's organic sense of form is best expressed in his houses. (*Adventures in the Human Spirit, Fourth Edition by Philip E. Bishop, pages 411-412.*)

Exercise 5.2

Fill in the blanks with an adjective in the following paragraph.

Sophia's _____ hobby is to read books and magazines. She reads _____ novels for extra credit during the summer for her summer school reading list. The _____ book she ever read was over 2,000 pages. Sophia managed to read this

_____ novel in less than three months. She read every day and managed to read at an _____ level. Sophia is also interested in writing her own novel someday. She hopes to write a _____ novel and possibly a _____ play before she graduates high school. When Sophia was in the _____ grade, she wrote a _____ poem for the local county fair. The poem entitled "My Greatest Accomplishment" won _____ prize in the county fair. The _____ poem was printed in the _____ newspaper and she received _____ hundred dollars for her entry. Hopefully, in the future Sophia will create _____ novels and will become a _____ writer.

Exercise 5.3

Fill in the blanks with descriptive pronouns that describe color, shape, or manner.

Krista and Kenley like to antique shop on Saturday afternoons. Recently, they purchased a _____ table to put in their dining room. They also found a _____ lamp that was accented with brass. Some Saturdays they don't find any antiques and other Saturdays they have a _____ day. Several weekends ago, they discovered an _____ shaped library table that was priced at $50.00. They purchased the _____ table and took it to an appraiser to see how much the table was worth. The appraiser estimated that the table was worth $150.00. Krista suggested that they place the table in the _____ bedroom in their house. Kenley agreed the _____ bedroom was the perfect spot for the table. Krista had a _____ feeling that the table was worth a lot of money. Now, Krista and Kenley will begin searching for a _____table to put in the same room.

Tip: There are three types of adjectives that describe and/or compare: positive, comparative, and superlative.

Types of Comparison

Adjectives	Definitions	Examples
Positive	used to describe a place, person, or thing (without making a comparison)	He is *tall*. Audrey is *thin*. She is *young*.
Comparative	used to compare two places, persons, or things (a comparison is made)	He is *taller* than his brother. Audrey is *thinner* today. She is *younger* than her sister.
Superlative	used to compare three or more places, persons, or things (a comparison is made)	He is the *tallest* of the boys. Audrey is the *thinnest* of her class. She is the *youngest* member of the family.

Tips to remember about positive, comparative, and superlative adjectives:

- An adjective of one syllable usually becomes comparative and superlative by adding *er* for the comparative form and *est* for the superlative form.
- An adjective of two syllables usually becomes comparative and superlative by adding *er* or *more* for the comparative form and *est* or *most* for the superlative form.
- An adjective of three or more syllables usually becomes comparative and superlative by adding *more* for the comparative form and *most* for the superlative form.
- An adjective forms negative comparisons by placing *less* or *least* before the comparative and superlative form.
- Not all adjectives follow the above methods for becoming comparative and superlative. An example:
  bad   worse   worst

Exercise 5.4

Each sentence in the following paragraph contains an incorrect positive, comparative, or superlative adjective. Draw a line through the incorrect positive, comparative, or superlative adjective and write the correct form above it.

Rachel is tallest than her sister Catherine. Since Rachel is the younger of three daughters,

the fact that she is the taller one of the group is amazing. Rachel's sisters are excellent

racquetball players. Out of the three, Rachel is the worse racquetball player. Catherine

and Hillary have more time to practice than their sister. Catherine has the less crowded

schedule out of all three girls. Hillary is fastest than Catherine on the court, but Catherine is the kinder out of the group. While Rachel may be the slower of her sisters, she is most

gracious than Hillary and is smartest than Catherine. Rachel says she doesn't mind being

the worse racquetball player since she is the more articulate out of her sisters. One day

Rachel hopes to be the better racquetball player out of her two sisters. She hopes to be

the faster one of the three.

Exercise 5.5

Fill in the blanks with the positive, comparative, or superlative form of the adjective in
parenthesis in the following paragraph.

In the small town of Smithville, a beauty pageant is held every year to name the (pretty)

_____ girl in town. The pageant officials also decide on the contestant who

is the (gracious) _____. The (soon) _____ the pageant

gets started, the more people that attend. When the pageant begins, the high school

gymnasium is the (crowded) _____. However, as it gets closer to time, the

gymnasium fills up quickly. Most Smithville residents find the pageant to be (good)

_____ and more entertaining than the county fair. Local merchants offer

prizes for the winners. The (good) _____ prize offered is a trip to the

mountains for the winner and her family. Perhaps the (big) _____ prize

offered is a television set from the local appliance store. Next year's pageant might be

held outdoors since the park is (crowded) _____ than the gymnasium.

Tip: Adjectives can sometimes be easily identified by their suffixes. Below are some of
the most commonly used suffixes.

Suffix	Example
ly	recently
y	dirty
some	handsome
ful	thoughtful

ary	primary
less	sunless
ic	scientific
en	wooden
al	conversational
able	forgettable
ible	tangible
ish	selfish
ous	gorgeous
ive	excessive

Exercise 5.6

Identify the personal, definite relative, indefinite relative, interrogative, or demonstrative adjectives (in italics) in the following paragraph. Above each adjective write **P** for personal, **DR** for definite relative, **IR** for indefinite relative, **I** for interrogative, and **D** for demonstrative.

Glenn and Bobby recently went on a fishing trip to Lake Ontario. They arrived at 10:00 a.m., at *which* time the fishing lure store was busy. Bobby decided *which* lures to buy for his fishing expedition. Glenn asked him, "*What* lure should I buy?" Bobby said, "*That* lure in front of you is the best." "*Whatever* bait you buy should be fine," suggested the store clerk. Glenn also purchased a homemade fried pie, the *very* dessert the bait store was famous for making. Bobby decided *which* fried pie to buy and Glenn asked, "*Which* flavor is the best?" "Was the pie *which* was on the top of the counter the best?" wondered Glenn. The store clerk said, "*Whichever* flavor you choose will be a good choice." After biting into a peach fried pie, Glenn agreed that no other pie would ever top it. "*Those* pies are wonderful," exclaimed Glenn. "*Your* place is terrific too," remarked Bobby. Every year, Glenn and Bobby return to the tackle and lure snack shop *whose* employees offer good food and service.

Exercise 5.7

Fill in the blanks with an appropriate adjective in the following paragraph.

Darrell decided to shop at the _____ mall near the _____ park on the

_____ side of town. Since he was shopping for his mother's birthday gift, Darrell

wanted to buy a _____ necklace. He wasn't sure if he wanted to buy a

_____ necklace or a _____necklace, but he did know that he wanted to

shop until he found the _____ gift. In the _____store, Darrell found a

_____ necklace, but he was afraid it would be too long for his mother. In the

_____ store, Darrell found _____bracelets, pins, rings, and necklaces.

Next to the necklace jewelry counter, Darrell saw a _____ ring that matched a

pair of _____ earrings that his mother already owned. Darrell thought that the

_____ ring would make a _____ gift, so he offered the _____

storeowner $200.00. The storeowner accepted the money and Darrell left the store with

the ring wrapped in a _____box with a _____ _____ bow on top.

Darrell's mother loved the _____ gift. She said that Darrell was the most

_____ person she knew.

Exercise 5.8

Fill each pair of blanks with two interesting adjectives that describe the nouns in the
following paragraph.

I saw many people that I recognized in the grocery store today. My _____,

_____ professor was in the vegetable aisle, sampling the organic carrots,

green bell peppers, and fresh radishes. My _____, _____

neighbor was in the bakery ordering a birthday cake for her grandson. She waved at me

as she sampled fresh baked cookies. The _____, _____ mail

carrier was with his wife down the frozen food aisle. They were buying frozen waffles and toaster pastries. My _____, _____ friend was shopping with her mother while my _____, _____ friend was busy searching for her wallet. My _____, _____ cousin was with her boyfriend buying dog food for Sparkles, her basset hound. Finally, on our way out of the grocery store, my mother and I saw her _____, _____ boss shopping for a company get-together. Our _____, _____ trip to the grocery store became a two hour event since we stopped to talk to everyone we knew.

Exercise 5.9

Underline all of the adjectives in the following paragraph.

Marsha recently bought a new red car. She had trouble deciding between a blue economy sedan and the red convertible that she always wanted. Since Marsha is a young energetic woman, she felt the sporty red car best fit her personality. The new car dealer felt she made the right choice. While Marsha knows her car insurance will be higher driving the red car, she can afford the payment since she paid for over half the car before driving it off of the crowded lot. Marsha works at the ice cream parlor to help make her monthly car payments. She asked her tall manager if she could work extra hours to help with her monthly payments. He agreed to offer her at least five more hours on the weekend. Marsha thanked her kind manager for allowing her to work longer shifts. Marsha figures that if she works at least two extra days each week, she will have plenty of money to afford her car payment. Marsha's parents have agreed to help her with her car insurance.

Exercise 5.10

Underline the adjectives in the following paragraph.

Dance is so closely allied with music that musical styles are often named for the dance they accompany. From the waltz to hip-hop, interpretative dance and beautiful music have evolved. The dance form of the minuet, which originated in France, was preserved in the eighteenth century symphonies of Mozart. In the 1970s, disco music fueled a popular dance revival among young people dissatisfied with rock-and-roll's informal dance styles. In the same way, the improvisational style of jazz has fostered the equally inventive form of jazz dance. A dance's form, much like the form of music or theater, is the artful combination of dancing gestures and movements. In a dance performance, a dancer's movements create a changing combination of line, motion, pattern, tension, and rhythm. More so than with any other art, the form of dance is perceptible only in performance. The three-dimensional energy and complexity of a dance performance cannot be fully captured by a system of notation or even by film, although filmed dance has been revived by the popularity of music video. (*Adventures in the Human Spirit, Fourth Edition by Philip E. Bishop, page 22*).

Chapter 6: Adverbs

What is an adverb?

An adverb is a word that describes a verb, an adjective, or another adverb. Adverbs answer: *how, how much, what, when who, where, why, to what extent, to what degree, with what concessions,* and *with what results.*

Tip: An *ly* ending usually indicates an adverb.

Tip: An adverb is usually located next to the word it modifies.

Sometimes an adverb phrase occurs when a prepositional phrase describes a verb.

Types of Adverbs	Definitions	Examples
interrogative adverbs	adverbs that ask questions	*Why don't you call when you arrive? Where is your favorite album?*
affirmative/negative adverbs	the only affirmative adverb=*yes* the negative adverbs=*no* and *not* (may also be part of a contraction)	*Yes, this is my home.* *No, it is **not** Sam's fault.* *Regina does **not (doesn't)** want a dog.*
intensifiers	answers the question *to what extent?* describes adjectives and adverbs	*Haley is **very** talented.* *She worked **tremendously** hard during the campaign.*
adverbs as nouns	usually names a time or place	*Working **at midnight** is difficult.*

Tip: Most adverbs end in *ly: quietly, anxiously, enthusiastically.*
   Some adverbs do not end in *ly: very, seldom, never, now.*

Exercise 6.1

Underline the adverbs in the following paragraph.

Since we had only four days to create a prom in our gymnasium, we anxiously started

hanging paper on the walls. The junior class is responsible for skillfully crafting a prom

set out of some lumber and paper supplies. The deadline is one week and is often missed

because there is so much work to be done. Several members of the junior class enthusiastically accept the challenge of building a major set in such a short period of time. Class members never feel confident that their work is good enough, despite how aggressively they work all week. When the last day of building occurs, the class nervously awaits as the senior class president gets a sneak peek of the prom. Once the senior class president gives his or her stamp of approval, the junior class silently feels a sense of relief. Working so diligently to complete the project, the junior class members often become closer to one another. Many members of the class have an opportunity to meet other classmates for the first time. The class members politely work with one another to achieve their one goal, a perfect prom.

Exercise 6.2

Fill in the blanks with an appropriate adverb in the following paragraph.

Savannah and Jenny _____ called their cousins when they found out they were going to Disney World. Their parents purchased tickets for the entire family to _____ travel to Florida. Savannah has _____ wished she could go to Disney World and began asking her parents to take her there when she was five years old. _____ did she imagine that for her high school graduation, a trip would be her gift. _____, a trip would be the best graduation gift she would ever receive. Jenny was also _____ thankful for the opportunity to visit the Florida-based theme park. She has many friends who have traveled to Disney _____. They _____ began packing their bags and _____ planned how they would spend their vacation at the many theme parks. They _____ thanked their parents for _____ planning and giving them such a wonderful gift. Savannah _____ claims that she will _____ forget this trip.

Exercise 6.3

Underline the adverbs and circle the adjectives in the following paragraph.

One contemporary revival grew directly out of pop art. Superrealism in painting faithfully reproduced in paint the qualities of the photographic image. Chuck Close was quite explicit in his aim to transfer photographic information to paint, often painting oversized portraits directly from photographs. Sculptor Duane Hanson sculpted mannequin-like figures faultlessly crafted of polymers to resemble breathing humans. Placed in airports or banks, Hanson's figures were often mistaken for real people. Another trend in art was to move outside the studio and find a new relation to nature and the social world. An outgrowth of minimalist sculpture, called earth art or land art, merged sculpture with the environment. Earth art was constructed of materials virtually identical to the surrounding natural site, often primeval landscapes in the desert or prairie. The best-known work of earth art was Robert Smithson's *Spiral Jetty*, a spiral form built from black basalt, limestone rocks, and earth in the Great Salt Lake of Utah. (*Adventures in the Human Spirit, Fourth Edition by Philip E. Bishop, pages 434-435*)

Tip: There are three types of adverbs that describe and/or compare: positive, comparative, and superlative.

Types of Comparison

Adverbs	Definitions	Examples
positive	used to describe a verb, adjective, or another adverb (without making a comparison)	Sue walks *fast*. Audrey talks *slow* in the morning. Tommy calls *late* at night.
comparative	used to compare two circumstances or two events	Sue walks *faster* than Tim. Audrey talks *slower* than Kim in the morning. Tommy calls *later* than Ron at night.
superlative	used to compare three or more circumstances or three or more events	Sue walks *fastest* when she is in a hurry. Audrey talks *slowest* in the morning. Tommy calls *latest* at night.

Tips to remember about positive, comparative, and superlative adverbs:

- Many adverbs become comparative and/or superlative by adding *er* and/or *est*.
- Some adverbs require *more* or *less* to form the comparative and *most* or *least* to form the superlative.

Exercise 6.4

Each sentence in the following paragraph contains an incorrect positive, comparative, or superlative adverb. Draw a line through the incorrect positive, comparative, or superlative adverb and write the correct form above it.

Kara talks fastest than her brother, Ken. Sometimes when Kara is talking, her mother tells her to talk slowest. Often, it is difficult to understand Kara on the telephone because she talks the faster on the phone. When talking to Kara in person, it is easier to understand her even though she talks fast. She has a tendency to talk fast to her friends than when she is talking in school. When the teacher calls on Kara, she answers most rapidly than her friend Heather. Heather talks slow than Kara, but Heather does not talk the slower in the class. Ben usually answers slower in the entire class. Ben, however, smiles happily because his answers are usually correct. He answers best than Kara and feels worse if he gets an answer incorrect. Kara volunteers less than her classmates to answer questions. Kara works better when she is not under the pressure of answering a question in front of her classmates.

What are double negatives?

A double negative occurs when two negative words are used in a sentence, when only one negative word is necessary.

Tips to remember to avoid a double negative:
- Do not use *not* with the words *hardly, none, no, nothing,* and *scarcely.*
- Do not use *not* with the words *but* and *only* to mean *no more than.*

Examples:

I didn't forget nothing in class today. (incorrect)
I didn't forget anything in class today. (correct)

I don't have but four dollars. (incorrect)
I have but four dollars. (correct)

Exercise 6.5

Underline the correct adjectives or adverbs in the following paragraph.

Dina and Sara always walk (quick, quickly) into their aerobic class. However, Sara usually arrives (soon, sooner) than Dina. As a result, the aerobic instructor believes that Sara is a (real, really) punctual person. When Dina arrives at the workout club, she (quiet, quietly) gets prepared to do aerobics. She stretches and warms-up (good, well) whereas Sara just starts to exercise (rapid, rapidly). Since Sara doesn't warm-up properly, she has seen (poor, poorly) results. Dina, however, has experienced (good, well) results after working out for only several weeks. Dina watches (anxious, anxiously) as her aerobic classmates advance in workout skill. She hopes to join the advanced class someday (soon, sooner). Dina can see (more, most) results since she has worked out with a professional trainer. Her trainer (positive, positively) encourages her to maintain a healthy and happy lifestyle.

Exercise 6.6

Write **ADJ** for adjective and **ADV** for adverb above the italicized words in the following paragraph.

Steve and Mike decided to take an *adventurous* vacation before returning to school in the fall. After looking on a map, the two decided to drive to the *sunny* shores of California. Since Mike had been to California several times in the past, he *reluctantly* agreed to go. Steve and Mike enjoy playing golf, so they *anxiously* called several golf courses in the California area. They decided to play golf at several *upscale* courses. Mike reminded Steve to pack his *golf* clubs and shoes because he *notoriously* forgets something when he plays golf. Steve believes that a *good* golfer always plays *patiently*. Mike just likes to have fun when he plays the *challenging* game. When Steve and Mike arrived at the *first* course in California, Mike hit the ball *aimlessly* and Steve laughed at his efforts. Then when Steve hit the ball, he hit the ball *well*. Mike realizes that Steve is a *better* golfer, but Mike still enjoys playing *different* courses. Steve has played golf since he was a teenager, so he has experience putting and chipping. When Steve putts, he hits the ball *slowly* and *smoothly*. He believes that having *enough* patience is the key to succeeding in golf. Perhaps this is why Steve plays *tremendously well*.

Exercise 6.7

Fill in the blanks with either an appropriate adjective or adverb as requested in the following paragraph.

Cathy and Sean recently bought their first home. They decided to buy a _____

adjective

home near the park. Since they have lived in a _____ apartment for several

adjective

years, Sean _____signed the closing papers. Cathy always wanted to live near a

adverb

_____ park where she could take their children to play on

adjective

the_____swing set and skate at the indoor _____ skating rink. Sean

adjective   adjective

_____packed their belongings and hired a moving company to help move the

adverb

larger pieces of furniture. Since Cathy likes her new kitchen the most, she decided to

decorate the walls with _____paint and _____portraits. Sean felt

adjective   adjective

the _____they moved in, the easier it would be to get settled. Since they left

adverb

their apartment a couple of months before their lease had expired, their landlord

_____ agreed to only charge them for half of the rent. Sean believed the rent

adverb

money was worth it to allow them to move into their _____,

adjective

_____ home early. The best parts of their neighborhood are their

adjective

_____neighbors and the _____garden in their backyard. Cathy and

adjective   adjective

Sean hope to raise their children in their _____ home.

adjective

Exercise 6.8

Fill in the blanks with an appropriate adverb in the following paragraph.

Beth and Savannah went shopping today for new school clothes. While they only had a

couple of mall gift certificates to spend, they managed their money _____

well. They traveled in and out of several stores very _____. Beth wanted

to walk around the mall _____, while Savannah wanted to walk

_____. Beth felt she had done very _____ at the mall since she

found three outfits. Savannah wasn't as lucky. She felt _____disappointed

with the fact that she was unable to find any outfits that fit. Beth agreed to help

Savannah shop _____ in a few days to find school clothes. Savannah felt

_____ happy for Beth who was _____successful in finding

several fall outfits. Both agreed that their time spent walking _____ around the

mall was fun. They were able to spend time together and they saw several of their friends

_____ shopping for bargains.

Exercise 6.9

Cross out any double negatives you find in the following paragraph. Above each double
negative, write the correction.

Cam doesn't hardly ever see a movie because he works the night shift at the local pizza

parlor. He only has one night off every week. Cam usually gets off work at 11:00 p.m.,

65

and the last movie begins at 10:00 p.m., so he rents movies from the local video store. He doesn't scarcely know how to tell his boss that he would like at least one weekend night off every month. Cam doesn't say nothing to his boss because he worries about his boss becoming angry. Cam's boss doesn't have no employee to fill in when Cam is off. His boss only has two people working, and his other employee can only work part-time. While the pizza parlor is busy most nights, Cam doesn't hardly make much money in tips. However, Cam likes his job because he gets to meet different people every day. He has worked at the pizza parlor for two years, and he hasn't asked for no raise, but his boss has offered to pay him more because Cam has been such a valuable employee.

Exercise 6.10

Underline the adverbs and the words they modify in the following paragraph.

When Hannah awoke this morning, she could hear the birds merrily chirping and the sun was brightly shining through her window. Hannah got up hurriedly and made her bed quickly. She was in a hurry to get dressed because today was her birthday. She had been anxiously waiting for this day to come for weeks. After she chose her outfit, she rapidly ran down the stairs to eat breakfast. When her parents saw Hannah at the breakfast table, they laughed hysterically because Hannah, in all of the excitement, had put her dress on backwards. Hannah was in such a hurry to frantically get dressed that she did not even notice the mistake. She was deeply embarrassed, but she too laughed at her obvious mistake. After breakfast, Hannah's parents set the table and began to hang party decorations. The colorful balloons floated aimlessly in the kitchen. The decorations filled the room and Hannah anxiously watched the clock until it was time for the party. When the guests slowly started to arrive, Hannah became very excited. Many of her friends graciously attended her party and she fortunately received many wonderful gifts. The day was perfect and Hannah exhaustedly slept well that night while dreaming about her perfect birthday.

Chapter 7: Prepositions

What are prepositions?

Prepositions are words that connect nouns or pronouns to other parts of a sentence. Prepositions show direction, position, and duration.

Below is a list of the most commonly used simple and compound prepositions.

Simple Prepositions

aboard	before	during	off	to
along	beyond	except	on	toward
against	behind	from	onto	under
after	below	for	out	underneath
across	between	in	outside	until
above	beneath	inside	over	unto
about	beside	into	past	up
alongside	besides	like	regarding	upon
at	by	near	round	with
as	but	nearer	since	within
around	concerning	nearest	through	without
among	despite	next	throughout	
amid	down	of	till	

Compound Prepositions

according to	due to	in spite of
as well as	except for	instead of
along with	from under	next to
as to	from between	owing to
apart from	from among	out of
as regards	from across	on account of
as for	in addition to	prior to
aside from	in case of	up to
because of	in lieu of	with the exception of
by means of	in front of	with reference to
by reason of	in place of	with regard to
by way of	in regard to	with respect to

When a preposition is combined with an object and any modifier that an object may have, a *prepositional phrase* is created.

Tip: If the prepositional phrase is placed at the beginning of a clause, then the prepositional phrase should be followed by a comma.

Exercise 7.1

Underline all prepositional phrases in the following paragraph.

Charles and his family recently purchased a cottage by the lake. Since Charles and his sons love to fish, they decided that driving a couple of hours to a lake home would be money well spent. Charles began to fish in the lake when he was just a little boy. His grandfather would take him on fishing expeditions instead of baseball games. Aside from never wanting to leave, the two suddenly realized that fishing would become their favorite hobby. In addition to the lake home, Charles also purchased a small pontoon boat for his children to ride at the lake. Despite the occasional months of hot weather, the lake home is the perfect retreat from the everyday hassles of city life. Until six months ago, Charles never realized how much he needed the rest and relaxation. In addition to stress, Charles felt as if he never made time for his family. With this new home, Charles is excited about having an opportunity to reconnect with his family. In front of his wife, Charles told his children that he would make every Sunday a family day. Sundays would become the days to spend time together as a family. With the exception of Charles' youngest daughter who likes to spend Sundays riding her bike, the family was ecstatic about spending much needed quality time together.

Exercise 7.2

Underline the prepositions in the following paragraph.

In 1509, Pope Julius II followed his architect's advice and commissioned a young painter to decorate his apartment chambers. The artist, known as Raphael, was already famed for a series of graceful Madonnas painted in Florence. Working under the Pope's patronage, Raffaello Sanzio became Renaissance Rome's busiest and most beloved artist. Besides painting, Raphael used his talents on projects for the Pope, such as the excavation of Roman ruins and the construction of the new St. Peter's Basilica. In a city of intrigues and jealousies, Raphael was loved for his good humor and modesty. When he died at thirty-seven, he was the most popular artist of the Renaissance. As a painter, Raphael was known for the clarity and spiritual harmony of his works, which eloquently embodied the High Renaissance style. His most famous work, the *School of Athens*, is a virtual textbook of Renaissance technique. The painting depicts a gathering of the great pagan philosophers. The two central figures are Plato, who points to the world of ideal forms above, and Aristotle, reaching for the natural world below. On either side, figures representing ancient philosophy are arranged in lively symmetry, balanced between the abstract and the practical. The painting's overall effect is of learning, tolerance, perfect harmony, and balance. (*Adventures in the Human Spirit, Fourth Edition by Philip E. Bishop, pages 213-214*)

Exercise 7.3

Underline the prepositions in the following paragraph. Above each preposition write **SP** for simple prepositions or **CP** for compound prepositions.

According to recent research, studies show that the facial patterns of some emotional expressions, such as fear and joy, are similar cross-culturally. But because nonverbal communication is learned largely through socialization, only an observer who knows the culture very well can detect leakage of other hidden emotions. If deception can be uncovered, then impression management may fail. Among many Asian cultures, including Korea, Japan, and Thailand, displays of emotion such as broad grins or angry outbursts are considered impolite. In addition, it is also rude to show disagreement with another person's behavior in these cultures. Middle Eastern and Latin cultures expect such displays as signs of interpersonal closeness. In the United States smiling is associated with friendliness and happiness, but not necessarily so in Korea. Smiling is a taken-for-granted cultural norm in most parts of the United States, especially by a shopkeeper hoping to make a sale. Some consequences of breaking norms of nonverbal behavior are even more unsettling. People who do not show emotions—referred to as flat affect by psychologists—in situations that call for emotional expression may be considered mentally ill because they violate taken-for-granted culture rules of nonverbal communication. (*Sociology, Third Edition by Linda L. Lindsey and Stephen Beach, page 156*)

Exercise 7.4

Underline the prepositions in the following paragraph. Above each preposition write **SP** for simple prepositions or **CP** for compound prepositions.

According to symbolic interactionists, society as a whole is constructed through the subjective meanings brought to all social interactions. They assert that we are not born with the social statuses of gender, race, social class, and the like. In addition, social interactionists emphasize that choices of behavior in social interaction are optional, but since race and gender cannot be disguised, people invariably use these categories to help structure their interaction. Class is less obvious and can be disguised or eliminated in a

71

variety of ways, such as learning appropriate class-based behavior. Eliza Doolittle, a character from the Broadway play *My Fair Lady*, was elevated to a much higher social class by changing her language, clothing, and "lower class" behavior. Professor Higgins may agree she is no longer the pitiful flower girl he found on the street, but she will always be a woman and relegated to the less-privileged category designated by the social construction of her gender. In regard to the play, the last line of *My Fair Lady* illustrates the class-gender distinction in terms of privilege when Professor Higgins calls out imperiously, "Eliza, bring me my slippers." (*Sociology, Third Edition by Linda L. Lindsey and Stephen Beach, pages 147-148*)

Exercise 7.5

Underline the correct prepositions in the following paragraph.

Socrates is one (of, for) the greatest philosophers belonging (to, from) the Western rational tradition. (In place of, In addition to) being a great philosopher, he has been a model and source (at, of) inspiration (off, for) many philosophers (unto, throughout) the centuries, including the stoics and the cynics who came before. Socrates actually wrote no philosophy himself, though Plato, one (of, for) his students, did incorporate many Socratic ideas (into, like) his writings. As many commentators point out, it is sometimes difficult to clearly distinguish (between, beside) Plato's original thought and what he borrowed (to, from) Socrates. Alfred North Whitehead, a famous twentieth-century philosopher, once suggested that all (of, at) philosophy is but a series of footnotes (to, upon) Plato. (From, To) an extent this is true, and insofar as Plato was strongly influenced by Socrates, perhaps Western rational philosophy should extend its series (to, of) footnotes a little further back (upon, to) Plato's mentor. Socrates had a reputation (to, for) being indifferent (of, to) fashion and what we sometimes call today the "creature comforts" (of, for) life. He believed in minimizing wants and needs (in, for) self-mastery. (*Experiencing Philosophy by Anthony Falikowski, page 49*)

Exercise 7.6

Underline the correct prepositions in the following paragraph.

(In regard to, In spite of) fashion, street fashion has tremendous influence (underneath, over) fashion trends. Most designers travel a great deal, pursuing information (on, outside) the latest trends, new color stories, and textile innovations. Inevitably, constant exposure (for, to) different cultures and the way people interpret fashions around the world influences fashion trends. Fashion (from, till) the street usually evolves (for, from) the ways young people experiment (for, with) existing garments, often recycling period pieces or customizing basics (near, like) denim garments and wearing them in new ways. Adding accessories typical (of, from) native costumes, wearing oversized garments, distressing clothes, and recycling vintage clothes are inexpensive ways to individualize fashion. The "grunge look" popular (for, with) today's youth has profoundly influenced high fashion. Creative people (in, from) the world (in, of) advertising, photography, and publishing are constantly (on, in) the lookout (for, in) the latest popular trends. They quickly document and integrate new looks (over, into) the international language (off, of) advertising and photography. Designers pick up on street trends firsthand or (outside, through) media images, and the look filters (over, into) the fashion cycle, particularly (of, in) the junior market, though high-fashion designers are also influenced (by, of) street fashions. (*Inside Fashion Design, Fifth Edition by Sharon Tate, page 99*)

Exercise 7.7

Underline the correct prepositions in the following paragraph.

Carley and Timmy recently purchased their first home (of, in) the town of Greenville. They were excited to move (by, into) their home because they had saved (in, for) two years to make the down payment. (According to, In spite of) Timmy, the home purchase went well. Carley and Timmy began searching (in, for) a home last fall. They contacted a local realtor and expressed their interest in searching (to, for) the perfect A-frame house. (Except for, Due to) low home interest rates, Timmy qualified (for, over) a first-time buyers' home loan. (Around, Among) the many houses they viewed, Carley and Timmy knew (in, at) first sight that the home they had purchased was perfect (over, for) them. (Outside, Inside) the home, trees cover a beautiful shady lot. (Outside, Inside) the home, faux painting adorns the walls and hardwood floors can be found (without, throughout) the home. (Because of, With the exception of) their hardworking realtor, Carley and Timmy's first offer to the seller was accepted. The day that Carley and Timmy found out that their offer had been accepted, they jumped up and down. Carley immediately called her family and shared the good news (for, with) her parents. Before they moved in their furniture, Carley's father painted one room and her mother helped clean the kitchen and bathrooms. (Upon, Since) moving (into, before) their new home, Carley and Timmy have discovered that they not only have a beautiful home, but they have friendly neighbors as well.

Exercise 7.8

Fill in the blanks with an appropriate preposition in the following paragraph.

The elements of a man's business suit were established _____ the beginning

_____ the twentieth century, and the evolution _____ fit and detailing _____

the century have formed the basis _____ restyling the business suit. The 1920s were

notable _____ the introduction _____ the Ivy League look and the natural-shoulder suit.

_____ the 1930s, the English drape suit, characterized by padded shoulders, a

fitted waistline, and wide lapels, was popular. The 1940s contributed a modified padded-

shoulder business suit silhouette and introduced many military-style garments _____

civilian use. _____ the 1950s, the natural-shoulder suit and Ivy League details

returned _____ popularity. The 1960s were a decade _____ experimentation

_____ the young generation, contrasted _____ conservative, Ivy League business

suits _____ the establishment. Men began to wear active sportswear _____ leisure

activities _____ the 1970s. Business suits were either conservative, natural-

shoulder silhouettes or the fitted and padded continental look; this trend continued

_____ the last decades _____ the twentieth century. Lifestyle changes have occurred

rapidly _____ the last 25 years, and men's clothing reflects the casual,

comfortable, sports-and-fitness orientation that continues to influence modern life.

(*Inside Fashion Design, Fifth Edition by Sharon Tate, page 357*)

Exercise 7.9

Fill in the blanks with an appropriate preposition in the following paragraph.

Ray and Stan recently traveled _____ Augusta, Georgia, _____ see the professional

Master's golf tournament. _____ Ray has played golf since he was a boy, he always dreamed _____ attending a professional golf tournament. Stan agreed ____

travel with Ray _____ he loves _____ watch Tiger Woods play golf ____

television. Ray invited Stan _____ winning tickets _____ a radio station contest. Ray

answered the question, "What golfer has won the most major tournaments in his career?"

Ray was the first correct caller who answered, "Jack Nicholas." Ray was given an all

expense paid trip _____ Georgia ____ the grand prize winner. When Ray and Stan

arrived _____ the Master's tournament, they met several professional golfers. Ray

stood _____ _____ _____Tiger Woods, and Stan shook hands _____ Phil

Mickelson. After the tournament, Ray and Stan had the opportunity to tour the Augusta

area. They spent three days playing golf and two extra days touring the sights _____ the

beautiful town. Stan was thankful _____ Ray _____ taking him _____ the trip _____ a

lifetime.

Exercise 7.10

Fill in the blanks with an appropriate preposition in the following paragraph.

_____ the fashion industry, coordinates are typically described _____ a closely

developed group _____ garments, carefully linked _____ color or detailing. These

garments are designed ____ an interrelated group to encourage the customer to complete

an outfit _____ buying several pieces. A typical coordinated group usually consists

_____ jackets, _____ a few accessory sweaters, blouses, pull-over sweaters, and T-

shirts. Basic and novelty pants and skirts, accessories, and sometimes dresses complete

the mix. The group can be rounded out _____ adding shorts, halters, and bandeaus

_____ the summer, and pantsuits, long skirts, vests and tunics ____ the fall. Current hot

items will be adapted _____ the coordinated group. To buy this complete package, the buyer will select many components so that the customer will have several possible outfits _____ which to choose. Each component will be bought ___ several colors and _____ a range _____ sizes. This will be an expensive purchase that will consume much _____ the "open to buy." The buyer usually purchases coordinated groups _____ large manufacturers who can ensure delivery and can provide cooperate merchandising programs. One problem _____ purchasing coordinates is that some odd pieces are left unsold. After most components _____ a group have been sold, the remainder must be marked down. (*Inside Fashion Design, Fifth Edition by Sharon Lee Tate, page 437*)

Chapter 8: Conjunctions

What are *conjunctions*?

Conjunctions are words that join a group of words together. There are two types of conjunctions: *coordinating* and *subordinating*.

What are coordinating conjunctions?

Coordinating conjunctions connect the same sentence parts together (example: nouns with other nouns, adjectives with other adjectives, clauses with other clauses, phrases with other phrases).

Coordinating Conjunctions:
- and   (*John **and** Jill walked to school.*)
- but   (*Susie is intelligent, **but** is often tardy.*)
- for   (*We were late **for** John overslept.*)
             *Tip: **For** is a conjunction when it means *because*; otherwise, it is a preposition.
- nor   (*Neither Sue **nor** Kirk remember the directions.*)
- or   (*Kadi **or** Sara will drive tomorrow.*)
- so   (*We made extra sandwiches **so** we wouldn't need to stop.*)
- yet   (*She wasn't angry, **yet** she said very little all night long.*)
             *Tip: **Yet** may be used in a compound subject or predicate.

Tip: The conjunctions *and, but* and *or* are used to connect the same parts of speech.

Examples:

Joining verbs: The chef cooked *and* served a wonderful dinner.

Joining nouns: Marsha *or* Courtney will arrive after lunch.

Joining adjectives: The mail carrier is polite, *but* doesn't remember my name.

Joining prepositional phrases: The girl had to call the doctor *and* go into his office for an appointment.

Tip: The conjunctions *for, yet* and *so* join main clauses (complete sentences) together. Note: A comma must be used before a conjunction when the conjunction is used to connect two main clauses.

Examples:

Joining clauses: She knew a storm was approaching, *for* the sky was turning dark.

Christina wants to accept the job offer, *yet* she fears a lower salary will make it difficult for her to live comfortably.

She forgot her book report, *so* she called her mother to bring the report to school.

Exercise 8.1

Underline the coordinating conjunctions in the following paragraph.

Christa and Breana celebrated their fifth birthday last Saturday. Neither Christa nor Breana have ever had a birthday party apart because the two girls are twins. Christa is taller than Breana, yet Breana was born twenty minutes earlier than her sister. The two girls share everything, but they don't look like one another. In fact, Christa has brown hair and Breana has blonde hair. They do have similar eyes, so people can usually tell they are twins. Every year for their birthday, they invite ten of their closest friends. Christa and Breana's mother bakes two separate cakes, for she wants the girls to each have an opportunity to blow out candles on the cakes. Christa likes chocolate cake, so her mother makes her a chocolate cake with fudge frosting. Breana likes white cake, so her mother makes her a white cake with cream cheese frosting. Both cakes are delicious, for they are homemade. During their most recent birthday party, Christa opened her gifts first, so Breana watched and helped her sister. Then Breana opened her gifts and Christa anxiously watched. Christa and Breana's father loaded up the gifts in the car. Neither Christa nor Breana left the party until the gifts were loaded and the decorations were taken down. The girls feel fortunate to have parents that create such wonderful parties in their honor.

Exercise 8.2

Underline the coordinating conjunctions in the following paragraph.

In 1900, Sigmund Freud published his study *The Interpretation of Dreams*, a work that revolutionized psychology much as Picasso transformed art. According to Freud, the mind was not the center of reason and self-mastery, but a battleground between unconscious desires and the oppressive demands of society. The family was not a sanctuary of innocent love, but a cauldron of incestuous attachments and murderous wishes. Freud applied his scientific analysis to subjects that were normally taboo, so many ideas have been created by Freud. His writings have given people a new vocabulary for understanding human thought, including now-familiar terms such as "unconscious," "ego," and "Oedipus complex." Every domain of the humanities, from surrealist art to philosophy and religion, has been affected by Freud's theories. Freud was the inventor of psychoanalysis, a method of treating mental illness by analyzing unconscious desires. One psychoanalytical method required a patient to talk freely about his or her thoughts and feelings. This "free association" of ideas revealed the unconscious thoughts behind the mental symptom and exposed the patient's thoughts to interpretation. (*Adventures in the Human Spirit, Fourth Edition by Philip E. Bishop, page 398*)

Exercise 8.3

Fill in the blanks with appropriate coordinating conjunctions in the following paragraph.

A job opening became available last week at the local bank. Over twenty people applied for the position, _____ only two applicants were called back for a second interview. Mr. Smith _____ Mr. Jones were the two favored applicants. Both applicants had exceptional work experience _____ creative ideas to bring to the bank. Neither

Mr. Smith _____ Mr. Jones had ever worked in the banking field. Mr. Smith

worked at an insurance agency, _____ had some experience in handling money

_____ loans. Mr. Jones had experience working in retail sales, _____ his father

_____ grandfather were bankers. The decision was a tough one, _____ the bank

president asked for the loan officer _____ the bank manager to attend the second

interview. The bank president asked if the job should be given to the applicant with the

most money experience _____ the most education. The loan officer _____ the bank

manager agreed that neither experience _____ education would make that big of a

difference. During the second interview, the bank president learned that another bank

branch had a job opening as well, _____ he was able to hire both Mr. Smith

_____ Mr. Jones for the same job, _____ at two different locations.

Exercise 8.4

Fill in the blanks with appropriate coordinating conjunctions in the following paragraph.

Glenn decided to run for president of his senior class. It is rumored that he will receive

many votes, _____ Glenn has the highest grade point average in his class. He is

honest _____ hardworking, _____ he is unsure about winning since Bobby is

also running for the position. Bobby is the quarterback of the football team _____

the center of the basketball team. He is involved in many activities in school,

_____ his grade point average is not as high as Glenn's. Neither Glenn

_____ Bobby would be a bad choice for president, _____ a problem does

exist since the two are best friends. Glenn _____ Bobby have known each other for

years _____ their parents are friends as well. Glenn would like to win the position,

81

_____ he feels Bobby would do an excellent job if elected. Bobby, while

campaigning, has said that Glenn is an excellent candidate _____ is his best friend.

Either Glenn _____ Bobby would be a positive influence on the senior class.

Perhaps the best part of this campaign has been the fact that both candidates are

supportive of one another, _____ regardless of who wins, a wonderful president will

be elected.

Exercise 8.5

Look at the italicized coordinating conjunctions in the following paragraph. If the conjunction is used correctly, write **OK** above it. If the conjunction is used incorrectly, draw a line through it and write the correct conjunction directly above.

Jana *and* Neal recently bought a car. It was the first time Jana had ever purchased a new

car, *or* she felt uncomfortable talking at car dealerships. Her first stop was the BMW

dealership, *so* a BMW had always been Jana's dream car. She test drove several vehicles

on the lot *but* didn't immediately feel comfortable in any one car. Neal agreed that he

didn't see one particular vehicle that he felt comfortable driving *yet* the two went to

another dealership. Jana was interested in test driving a sports utility vehicle, *so* Neal

suggested that they look at Ford Explorers. Jana drove a silver Ford Explorer *but* wasn't

convinced that she could drive a vehicle that size. Neither Jana *nor* Neal felt comfortable

in a sports utility vehicle, *yet* they liked driving a Ford. They decided to test drive a Ford

car *or* after driving through town in a sedan, Jana decided that she truly liked the BMW

X3. She felt the X3 was the perfect size vehicle, *so* they returned to the BMW dealership

and test drove several different styles of the X3. Jana found a light blue X3 that she felt

was the perfect vehicle for her *yet* Neal agreed it was the perfect car for Jana. After test

driving vehicles all day, they purchased their first BMW.

What are subordinating conjunctions?

Subordinating conjunctions connect subordinate clauses to independent clauses (complete sentences). Subordinating conjunctions often introduce adverb clauses. When a subordinate clause begins a sentence, a comma must be used to separate the subordinate clause and the independent clause. When the subordinate clause comes after the independent clause in sentence, a comma is usually not used to separate the subordinate and independent clauses.

Subordinating Conjunctions:

when	*whenever*	*where*
wherever	*because*	*unless*
until	*till*	*though*
although	*even though*	*as though*
while	*before*	*after*
as	*if*	*as if*
as long as	*as soon as*	*whether*
so that	*provided*	*provided that*
except that	*in order that*	*whereas*
than	*since*	

Examples:

(subordinate clause in the middle of the sentence): *Coffee,* **which is derived from coffee beans***, contains caffeine.*

(subordinate clause at the beginning of the sentence): **Before we leave for work,** *we need to make sure the front door is locked.*

(subordinate clause at the end of the sentence): *We drank hot chocolate* **since it was cold outside.**

Tip: Notice that when the subordinate clause comes at the end of a sentence no comma is needed in between the two clauses.

Exercise 8.6

Underline the subordinate clauses in the following paragraph.

Whenever Jim is around, people seem to always have fun. Jim is the kind of guy that

doesn't know a stranger. In fact, he may be the friendliest person I know. As long as

people are willing to listen, he tells the funniest stories. Provided that he isn't busy with his job or other hobbies, Jim enjoys spending leisure time visiting with friends. He usually spends his Saturdays, if time permits, playing basketball with his four best friends. The four men have played basketball every Saturday since they were in high school. Because they have such a good time on Saturday mornings, they often play football on Sunday afternoons. Even though they all live several miles away from the gym, they make it a point to play sports every week. Whenever he can, Jim tries to invite his friends and their wives to his house for outdoor cookouts. Jim loves to grill outside provided that the weather is nice. Altogether, Jim is a well-rounded, likeable guy and his friends think he is truly a supportive, kind friend.

Exercise 8.7

Underline the subordinate clauses in the following paragraph.

Before Whitney starts her new job, she has to spend several days in orientation. Because her job requires meeting new people on a continuous basis, proper training is a must. Her job, which begins next Monday, will require some travel. Whitney will be reimbursed for her travel provided that she completes the proper travel reimbursement forms. Even though her job will require travel, she will not travel every week. Some of her travel will require flying unless she can drive the distance in one day. Perhaps the best part of Whitney's new job will be the locations that she will be required to visit. Her company has branches in Hawaii, London, and Miami. Even though Whitney loves to travel, she is afraid that traveling will be difficult at times. Since Whitney has children, she is afraid that she will miss her husband and children when she has to travel overnight. As long as her husband and children pay their own travel expenses, Whitney is allowed to have them travel with her on an occasional business trip. Her children are looking forward to going to Hawaii provided that they will travel with her to the beautiful island.

Exercise 8.8

Fill in the blanks with appropriate subordinating conjunctions in the following paragraph.

_____ Megan leaves the house in the mornings, she is responsible for feeding the family dog. _____ the dog was given to Megan for her birthday, she promised her mother that she would take care of him. Megan feeds the dog every morning at the same time _____ _____ he doesn't oversleep. _____ her alarm clock goes off in the morning, the dog immediately jumps on top of Megan and licks her face. _____ _____ the cheerful dog wakes Megan up every morning, she loves to walk him. The dog greets Megan at the front door when she arrives home _____ he is asleep on the couch. _____ Megan has her friends over after school, her dog gets so excited that he barks nonstop. Megan's friends think that her dog is funny and they encourage him to bark and run quickly through the house. _____Megan's friends love to see her dog run through the house, her mother doesn't like the commotion that the dog causes. Megan's mom loves the dog _____ _____ she didn't agree with Megan's father about buying a dog. She felt a dog would be too difficult to take care of _____ they all have busy schedules. _____ the dog requires care and hard work, Megan and her family loves him very much.

85

Exercise 8.9

Look at the italicized subordinating conjunctions in the following paragraph. If the conjunction is used correctly, write **OK** above it. If the conjunction is used incorrectly, draw a line through it and write the corrected conjunction directly above.

Coffee shops have become popular all over America. *Although* not everyone likes to drink coffee, coffee shops have become the coolest places in town to hang out. Coffee drinks are delicious cold *as long as* the outside temperature is hot. *Where* coffee houses serve tea, people who don't drink coffee also stop by from time to time. Poetry readings and books for sale in coffee shops have also made them popular places. *Although* coffee shops specialize in coffee, most also serve hot sandwiches and snacks. *Than* coffee is served, people enjoy reading. Several businesses have opened coffee shops in the middle of their bookstores. Most people like to read in coffee shops *except when* occasionally the coffee shop gets busy and then noisy. This can make it difficult to read *since* people receive their coffee. *Because* of the recent popularity of coffee shops, book clubs and reading lists have once again become popular. Coffee and reading seem to mix well together. *Since* socializing over coffee has become the cool thing to do, hopefully reading will also remain a cool activity.

Exercise 8.10

Look at the italicized conjunctions in the following paragraph. If the conjunction is a coordinating conjunction, write **C** above it and if the conjunction is a subordinating conjunction, write **S** above it.

Mary was looking forward to leaving for college, *but* she was also afraid. *Since* this would be the first time she ever lived alone, Mary was nervous about leaving her small town. *Even though* her parents will only live two hours away, Mary still worries that she will have no friends and that she will have a hard time living on her own. Leigh *and*

Regina are also going to the same college. The three girls went to high school together, *but* they don't really know each other very well. *Since* they will be attending the same college, they have called each other several times over the summer. Mary, *provided that* her roommate still attends, will room with a girl from another state. Mary is excited about the possibility of meeting new friends. *Because* she is from a small town, Mary chose a college that has a small student body. The college is in a town that is similar to the town where Mary was raised. Mary's mother has promised to visit *whenever* possible. Mary's mom *and* dad are excited about the new possibilities college has to offer.

What are the most popular forms of punctuation?

commas	*colons*	*semicolons*
periods	*question marks*	*exclamation points*
quotation marks	*hyphens*	*dashes*
apostrophes	*parentheses*	*virgules*

Commas

What are commas and when are they used in writing?

Commas are used a number of ways. By following the simple rules below, using commas properly can be easy to accomplish.

Use a comma in a series:

Place a comma in between three or more sentence parts (such as phrases or clauses).

Tips: Remember to place a comma before the conjunction, but not after the last word, phrase, or clause. Commas are not used when equal sentence parts are all joined by conjunctions.

Examples: *Steve needs to bring pencils, paper, and erasers to the examination room.*

Sandy was asked to cook dinner, clean the kitchen, and prepare dessert.

Use a comma with adjectives in a series:

Two similar types of adjectives not connected by *and* should be separated by a comma.

Tips: If two adjectives are connected by a conjunction (such as *and*) a comma is not needed.

Examples: *The movie is a humorous, light-hearted story.*

The concert was a loud, popular show.

Use a comma to set off an appositive:

An appositive occurs when words are restated in different words. The restatement is called an appositive. Use a comma to set off an appositive.

Tips: If the restated name or item is one of several possibilities, then it is not set off with commas. Reflexive pronouns (such as *myself, herself*) are not set off by commas. Example: Deborah feels tired today, but I myself feel terrific.

Examples: *My sister, Kadi, is a teacher.* (correct: Kadi is the only sister.)

My sister Kadi is a teacher. (correct: Kadi is one of several sisters.)

Use a comma when using calendar dates, years, and weekdays:

Commas are used with dates on a calendar, years, and with weekday combinations. Commas are also used to separate time and a time zone.

Tip: Commas are optional in between a month and a year.

Examples: *August, 2004, is the baby's birthday.* (correct)

August 2004 is the baby's birthday. (correct)

Our daughter got married on Saturday, July 18, 2004.

The plane will arrive in Nashville at 2:20 p.m., CST.

Use a comma with cities and states:

Commas are used in between a city and state and after the state.

Tips: One of the most common errors made with commas is the deletion of a comma after the state name. A comma should always be placed after the name of a state, except if the state name is the subject of a sentence. A comma should never separate a subject from its verb.

Examples: *We visited Nashville, Tennessee before returning home.*

Their summer home in Gulf Shores, Alabama is a beautifully decorated mansion.

Use commas with independent and dependent clauses:

Commas are used to connect an independent clause to a dependent clause. Two independent clauses may be joined by a comma, but a comma plus a conjunction must be used. A dependent clause that gives additional information within a sentence should be set off by commas.

Tips: An independent clause is a complete sentence, while a dependent clause is an incomplete sentence. Two independent clauses should never be joined by a comma without a conjunction.

Examples: *The party should start around noon, but the guests will start arriving at least an hour earlier.* (correct: two independent clauses joined by a comma and conjunction.)

Joan will, if time allows, call ahead to the restaurant. (correct: a dependent clause that provides additional information is set off by commas, also known as a nonrestrictive clause.)

Use commas after introductory clauses, phrases, or words:

Commas are used to separate a dependent clause from an independent clause when the dependent clause is an introductory clause.

Tip: A comma is used after introductory words (such as *although, since, before, while.*)

Examples: *While Stan normally arrives early, his wife is never punctual.*

Although Jayce is older than his brother, he dresses and acts younger.

Use commas with direct addresses of people, degrees, and abbreviations:

Commas should set off the name or title of a person. Commas should set off college degrees and abbreviations.

Examples: *Michael Jones, C.P.A., recently began working at a new firm.*

Smith, Williams, and Wyatt, Inc., will have an open house in September.

Thanks for the all help with the birthday party, Sally.

We are thankful, Reverend, to have you as part of our community.

Use commas with direct quotations:

Quotations should always be set off by commas.

Tip: Notice that periods and commas at the end of sentences should be inside the quotation marks.

Dr. Jones said, "The cause of your headaches is due to stress."

"The cause of your headaches is due to stress," said Dr. Jones.

Use commas with closings:

Commas are used after a closing in a letter.

Sincerely,   Your truly,   Best wishes,

Exercise 9.1

Insert commas as needed in the following paragraph.

Our next-door neighbor Mrs. Golden recently traveled to Europe. She had always planned to travel to Europe in August 2004, but she had to cancel because of work. Finally she was able to fly to Europe with her daughter in November 2004. Their first stop was a fun exciting country. They began their trip in France where they shopped toured sights and dined at outdoor cafes. Since Paris France is a popular tourist attraction the hotel where Mrs. Golden stayed was busy. After a trip to the Eiffel Tower Mrs. Golden and her daughter traveled by train to Germany. While in Germany they toured several museums attended several music festivals and ate at many unique restaurants. Heidelberg Germany was by far their favorite city to visit. While in Heidelberg Mrs. Golden met a famous European actor. The highlight of their trip was touring the Tate Gallery in London England. At the Tate Gallery many nineteenth-century paintings were on exhibit. The art gallery director Mr. Redding suggested that many paintings in the gallery are worth more than a million dollars. Hopefully Mrs. Golden and her daughter will make their trip an annual event.

Exercise 9.2

Insert commas as needed in the following paragraph.

On May 25 2004 Christina graduated from college with a degree in business. Her parents grandparents and brothers attended the ceremony. Her favorite professor William Sneed also attended the event. William Sneed Ph.D. is the chair of the business department. When Professor Sneed saw Christina at graduation he said "I am so proud of you." Christina felt that Professor Sneed was the most helpful instructor at the college. After graduation Christina approached Professor Sneed and said "Thank you for always encouraging me to finish my degree." Christina now hopes to attend graduate school in the fall. If she does attend graduate school she will be the first person in her family to ever complete a graduate degree. After the graduation ceremony Christina's family hosted a party in her honor. She received a clock a briefcase and a collection of several books as graduation gifts. The day was perfect and Christina was thankful to her family for helping her celebrate.

Semicolons and Colons

What are semicolons and how are they used?

Semicolons are used in the following ways:
- to separate two independent clauses (two complete sentences) that do not have a conjunction. (In the example below, a semicolon functions like a period.)
Example: *We traveled to the grocery store; we bought food for the party.*

- to separate items where internal commas are placed.
Example: *We called offices in Austin, Texas; Louisville, Kentucky; and Chattanooga, Tennessee.*

Tips: If a semicolon is needed at the end of a quotation, the semicolon goes outside the quotation marks. Semicolons are also used before conjunctive adverbs and a comma is used after the conjunctive adverb.

Examples: *John said, "We will be late for the premier"; the group is always tardy.*

We fished for two hours; therefore, we decided to postpone our skiing adventure.

What are colons and how are they used?

Colons are used in the following ways:
- to introduce lists or statements.
Example: *Success in school requires the following: a good dictionary, a calculator, and a notebook.*

- between a title and subtitle of a publication.
Example: *Writing: Portfolio Style*

- on a work(s) cited and/or consulted page, use a colon between the city of publication and the publisher's name.
Example: *Upper Saddle River: Prentice Hall, 2004.*

Exercise 9.3

Insert semicolons and colons as needed in the following paragraph.

Leigh discovered this summer that she has a love for reading. At the beginning of the summer, she decided to form a book club she invited many of her friends to join. Forming a book club requires the following at least three members, a variety of novels, and a meeting place, such as a coffee house or library. Leigh started by calling her closest friends. She called Bella and said, "Please join our book club" Bella never hesitated. Bella helped Leigh build the group and the club held their first meeting a week ago. When the group met, they decided to let Leigh choose the first novel. She had trouble deciding, so she asked for the group to buy the following *Wuthering Heights, The Pearl,* and *Mother Night.* The group agreed to begin with *Wuthering Heights* Leigh was responsible for leading the first discussion. Since beginning the book club, Leigh has read many wonderful books she is glad that the group was able to come together and she hopes to continue meeting monthly for many years to come.

Exercise 9.4

Insert semicolons and colons as needed in the following paragraph.

Science impacts our everyday world. Late in 2002, a Canadian chemist created quite a stir at a press conference she announced that her company had cloned a human being. Now, set aside for the moment the fact that no evidence was ever offered for this claim just consider the announcement. Average citizens may not have understood exactly how the company carried off its supposed feat, but they had a rough idea of what the company was claiming that it had produced one human being who was a genetic copy of another. Moreover, they understood that this person was conceived not through sex but through genetic manipulation in the laboratory. Though this announcement may have been surprising, it was not startling for the first time, it caused people to have some context in which to place cloning. The remarkable thing is how far the concept of cloning had to come to reach this common-knowledge status. Here at the start of the twenty-first century, scientific innovations are moving with breathtaking speed people will now hear more about cloning on a daily basis. (*Biology: A Guide to the Natural World, Third Edition by David Krogh, page 3*)

Dashes and Hyphens

What are dashes and how are they used?

Dashes are used in the following ways:
- to set off parenthetical elements.

Example: *Two months ago—from the advice of my father—I opened a savings account.*

- to create a break in thought.

Example: *Let's call home—after we eat dinner.*

What are hyphens and how are they used?

Hyphens are used to form compound words, with some prefixes and suffixes, at the end of a typed or handwritten line, with spelled-out numbers, and to indicate spelling a word letter by letter.

Tips: A hyphen should be used for most compound modifiers that precede a noun. A hyphen should not be used for most compound modifiers after the noun.
Example: *four-inch square* (hyphen)   *a square of four inches* (no hyphen)

Do not use a hyphen when a compound modifier starts with an adverb ending in *–ly.*
Example: *happily married groom* (no hyphen)

Do not use a hyphen when a compound modifier is in the form of a comparative or superlative.
Example: *most significant meeting* (no hyphen)   *least attractive person* (no hyphen)

Do not use a hyphen when the compound modifiers are foreign.
Example: *ad miscordium logical fallacy* (no hyphen)

Do not use a hyphen with a possessive compound modifier.
Example: *a long week's salary* (no hyphen)

- hyphens are used to form compound words. The hyphen connects a compound word together, making it one unit.
Example: *My sister-in-law is older than my sister.* (compound noun)
The four-inch box was too small to ship the gift. (compound modifier)

- hyphens are used after the prefixes *all, ex,* and *self.* (Note: do not use a hyphen with *self* when the prefix is a root word.) See other tips below for using hyphens with prefixes and suffixes.
Tip: Use a hyphen before the suffix *elect.* Use a hyphen between a prefix and the first word of a compound word. Use a hyphen when two or more prefixes apply to one root word. Use a hyphen when a prefix comes before a number or before a word that starts with a capital letter.
Example: *My mother won an all-expense paid trip to Mexico.*

- hyphens are used between two-word numbers, between two-word fractions, and in a compound modifier formed from a number and a word.
Example: *We had twenty-two percent of the committee present.*

Beth offers a fifty-minute aerobics class every Saturday.

Two-thirds of the student body will pass the exam.

- hyphens are used at the end of a typed or written line. However, a very short word or one-syllable words should not be hyphenated. Words should be divided between syllables.

Example: *Many people feel that omitting the third step of the procedure will hurt the process for others who may follow.*

Exercise 9.5

Insert dashes and hyphens as needed in the following paragraph.

Tommy's sister in law recently accepted a new job in Nashville. The committee decided to award her the job after taking a vote. Over two thirds of the committee agreed that Karen was the right person for the job. Karen was thrilled when she received the news. She called her in laws to share the news. Thirty minutes later at the insistence of her family she went out to eat to celebrate. Karen made sure to thank the committee for their decision especially the president elect who helped Karen with her resume. Perhaps the best part of her new job is that she will receive a pay raise of around thirty five percent. With her new job, she will be able to travel two or three times a year. When Karen starts her new job, she will be working in the second, third, and fourth floor courtrooms with Judge Wheeler. Karen is glad that her brother in law, who is a lawyer, encouraged her to attend paralegal school.

Apostrophes

What are apostrophes and how are they used?

Apostrophes are used to show possession, in place of eliminated letters in contractions, and to form the plural of abbreviations.

Apostrophes are used to show ownership.

- Tips: Add *'s* to nouns that do not end in *–s*.

Example: *She saw her mother's friend at the grocery store.*

The children's coats are located in the classroom.

Josh's car needs to be washed.

- Add *'s* to singular nouns that end in *–s.*
Example: *Tim Jones's car is not running properly.*

The business's weekly reports are inaccurate.

- Add only an apostrophe to plural nouns that end in *–s.*
Example: *The girls' purses were on the floor.*

Two months' work is what the construction crew lacks.

- Add *'s* to the last word in a compound word or phrase.
Example: *Her brother-in-law's workload is very demanding.*

His mother-in-law's house needs painting.

- Add *'s* to each noun in individual possession.
Example: *Samuel's and Deborah's houses are located in Canterbury subdivision.*
(Note: Samuel and Deborah each own a separate home.)

Krista's and Jen's cars are both red.

- Add *'s* to only the last noun in a group or joint possession.
Example: *Samuel and Deborah's house is located in Canterbury subdivision.*
(Note: Samuel and Deborah own their house together.)

Krista and Jen's car is red.

Apostrophes are used in place of letters in contractions.

- Use an apostrophe in contractions where letters are eliminated.
Example: *It's not fair for the game to start late.*

We can't seem to arrive on time.

- Use an apostrophe to indicate the plural of an abbreviation.
Example: *Ella earned three A's on her report card.*

Jeff earned two M.B.A.'s at two different universities.

Exercise 9.6

Insert apostrophes as needed in the following paragraph.

Jack and Janas house is a beautifully restored Victorian home. They purchased the home at an estate auction last October. Since the house needs some work, they wont move in until summer. Janas dream has always been to own a Victorian home. When Jana was growing up, she lived in a Victorian home in a small town in Kentucky. She loved her parents house and vowed to own a similar type of home someday. In most Victorian homes the bedrooms are smaller than in a standard house, but Jana and Jacks home is a little different. Their childrens bedrooms are just as large as the master bedroom. Also, the house features large closets. Overall, they dont have a lot of work to do on the home before moving, so theyll move during the month of May. Many of Janas neighbors have come by to welcome the new family to the subdivision. Martha and Bob Jones, Jack and Janas next-door neighbors, have already been over to welcome the family. The Jones house is similar to Jack and Janas. They are both southern Victorian homes with beautiful wraparound porches in the front. Jack and Jana know they will enjoy their new home.

Exercise 9.7

Insert apostrophes as needed in the following paragraph.

Carolyn is going to her first job interview tomorrow morning. Since she just graduated from college, she is nervous about interviewing. Dr. Cantrell, her biology professor, told her about the job possibility. Dr. Cantrells advice was to prepare a strong resume, which wasnt difficult for Carolyn to do since she received help from Mr. Richards in the career department. Carolyn graduated with all As with a degree in biology. She hopes to follow in her fathers footsteps and teach high school biology. Carolyns father has tried to advise her in the biology field, but he agrees that the field has changed a lot in the past thirty years. Carolyns mother offered to practice interviewing with her, but Carolyn didnt think that practicing was necessary. She believes that she wont feel too nervous once the interview begins. Carolyns attitude about interviewing has been positive overall. She believes that the right job will come along for her. She hopes that a teaching position will make her happy.

Quotation Marks

What are quotation marks and how are they used?

Quotation marks should be used in the following ways:
- when directly quoting exact words of prose or poetry from a source.

Example: *Sullivan suggests that "The best way to overcome a bad virus is bed rest" (22).*

- when quoting spoken words or dialogue

Example: *"Do you have the time?" asked the older gentleman.*

- when referring to titles of short published works.

Example: *"The Case Against School Violence" by John Larkin*

- when referring to song titles.

Example: *"White Christmas"*

- when indicating technical terms, foreign or translated words, and words meant to be ironic.

Example: *Many people confuse the words "accept" and "except."*

When should quotation marks not be used?

Quotation marks should never be used:
- around slang or clichés.
- around words just to draw attention to them.
- around indirect quotations or paraphrases.

Tips: Commas and periods should be enclosed inside quotation marks. Colons and semicolons should not be enclosed inside quotation marks. Other marks of punctuation may be either inside or outside of quotation marks depending on the function.

Exercise 9.8

Insert quotation marks as needed in the following paragraph.

Mary recently had a dinner party to celebrate Tom's birthday. Several people from her office attended. Since it was a surprise party, Tom was shocked when he opened the front door and saw his friends. His friends shouted, Surprise! Tom laughed and responded, You got me! He was truly surprised. After the guests entered, they began to sing Happy Birthday. Tom's face turned bright red from embarrassment. I am thankful, he said, to have so many wonderful friends who care about me. Tom's friends wanted to make sure that Mary received the credit for putting the whole party together, so his friends began to cheer, Mary, Mary. Mary smiled and said, It was my pleasure to organize this party for Tom since he is such a terrific guy. After the speeches were made, the band played the slow song You Look Wonderful Tonight, and Mary and Tom began to dance. Tom thanked Mary for her hard work and said, I am so proud to have you for my best friend. No one on earth, Tom said, knows me as well as you. Mary blushed, for she has strong feelings for Tom. As the song was coming to an end, Tom lightly kissed Mary's cheek and Mary said, Wow!

Parentheses and Virgules

What are parentheses and how are they used?

Parentheses interrupt a sentence's structure in order to add information. Parentheses and dashes are similar in that both interrupt a sentence's structure to add information, but whereas dashes cause attention to whatever they set off, parentheses try to de-emphasize any additional attention.

Parentheses may be used to set explanations, definitions, and examples apart from other information in a sentence. Parentheses may also be used to enclose numbers or letters in a list of items.

Tips: Commas should always go outside of parentheses. Sometimes brackets are mistakenly used as parentheses. Note: Brackets are used to enclose words that are inserted into quotations to make the wording flow smoothly.

Example: *Though many cities (Nashville, for example) have agreed to start recycling programs, the projects may be halted because of financial resources.*

At today's meeting we will discuss (1) payroll taxes, (2) health benefits, (3) vacation planning, and (4) insurance premiums.

What are virgules and how are they used?

Virgules, also known as slashes, are used when quoting three or fewer lines of poetry to divide one poetic line from another.

Tip: When using a virgule to divide lines of poetry, a space should be left before and after the virgule.

Virgules are also used to separate numerators from denominators in numerical fractions. A space before and after the virgule is not needed with numerical fractions.

Example: *Robert used 1 ½ cups of milk to make his famous homemade cake.*

We used ¾ of the oil for the lawnmower.

Exercise 9.9

Insert parentheses and virgules as needed in the following paragraph.

Jena wanted to make homemade cinnamon rolls for her husband's birthday breakfast.

She called her grandmother for the recipe. Jena's grandmother told her that the secret of

making wonderful cinnamon rolls is to let the dough rise also known as dough growing to

have fluffy results. Jena made sure to follow the recipe exactly as written because last

time she attempted to make them she only used 1 4 cup of yeast instead of 1 2 cup. This

time she followed the recipe exactly, but she was nervous about rolling out the dough.

Her grandmother told her that once the dough had risen she would need to punch the

dough also known as pushing the dough down in order to get the right texture. Jena

divided the dough and took 1 3 of the dough to knead. Jena kneaded the dough also referred to as working the dough for several minutes before rolling the dough. She then stuffed 1 2 of the dough with brown sugar, nuts, and cinnamon before stuffing the other 1 2 of the dough. After she baked the rolls, she frosted the rolls also known as icing the rolls before they cooled. The cinnamon rolls were a huge hit with her family, and her husband said they were the best cinnamon rolls he had ever eaten.

Periods and Question Marks

What are periods and question marks and how are they used?

Periods

Periods are used to mark the end of sentences that are not questions or exclamations. Periods are also used to mark the end of an abbreviation. Periods also mark the barriers in between decimals and in between whole numbers.

Example: *The dinner was postponed due to bad weather.*

The temperature outside is 98.5 degrees

Joshua had 12.5 pages of the manuscript completed.

Question Marks

Question marks are used at the end of a direct question.

Example: *What time does the ceremony begin?*

How many cars need washing?

Exclamation

An exclamation is either a word or a group of words that show strong emotions.

If an exclamation shows mild emotion then it should be set off by a comma. If an exclamation expresses strong emotion then it is set off by an exclamation point. An exclamation point comes at the end of a sound.

Exclamation Points

Exclamation points are used after a word, phrase, or sentence that shows emotion.

Example: *Ouch! The bee sting hurts!*

I am getting married today!

Exercise 9.10

Insert periods, question marks, and exclamation points as needed in the following paragraph.

Jon was at work when he received the news   The phone rang, and when he answered the voice on the other end of the phone said, "Is this Jon, the luckiest man in the world   " Jon then found out that he had won an all expense paid vacation to London "Wow I won " screamed Jon "Yeah " cheered Jon   He was so excited that he called his mother   Jon will leave in a few weeks from Dallas, Tex and will then fly back into New York before driving home to Memphis, Tenn, in a rental car   "How many people entered the contest ", Jon wondered   Out of 2,500 people, Jon won   When the radio station manager brought the plane tickets and the hotel reservations, Jon screamed. "Thank you   Thank you   Thank you   ", Jon cheered   Jon's wife is equally as excited   She has dreamed about taking a European vacation for years   When she heard the news, she began researching London on the Internet   She found information about restaurants and tourist attractions   She also learned the average temperature in Europe in the fall is 70 5 degrees   She is looking forward to taking a dream vacation with her husband

Chapter 10: Fragments

What is a fragment?

A sentence fragment is only part of a sentence that lacks a subject, a verb, or both. Sentence fragments often look like sentences because the first word may be capitalized and the end of the fragment may contain an ending mark of punctuation (period, question mark, exclamation point). There are five common types of fragments: *subordinating word fragments, added-detail fragments, -ing and to fragments,* and *missing-subject or verb fragments.*

Subordinating Word Fragments

What are subordinating word fragments?

Subordinating word fragments occur whenever a sentence begins with a subordinating word. The following words are examples of subordinating words.

Subordinating Words		
after	*although*	*as*
because	*before*	*even if*
even though	*how*	*if*
in order that	*since*	*so that*
that	*though*	*unless*
until	*what*	*when*
where	*whether*	*which*
whatever	*whenever*	*wherever*
whichever	*while*	*who*
whose		

Tips: To correct a subordinating word fragment, either join the fragment to the complete sentence that falls before or after the subordinating word fragment, or rewrite the phrase in a complete sentence.

Example: *Although she is usually on time.* (incorrect)

Although she is usually on time, she was late for the wedding. (correct: the subordinating word fragment is joined to a complete sentence.)

Exercise 10.1

Underline the subordinating word fragments in the following paragraph. Then directly below, rewrite the paragraph correcting the subordinating word fragments.

When Betsy decided to become a nurse. She investigated several nearby colleges in her community. Although she already has a degree in finance. Betsy decided a year after graduating from college that she wanted to become a nurse. Betsy fears that nursing school might be too expensive. Even though she has received a partial scholarship. While Betsy's parents have agreed to help her with expenses. She wants to avoid having to rely on her parents for help. Betsy works part-time at a bank. So that she can earn extra money for books and supplies. Thankfully, her parents still let her live at home. Though she doesn't have to worry about making a house payment. She still tries to give her parents extra money at the end of the month to help with bills. Even though she feels a little guilty for still living at home. Betsy still wants to be a nurse. Her parents are happy to help her in her career choice. Because they know the importance of loving a job. Betsy's father understands her love for nursing. Because he is a nurse. Betsy wants to follow in his footsteps. So that there will be two nurses in the family someday.

Rewrite of Exercise 10.1

_____

_____

_____

_____

_____

_____

_____

_____

_____

_____

_____

_____

Exercise 10.2

Underline the subordinating word fragments in the following paragraph. Then directly below, rewrite the paragraph correcting the subordinating word fragments.

Because of the recent addition of several factories. The town of Spring Hill has grown dramatically. The population doubled. Because of the recent opening of a textile plant. Since the rise in population. The town has recently decided to build another elementary school, doubling the size of the original building. Even though a new middle and high school are also needed. Spring Hill only has enough funding for one new school project this year. The city is also building a brand new city hall building. Unless the funding for this project falls through. Whenever funding is not enough. The townspeople will have to come up with additional ways to fund the project. One recent idea that the city council came up with was to hold a city clean-up auction. The auction will be held on the town square, and any town citizen will be able to auction any goods, with proceeds going to the building fund. Until the idea has passed the city council. The auction is on hold. Although the auction seems to be favored by most Spring Hill citizens. Some townspeople don't believe the money raised will be enough.

Rewrite of Exercise 10.2

_____

_____

_____

_____

_____

_____

_____

_____

_____

_____

_____

Added-Detail Fragments

What are added-detail fragments?

An added-detail fragment does not contain a subject or a verb. Most added-detail fragments often begin with the following words: *also, especially, except, for example, including,* and *such as.*

Tips: An added-detail fragment can be corrected by adding a subject or a verb. Another solution is to add the fragment to the sentence that comes directly before it.

Example: *We were excited about going to Disney World. Especially going to Epcot.* (incorrect)

We were excited about going to Disney World, especially going to Epcot. (correct)

Exercise 10.3

Underline the added-detail fragments in the following paragraph. Then directly below, rewrite the paragraph correcting the added-detail word fragments.

Fred recently won money playing in a local golf tournament. Fred began playing golf in high school but really began enjoying the sport in college. Especially his sophomore year. Fred has been a successful golfer since he plays every other day. Except on Saturdays when he spends time with his family. Fred feels that the game of golf helped him to connect with his father. Especially since his father loved the sport as well. Fred and his father would spend many mornings on the golf course and would talk about their lives. Especially about work and school. Fred's father has introduced him to some famous golfers. Including Jack Nicklaus and Arnold Palmer. Since Fred's father worked in sports sales, he was able to take Fred to several golf charity events a year. Fred will always cherish the golf memories with his father. Especially the weekend trips they would take to different golf courses around the nation. Fred hopes to pass his love of golf on to his own children. Especially his son. Because of his love for the sport, Fred will continue to build a relationship with his children and hopefully his grandchildren.

Rewrite of Exercise 10.3

_____

_____

_____

_____

_____

_____

_____

_____

_____

_____

_____

_____

Exercise 10.4

Underline the added-detail fragments in the following paragraph. Then directly below, rewrite the paragraph correcting the added-detail word fragments.

The most celebrated literary work of the Middle Ages is the epic poem *The Divine Comedy* by the Italian poet Dante Alighieri. Born in Florence in 1265, Dante was involved in politics as well as literature. Especially in writing poetry. Dante was exiled from his home city, never to return. Including the place he was born. *The Divine Comedy* was completed in Ravenna shortly before Dante's death. In the poem, Dante makes numerous references to the politics of his day. Especially to the rivalry between the Guelphs and Ghibellines, two opposing Florentine political parties, that left him in exile from this native city. The influence of Dante's *Divine Comedy* can hardly be exaggerated. It was first mentioned in English by Chaucer in the fourteenth century, and in the twentieth century, it has continued to influence poets such as T.S. Eliot. Dante still continues to influence upcoming writers. Especially poets who are in the beginning stages of their writing careers. Dante will always be remembered for writing *The Divine Comedy*. Including his vivid creativity. *(Arts and Culture: An Introduction to the Humanities by Janetta Rebold Benton and Robert DiYanni, pages 277-279)*

Rewrite of Exercise 10.4

_____

_____

_____

_____

_____

_____

_____

_____

_____

_____

_____

-ing Fragments

What are –ing fragments?

When a word that ends in *–ing* appears at the start (or close to the start) of a clause and stands alone as a sentence, a fragment will usually form.

Tips: Most *–ing* fragments may be corrected when the fragment is attached to the sentence that follows it. A subject may be added while changing the verb to another correct form. If the fragment occurs with the word *being*, then changing the verb to the form of *be* will eliminate the problem.

Example: *She waited in the restaurant. Hoping to see him.* (incorrect)

She waited in the restaurant, hoping to see him. (correct)

Exercise 10.5

Underline the *-ing* fragments in the following paragraph. Then directly below, rewrite the paragraph correcting the *-ing* word fragments.

Henry called for reservations at the new restaurant called Escape. Hoping to be seated before seven o'clock. The new restaurant recently opened. Featuring fresh seafood. Attempting to broaden his taste for different foods. Henry decided to invite his family to join him. Henry has never been a huge seafood fan, but he felt ready to try this restaurant. Hoping he would find something on the menu to his liking. Not realizing that Escape was already on a three-day wait. Henry was told it would be two weeks before he and his family would be able to dine there. Being disappointed. Henry understood that the wait would be long, so he made the reservation for two weeks later. After Henry hung up the phone, he realized that two weeks would be perfect because his mother's birthday would be around the same time. Confirming the reservations with his family. Henry called his mother and told her that going to Escape would be her birthday celebration. She was excited to hear that Henry had already remembered her birthday. Knowing that last year Henry forgot his mother's birthday. She was delighted that he made the reservation.

Rewrite of Exercise 10.5

_____

_____

_____

_____

_____

_____

_____

_____

_____

_____

_____

_____

_____

Exercise 10.6

Underline the *-ing* fragments in the following paragraph. Then directly below, rewrite the paragraph correcting the *-ing* word fragments.

In the early 1890s, the Impressionist style of painting was widely accepted. Challenging the mainstream of art. The Post-Impressionists became the next group of talented artists. The term Post-Impressionist is, in fact, an extremely broad one to define. Meaning "to work in isolation." The Post-Impressionist artists did not band together. Not completely rejecting Impressionism. Post-Impressionists considered Impressionism too objective, too impersonal, and lacking control. They did not think that recording a fleeting moment or portraying atmospheric conditions was sufficient. Placing greater emphasis on composition and form, on the "eternal and immutable," what Baudelaire described as the "other half" of art. The Post-Impressionists worked to control reality, to organize, arrange, and formalize. The Post-Impressionist painters wanted more personal interpretation and expression, greater psychological depth. Shaping the art world as we know it today. The Post-Impressionists were responsible for creating an art movement that is still enjoyed, admired, and imitated in today's artistic movements.

(Arts and Culture: An Introduction to the Humanities by Janetta Rebold Benton and

Robert DiYanni, page 487)

Rewrite of Exercise 10.6

_____

_____

_____

_____

_____

_____

_____

_____

_____

_____

To Fragments

What are *to* fragments?

A *to* fragment occurs when the word *to* appears at or near the start of a clause.

Tip: The easiest way to correct a *to* fragment is to attach the fragment to the sentence that comes before or after it.

Example: *To avoid making my parents angry. I studied for the history exam.* (incorrect)

To avoid making my parents angry, I studied for the history exam. (correct)

Exercise 10.7

Underline the *to* fragments in the following paragraph. Then directly below, rewrite the paragraph correcting the *to* word fragments.

Perhaps the most influential architect of the twentieth century was American Frank Lloyd Wright, a student of Louis Sullivan. To study and design with Sullivan. Wright was fortunate to learn from the best. Early in his career, in the first decade of the twentieth century, he designed what he called "prairie houses." To design his prairie house. Wright embodied the idea that the character of a building must be related to its site and blend with the terrain. To imitate the prairie on which it stands. Wright used shapes related to the surrounding landscape. The Robie House is low and flat, stressing the horizontal as it seems to spread out from its walls. To make the house seem part of the surrounding natural environment. Wright used extensive windows and broad reinforced concrete cantilever overhangs to relate interior and exterior. The brick used to build the house is made from sand and clay from a nearby quarry. To demonstrate his love of natural materials. Wright will be remembered for being an organic architecture. Wright considered his building organic, but his critics said his buildings were sometimes too impersonal. *(Arts and Culture: An Introduction to the Humanities by Janetta Rebold Benton and Robert DiYanni, page 586)*

Rewrite of Exercise 10.7

_____

_____

_____

_____

_____

_____

_____

_____

_____

_____

_____

_____

Exercise 10.8

Underline the *to* fragments in the following paragraph. Then directly below, rewrite the paragraph correcting the *to* word fragments.

Joan recently received a computer for her birthday from her grandchildren. To help her set up the computer. Her grandson, Michael, agreed to spend a few nights at his grandmother's house. Joan was very reluctant. To have a computer in her house. She has never been the type of person to work well with computers. She decided on having a computer installed at her house. To have the ability to e-mail her family members. Since she will now have a computer at home, she will be able to send and receive pictures of her great-grandchildren. To help his grandmother with simple computer tasks. Michael bought Joan a book about how to use everyday functions on a computer. With Michael's help, Joan hopefully will be able to check e-mail, use the word processor features, and create a budget on her computer. Michael has shown his grandmother how to use the computer. To really know how to use all of the features. Michael told his grandmother that it simply takes lots of time and practice. With the help of Michael, Joan did send her first e-mail. To show the latest picture of her great-granddaughter, Hannah. Joan is excited about having the opportunity to communicate with her family in such a quick and efficient way.

Rewrite of Exercise10.8

_____

_____

_____

_____

_____

_____

_____

_____

_____

_____

_____

_____

Missing-Subject Fragments

What is a missing-subject fragment?

Missing-subject fragments occur when a subject is missing from a complete sentence.

Tip: One way to correct a missing-subject fragment is to simply add a subject. Remember a subject may be either a noun or pronoun. Another way to correct a missing-subject fragment is to attach the fragment to the preceding sentence.

Example: *Kara separates clothing. But never does laundry.* (incorrect)

Kara separates clothing, but never does laundry. (correct)

Exercise 10.9

Underline the missing-subject fragments in the following paragraph. Then directly below, rewrite the paragraph correcting the missing-subject fragments.

Candace recently became engaged to her boyfriend of four years. She has begun to prepare for the big day. But is nervous about expenses. Candace's parents agreed to help her with expenses. And hope to help with the planning as well. Candace has decided to have an outdoor wedding. Then a reception under outdoor tents. Jim, Candace's fiancé, agrees with Candace's wedding decisions. He is thrilled that she is taking on the headache of planning this major event. Candace decided on having the wedding in her parents' backyard. But worries about the chance of rain. Candace decided to have a rented room in case her outdoor plans fall through. The caterer agreed to set up under a tent at Candace's parents' home. But will charge extra for setting up outdoors. They have agreed to serve some hot and cold foods. And will serve buffet-style to guests. Finally, the photographer agreed to reserve Candace's wedding date. But needed a small deposit. Candace's mother helped her with the deposit. And helped with other costs as well. Candace feels fortunate to have parents who are willing to help so much.

Rewrite of Exercise 10.9

_____

_____

_____

_____

_____

_____

_____

_____

_____

_____

_____

_____

_____

Exercise 10.10

Underline the missing-subject fragments in the following paragraph. Then directly below, rewrite the paragraph correcting the missing-subject fragments.

Jennifer had a minor fender bender in the parking lot where she works yesterday. A gentleman hit her front fender. But didn't realize he had hit it. Jennifer got out of her car to see the damage. But didn't see who hit her car. The man who hit Jennifer's car saw Jennifer in his rearview mirror. And decided to stop. It was then that Jennifer told him her car had been hit. The man felt terrible about hitting Jennifer's car. But didn't know what to do. Jennifer suggested that they call the police to fill out an incident report. Jennifer made the call on her cell phone. And waited for the police to arrive. When the police officer arrived, he was relieved to discover that no one was hurt. Jennifer said they were lucky. Everyone was fine. Except for the man who had a little pain in his shoulder. The man apologized over and over again for hitting Jennifer. And causing an accident. Jennifer graciously accepted the man's apology. But realized the damage to her car would be expensive. Luckily both Jennifer and the man have the same insurance agent, so they won't have to meet a deductible.

Rewrite of Exercise 10.10

Run-On Sentences

What are run-on sentences?

A run-on sentence happens when two complete sentences or independent clauses are joined together without a break between them. There are two types of run-on sentences: *fused sentences* and *comma splices*.

Example: *Cathryn is on a low-carb diet we ordered pizza for dinner anyway.* (incorrect)

There are several ways to correct run-on sentences.

- A comma and a coordinating conjunction (*and, but, for, or, nor, so, yet*) may be added to join the two complete sentences.

  Example: *Cathryn is on a low-carb diet, but we ordered pizza for dinner anyway.*

- A period may be placed in between the two complete sentences. Tip: Make sure to capitalize the first letter of the word that begins the second complete sentence.

  Example: *Cathryn is on a low-carb diet. We ordered pizza for dinner anyway.*

- A semicolon may be placed in between the two complete sentences. Tip: The first letter of the word that begins the second complete sentence is not capitalized (unless it is the word *I* or is a proper noun) after a semicolon.

  Example: *Cathryn is on a low-carb diet; we ordered pizza for dinner anyway.*

- A transition (such as a conjunction or conjunctive adverb) may be placed in between the two complete sentences. Tip: A comma should be used after the conjunctive adverb.

  Example: *Cathryn is on a low-carb diet; however, we ordered pizza for dinner anyway.*

Fused Sentences

What are fused sentences?

A fused sentence is a type of a run-on sentence in which two complete sentences are fused together without a break (*period, semicolon, comma and conjunction*).

Exercise 11.1

Correct each run-on sentence by inserting a comma and a coordinating conjunction to join the two complete thoughts together.

America's foremost Romantic landscape painter in the first half of the nineteenth century was Thomas Cole. He emigrated from England to the United States at seventeen by 1820, he was working as an itinerant portrait painter. On trips around New York City, Cole sketched and painted the landscape, which quickly became his chief interest his paintings launched what became known as the Hudson River School. With the help of a patron, Cole traveled in Europe between 1829 and 1832. In England, he was impressed by Turner's landscapes in Italy, the classical ruins aroused his interest in a subject that also preoccupied Turner: the course of empire. In the mid-1830s, Cole went on a sketching trip that resulted in *The Oxbow*, which he painted for exhibition at the National Academy of Design in New York. Cole considered it one of his "view" paintings the painting was monumental. The painting shows the top of Mount Holyoke in western Massachusetts, a spectacular oxbow-shaped bend in the Connecticut River appears in the background. Cole contrasts a dense, stormy wilderness to a pastoral valley the fading storm suggests that the wild will eventually give way to the civilized. *(Art History Revised, Second Edition by Marilyn Stokstad, page 960)*

Exercise 11.2

Correct each run-on sentence by inserting a period to seperate the two complete thoughts together. (Remember to capitalize the first letter of the word that begins the sentence.)

A new law has recently been put into place in the state of Tennessee all passengers under the age of four are still required to ride in a car seat. All passengers under the age of nine are now required to ride in a child booster seat this law was passed to ensure the safety of small children over the age of four traveling on Tennessee roads and highways. The new law comes into effect as vehicle standards and lengths of average commutes have changed over the years. Today, more people are commuting longer distances to work this causes more children to ride in vehicles for longer periods of time than twenty or thirty years ago. Another significant difference in vehicle safety today is the installation of car air bags designed to prevent serious injuries during an automobile accident, air bags can sometimes harm a child by deploying from a minor fender bender or accidentally. Recent studies have shown that air bags deploying into the faces of small children, especially in the front seat of a vehicle, cause serious harm to children now the law states that children under the age of nine must ride in booster seats and in the backseats of vehicles to ensure they are protected from injuries sustained in an accident or by air bags this law will hopefully help to eliminate the number of injuries and deaths per year caused by accidents and air bags releasing onto children.

Exercise 11.3

Correct each run-on sentence by inserting a semicolon to join the two complete thoughts together.

In 1848, seven young London artists formed the Pre-Raphaelite Brotherhood in response to what they considered the misguided practices of contemporary British art. Instead of the conventions taught at the Royal Academy, the Pre-Raphaelites advocated a naturalistic approach of early Renaissance masters they concentrated on the Renaissance masters of northern Europe. The use of naturalism is best represented in one of the leaders of the Pre-Raphaelite movement, William Holman Hunt. A well-known painting by Hunt is *The Hireling Shepherd* Hunt painted the landscape portions of the composition outdoors, an innovative approach at the time, leaving space for the figures, which he painted in his London studio. The work depicts a farmhand neglecting his duties to flirt with a woman while pretending to discuss a death's-head moth that he holds in his hand meanwhile, some of his employer's sheep are wandering into an adjacent field, where they become sick or die from eating green corn. Hunt later explained that he meant to satirize pastors who, instead of tending their flock, waste time discussing what he considered irrelevant theological questions the painting can also be seen as a moral lesson on the perils of temptation. The woman is cast as a latter-day Eve, as she feeds an apple—a reference to humankind's fall from grace—to the lamb on her lap and distracts the shepherd from his duty. (*Art History Revised, Second Edition by Marilyn Stokstad, page 977*).

Exercise 11.4

Correct each run-on sentence by inserting a conjunctive adverb or a conjunction and a comma to join the two complete thoughts together.

Cynthia and Tim recently found out they are expecting their first child. When they found out the news, they were so excited they were also somewhat scared. Cynthia is afraid of the unknown, what labor will be like and what to do once she comes home with the baby. They told their doctor that they were a little afraid he told them that fear was a normal emotion to experience when expecting a child. He advised them to take parenting classes at the YMCA the local hospital offers a class specifically designed for first-time parents. Cynthia and Tim enrolled in the class they scheduled a tour of the hospital's maternity ward. They started to feel a little more confident after taking the class and touring the building they still had some fears about what to do when they arrived home with their baby. Tim's mother agreed to stay at their house for the first two weeks Cynthia's mother agreed to stay the following two weeks. Tim decided to take a week's vacation when the baby arrived Cynthia decided to take four months off. While they still feel nervous about having a baby, they are excited and look forward to holding their baby for the first time.

Comma Splices

What are comma splices?

A comma splice is a type of a run-on sentence in which two complete sentences are joined together by a comma.

Exercise 11.5

Correct each comma splice by inserting a coordinating conjunction after the comma to join the two complete thoughts.

Marsha decided to throw a Halloween party for all of her daughter's friends. She invited all of the children in the neighborhood, she invited the parents to attend as well. Since Marsha loves Halloween, she looks forward to having a party in October every year. This year she has decided to have an apple-bobbing contest, she also plans to hang a Halloween piñata for the kids to hit with a broomstick. Katie, Marsha's little girl, has decided to dress up as a princess, Marsha will dress to match her daughter. Marsha has also requested that the neighborhood children dress up as their favorite character or person, she has encouraged their parents to do the same. Marsha also plans to make popcorn balls and caramel apples for all of the children and their parents, she learned how to make Halloween goodies when she was a little girl from her grandmother and mother. She also plans to give each child a Halloween treat bag to be filled with candy. Marsha loves the fall weather and Halloween, she becomes sad when the holiday is over because it means she will have to wait another year to see her beautiful daughter dressed up with her friends once again.

Exercise 11.6

Correct each comma splice by inserting a period to separate the two complete thoughts together. (Remember to capitalize the first letter of the word that begins the sentence.)

Feminist art emerged in the context of the Women's Liberation movement of the late 1960s and early 1970s, a major aim of feminist artists and their allies was increased recognition for the accomplishment of women artists, both past and present. A 1970 survey revealed that although women constituted half of the nation's practicing artists, only 18 percent of commercial New York galleries carried works by women. Of the 143 artists in the 1969 Whitney Annual, one of the country's most prominent exhibitions of the work of living artists, only eight were women, the next year, the newly formed Ad Hoc Committee of Women Artists, disappointed by the lukewarm response of the Whitney's director to their concerns, staged a protest at the opening of the 1970 Annual. To focus more attention on women in the arts, feminist artists began organizing women's cooperative galleries, while feminist art historians wrote in books and journals about women artists and the issues raised by their work, feminist curators and critics promoted the work of both emerging women artists and long-neglected ones, such as Alice Neel, who had her first major museum retrospective at age seventy-four. *(Art History, Revised Second Edition by Marilyn Stokstad, page 1124)*

Exercise 11.7

Correct each comma splice by inserting a semicolon to join the two complete thoughts together.

The town of Mayfield recently declared the last day of summer as community clean-up day, this day will be set aside for community members to clean up around the downtown area. One area that will be cleaned and addressed this year will be the planting of new fall flowers. Also, many merchants will plant seasonal flowers in flower boxes outside their stores, many store owners have also agreed to paint the exterior of their building if needed. The mayor of Mayfield has also agreed to fund a new project for new streetlights, replicas of street lights from the 1950s. The most exciting project scheduled during the clean-up day is the installation of a fountain on the square, the fountain will operate year-round as weather permits. The funding for this project will come from donations and fund-raisers that have been held over the past year, the largest amount of funding will come from the water plant in Mayfield. After the town citizens spend all day cleaning and building, they will hold a square dance and carnival on the square. Everyone in town is looking forward to the big day, they can't wait to celebrate at the dance and carnival in the evening.

Exercise 11.8

Correct each comma splice by inserting a conjunctive adverb or a conjunction after a comma to join the two complete thoughts together.

The English novel as we think of it today came into being during the eighteenth century, it focused on particular people doing particular things in everyday and ordinary circumstances, its popularity among the reading public was enormous. Here were characters like the readers themselves, suddenly elevated to the level of heroes and heroines, admired or despised by all. One of the most important novelists of her day, Jane Austin was the daughter of a clergyman and spent the first twenty-five years of her life at her parents' home in Hampshire, where she wrote her first novel, *Northanger Abbey*, none of these works was actually published until the second decade of the nineteenth century, when Austen was almost forty. She came from a large and affectionate family, her novels reflect a delight in family life, they are essentially social comedies. Above all else, they are about manners, good and bad, they advocate the behavioral norms by which society deemed decent and should operate. They are also deeply romantic books that have marriage as their goal and end, Jane Austen was not so naïve as to believe good marriages could come from alliances built solely on social advantage, it is her scenes showing romantic love, not expedient matrimony, that draw the reader's sympathy. (*Arts and Culture: An Introduction to the Humanities, Second Edition by Janetta Rebold Benton and Robert DiYanni, pages 418-419*)

Exercise 11.9

Correct each comma splice or fused sentence by one of three ways: (1) inserting a conjunctive adverb or a conjunction after a comma, (2) inserting a semicolon, or (3) inserting a period.

James Joyce accomplished for modern fiction what T.S. Eliot did for modern poetry, he changed its direction by introducing startling innovations. Like Eliot, who employed abundant and wide-ranging literary and historical allusions in *The Waste Land*, Joyce, in his monumental *Ulysses*, published in the same year, complicated the texture and structure of his narrative with intricate mythic and literary references. Joyce used a stream of consciousness narrative technique to take readers into the minds of his characters his innovations include shifting abruptly from one character's mind to another; moving from description of an action to a character's response to it; mixing different styles and voices in a single paragraph or sentence; combining events from the past and the present in one passage. Joyce uses stream of consciousness to recreate the early memories of his protagonist partly by imitating the toddler's baby talk and partly by emphasizing the sights, smells, and tastes of a young child's consciousness, despite the modernist style, Joyce still casts his novel as the traditional novel of education, the preferred genre of eighteenth- and nineteenth century novelists. *(Arts and Culture: An Introduction to the Humanities, Second Edition by Janetta Rebold Benton and Robert DiYanni, page 530)*

Exercise 11.10

Correct each comma splice or fused sentence by one of three ways: (1) inserting a conjunctive adverb or a conjunction after a comma, (2) inserting a semicolon, or (3) inserting a period.

July recently marked Sara Fuller's anniversary at work, it has been eight years since she first started working at Pillar and Associates, a New York law firm. Sara began her job at Pillar as a paralegal unsure what she wanted to do as a career since she had trained to be a paralegal, she decided to work in law until she could decide which direction she wanted her life to take. After working at Pillar for a year, Sara decided to return to school, this time she attended law school at night. The program was difficult, but she managed to attend class three nights a week and study every weekend, it took Sara over four years to complete her law degree, she finished with top honors. After finishing law school, Sara was bombarded with offers to work at other law firms, but she felt that Pillar and Associates had treated her so well that she wanted to stay with the firm, even though many offers were for more money, Sara decided to build her career at Pillar. Mr. Pillar was so surprised and pleased that Sara decided to stay that he increased her pay considerably and gave her many wonderful new benefits Sara was thankful to Mr. Pillar and realized that she made the right decision. Today, Sara has recently made partner at the firm the door to the office now reads Pillar, Fuller, and Associates.

Chapter 12: Dangling/Misplaced Modifiers

Dangling Modifiers

What is a dangling modifier?

A dangling modifier is a phrase or clause that does not correctly modify a word(s) in a sentence. A modifying phrase (that contains a verbal) that comes at the beginning of a sentence should be followed by a comma. After the comma, the word that the modifying phrase describes should follow. Modifiers, whether single words, phrases, or clauses, should be directed to the words they modify.

Example: *Opening the window to let some fresh air in, the car swerved into the oncoming lane.* (incorrect: it appears in this sentence that the car instead of the driver opened the window)

When the driver opened the window to let some fresh air in, the car swerved into the oncoming lane. (correct)

Example: *After shopping at the store, presents were wrapped.* (incorrect: it appears in this sentence that presents shopped at the store)

After shopping at the store, I wrapped presents. (correct)

Dangling modifiers are corrected by revising the sentence several ways: (1) adding a noun or pronoun in the subject of the sentence, (2) adding a noun or pronoun in the modifier of the sentence, or (3) adding additional words and rewriting the entire sentence.

Exercise 12.1

Underline the dangling modifiers in the following paragraph.

Jack recently received his second speeding ticket in two months. He was caught driving nine miles over the posted speed limit. While driving quickly, the speed limit sign appeared. Jack tries to be conscious of his speed, but sometimes he gets distracted. Dancing to the music of the radio, the siren loudly blared. When Jack heard the siren, he immediately pulled his car over. After accepting the speeding citation, the car was parked on the side of the road. The officer politely questioned Jack about his careless driving habits. Jack promised to slow down and to attend driving school in lieu of having the citation on his permanent record. While negotiating the hours of driving school, the speeding citation flew out of the window. The police officer grabbed the citation and placed it back in Jack's hands. Immediately after talking to the officer, the car started. Jack shook hands with the officer and thanked him for his courtesy. The officer told Jack to slow down and to drive safely. While waving goodbye, the car traveled on the highway. Hopefully, Jack has learned his lesson.

Exercise 12.2

Dangling modifiers are italicized in the following paragraph. On the spaces provided below, rewrite the paragraph eliminating any dangling modifiers.

When only eight years old, my grandmother took me shopping at Macy's. It was the first time I had ever been to New York. I remember feeling excited seeing the tall skyscrapers for the first time. When I traveled to New York, it was the first time I had ever traveled without my parents. *While fidgeting with the seatbelt,* the airplane landed. I saw my grandmother at the terminal and ran to give her a hug. *Before leaving the airport,* the luggage was missing. We watched the conveyor belt go around and around and finally my luggage appeared. *Being tired,* the chair at the airport lounge looked inviting. My grandmother and I sat down and rested a while before taking a taxi to Macy's. The department store was the biggest store I had ever seen in my life. *Immediately after walking through the door,* my money was gone. I spent most of my money that I had saved on new clothes, shoes, and souvenirs to take home for my family. *Walking around the aisle,* the shelves were almost empty from all the shoppers. I, like many other shoppers, left that day with many shopping bags on my arm. I am thankful that I had the opportunity to travel to spend time with my grandmother. Now as an adult, I am very fond of New York and I try to visit whenever I have the chance.

Rewrite of Exercise 12.2

_____

_____

_____

_____

_____

_____

_____

_____

_____

_____

_____

_____

_____

Exercise 12.3

Write complete sentences in the following paragraph using the italicized modifiers. Remember that each modifier should be followed by a word that it can clearly modify.

The latest consumer reports show that online shopping is one of the most used forms of

shopping today. *Surfing the Internet*, _____

_____. Most people shop online because of convenience. It is estimated

that online shopping saves the average consumer at least two weeks at the mall per year.

*Shopping online,*_____.

One large concern with online shopping is the safety of credit card information. *Monitoring all transactions,* _____. Many online credit card scammers have been caught, but these scammers are creative and dangerous. *To avoid being caught,* _____ _____. Several online businesses have begun monitoring credit card transactions by offering secure online payment services to their customers. *Screening all transactions,* _____.

In the future, punishment for credit card scammers will be harsher, hopefully eliminating the problem altogether.

Exercise 12.4

Underline the dangling modifiers in the following paragraph.

While vacationing in Las Vegas, Nevada, I saw many tourist sites. Strolling down Las Vegas Boulevard, the architecture of the hotels impressed me. We saw hotels that resembled the Eiffel Tower, the Statue of Liberty, and even a castle. The restaurants in Las Vegas were unique as well. At one restaurant they served homemade dinner rolls by throwing them in the air for all the patrons to catch. Being hungry, the rolls looked delicious. I ate four rolls before eating my meal. Another fun activity to do in Las Vegas is to attend several shows. The shows often attract more tourists than the casinos located in every hotel. Watching the Celine Dion concert, the chairs were uncomfortable. However, we were tired so we were glad to have the opportunity to sit for awhile. After walking all day, a concert is soothing. The concert was truly spectacular. After the concert, we stopped at a corner café for coffee and dessert. Immediately after eating dessert, the temperature began to drop. On our walk back to the hotel, it began to rain.

Since we were tired, we decided to wait until the next day to finish touring Las Vegas.

Misplaced Modifiers

What is a misplaced modifier?

A misplaced modifier is a phrase or clause that correctly modifies a word(s), but the modifier is misplaced in the sentence so that it seems to modify something that is not meant to be modified.

The difference between a dangling modifier and a misplaced modifier is that a dangling modifier cannot fit logically into a sentence. A misplaced modifier can logically fit into an existing sentence.

The easiest way to correct a misplaced modifier is to move it from its original position to another part of the sentence where it makes clear, logical sense.

Example: *There is a birthday card sent by Susan in your backpack.* (incorrect)

There is a birthday card in your backpack sent by Susan. (correct)

Exercise 12.5

Underline the misplaced modifiers in the following paragraph.

Miss Thompson recently began teaching the first grade. Teaching has always been Miss Thompson's dream. Miss Thompson has wanted to teach young children since she was in elementary school. Miss Thompson met her class for the first time last Wednesday. She told the children what to expect with a smile. She wanted to teach the children how to read and how to add numbers together. The students gave a welcome card to the principal of the school in a rush. They also gave Miss Thompson flowers on the first day of school. The principal welcomed the students from the main office. The students attended the school early in the morning who wanted breakfast. After breakfast, Miss Thompson read to the students until all the other students arrived. The best part about being in Miss Thompson's class on that day was activity time. She gave out stickers and other prizes wearing a silly hat. Miss Thompson also sang funny songs to the class with a ukulele. She hopes someday that her students will look back at the time spent in her class with fond memories.

Exercise 12.6

Misplaced modifiers are italicized in the following paragraph. On the spaces provided below, rewrite the paragraph eliminating any misplaced modifiers.

Fred recently attended a leadership conference in Birmingham, Alabama. *The conference spokesperson delivered his speech wearing a three-piece suit. The spokesperson emphasized that appearance was important when working in management.*

 Fred joined the leadership conference club managing a district sales office. When Fred first began managing people, he realized that good management requires hard work and skill. *He decided to learn more about management on the day he began his job.* By joining the leadership conference club, Fred feels more confident about his job. He finds that good management doesn't happen instantly. *The spokesperson suggested that building relationships with employees requires time with lots of leadership experience.* From his most recent conference, Fred decided to hold a barbeque to reward his employees' hard work. *He noticed more happiness in the work place walking through the offices.* Fred will continue to create a positive work force. He believes that the key to success is having happy employees.

Rewrite of Exercise 12.6

_____

_____

_____

_____

_____

_____

_____

_____

_____

_____

_____

_____

Exercise 12.7

Several sentences in the following paragraph contain misplaced modifiers. Rewrite the following paragraph below correcting any misplaced modifiers.

Patty recently joined a gardening club in her community. The purpose of the club meetings is for members to discuss their flower and food gardens. Patty was interested in joining because she has planted several rose gardens in her yard. A beautiful flower garden was planted by her brother, Dennis, behind the deck. This is how she began to appreciate flowers. The gardening club sent Patty a membership invitation. Patty accepted the invitation and decided to join the group immediately. While planting her roses, Dennis noticed that the ground seemed very hard. Patty reminded him that it had been several days since it had rained. Patty believes that the secret to growing beautiful roses is a good amount of rain. Since she joined the gardening club, Patty has learned many secrets to growing beautiful roses. Next year, she hopes to enter the fair with confidence. She believes that perhaps her roses might win the coveted first prize ribbon. Patty hopes to continue growing roses for a long time to come.

Rewrite of Exercise 12.7

_____

_____

_____

_____

_____

_____

_____

_____

_____

_____

_____

Exercise 12.8

Underline the misplaced modifiers in the following paragraph.

Clara decided to cook a large Italian dinner for Christmas dinner this year. Since Clara is Italian, she wanted to surprise her parents with the special dinner. She served homemade spaghetti to her parents, loaded with mushrooms and peppers. She also decided to surprise her grandparents with manicotti. Since the trick to making manicotti is to boil the noodles for the proper length of time, she was nervous about creating the Italian feast. After boiling the noodles for nine minutes, Clara added garlic to the sauce. She had never stuffed manicotti noodles before. She called her sister for help. Her sister had cooked several Italian dinners before. Clara brought the manicotti to the table. Her father cheered with excitement. Clara's sister brought spaghetti to the table with fresh herbs and mushrooms. Clara's parents appreciated all of her hard work. Clara found some old pictures in the closet of her mother in the kitchen. She, too, made wonderful Italian dinners when she was younger.

Exercise 12.9

Underline the dangling modifiers and misplaced modifiers in the following paragraph.

Jim and his brother found an old scrapbook in the attic that was dusty. Since they were cleaning the attic, they found lots of boxed pictures and letters. The scrapbook featured pictures of his father that was maroon. The pictures were from holidays, birthday parties, and family vacations. One picture featured a vacation to Yellowstone National Park that was black and white. It was a picture of Jim's father with his parents. He was eight years old in the photo. Jim also found a journal in a box that was handwritten by his grandmother. Jim's grandmother wrote in her journal nearly every day her real life experiences. One entry discussed a surprise party for his grandmother in the journal. Her many friends were invited to attend. Jim also found his father's tuxedo from his wedding day. The tux fit Jim like a glove from his wedding. Jim and his brother laughed at how out of style the jacket appeared. Jim and his brother had a good time looking through lots of different boxes.

Exercise 12.10

Underline the sentences that contain either dangling modifiers or misplaced modifiers in the following paragraph.

Nicki and her mother organized a recent food drive for their community. Nicki attended organizational meetings to develop the program for about eight months. With the help of her mother, she was able to find over 50 volunteers. The volunteers offered to work whenever possible. Nicki organized the drive wearing a food drive T-shirt. When a local newswoman saw Nicki's shirt, she felt it was important to feature Nicki's group on television. The volunteers raised over 75 cases of food for the homeless. Nicki's mother was proud of her accomplishment. After celebrating the victory, the telephone rang. It was the mayor of St. Louis. He called to thank Nicki and her friends for their hard work and consideration. Trying to thank the mayor, her heart pounded. She was nervous talking to the mayor, and she thanked him for taking the time to call. Nicki felt wonderful about the difference she was able to make in the lives of others. She hopes to continue the food drive in the future.

Chapter 13: Parallelism

What is parallelism?

Parallelism (also known as parallel form) occurs when words, phrases, or clauses within a sentence grammatically match.

Example: *Trey loves skiing, exercising, and to run.* (incorrect: *to run* is not parallel with *skiing* and *exercising*).

Trey loves skiing, exercising, and running. (correct)

Example: *She presented a wonderful conference, a delicious lunch, and her reading packet was worthwhile.* (incorrect: *and her reading packet was worthwhile* is not parallel with *a wonderful conference* and *a delicious lunch.*)

She presented a wonderful conference, a delicious lunch, and a worthwhile reading packet. (correct)

Exercise 13.1

Fill in the blanks with a word, phrase, or clause that matches the others in parallel form.

On our vacation to the lake, we plan to ski, to fish, and to _____. Last time we traveled to the lake, we felt somewhat unprepared. We didn't know what to expect, but this time we have packed blankets, carried food, and _____. We hope to do some shopping this trip because many of the stores near the lake offer unique shells, lovely trinkets, and _____. We hope that our mother will leave her work at home. Last time we traveled to the lake, Mom brought reports to be filed, memos to be signed, and _____. Dad says that we will spend more family time together. He has planned to host a cookout, to play some board games, and to _____. Our sister is bringing her puppy to the lake with us. Her puppy is rambunctious, courageous, and _____. He wants to play all the time and my sister plans to let him run around the dock. This trip will be challenging, relaxing, and _____ for our family who all work too much. I plan to bask in the sun, swim in the lake, and

_____. We all agree that we need a vacation.

Exercise 13.2

Fill in the blanks with a word, phrase, or clause that matches the others in parallel form.

Wallington and Associates recently held an annual golf tournament to raise money for

breast cancer awareness. Participants receive a free box of golf balls, a free lunch, and

_____. Thomas Wallington is in charge of the tournament

this year. He has collected donated prizes to give to the winners. The prizes include a

Nike golf club, a Jamaican vacation, and _____. When the

participants arrived at the registration table they were asked to fill out an information

card, to collect a complimentary lunch card, and to_____.

The golf tournament participants include bankers, lawyers, and _____. The

tournament allows participants to meet new people, to eat delicious food, and to _____

_____. At the closing reception, Thomas Wallington's

colleagues congratulated, thanked, and _____ him for all of his work in

organizing the event. Thomas felt relieved, thrilled, and _____ after the

tournament was over. Wallington and Associates raised several thousand dollars for

breast cancer awareness.

Parallelism with Paired Expressions

There are paired expressions that require parallel words, phrases, or clauses to follow
each half of the pair. The following are the most common paired words:
- *neither, nor*
- *either, or*
- *both, and*
- *not only, but also*
- *rather, than*

Example: *He is neither friendly nor angry.*

Either the girl is sick or tired.

Both reading and studying are important skills to learn in college.

The band is not only enjoyable but also loveable.

He would rather ride a horse than drive a bike.

Exercise 13.3

Fill in the blanks with the needed words to form parallel units in the following paragraph.

Karen, a local horse trainer, recently entered her horse in the Kentucky Derby. Neither her assistant horse trainer _____ her assistant veterinarian technician has ever entered a horse in a major contest. They have decided to enter Bread-N-Butter, a beautiful brindle stallion. Bread-N-Butter not only runs quickly _____ runs smoothly. Both the trainer _____ the technician have high hopes for the horse to win. Karen would rather watch from the stands _____ watch from the ground level. This is not only the most exciting race Karen has ever witnessed _____ the most challenging. Karen hopes that Bread-N-Butter will at least finish the race in the top ten. If the horse does finish in the top ten, Karen will still win a substantial amount of prize money. Both courage _____ strength will help the horse win. Karen is either nervous _____ scared because as the race gets closer she is acting weird. While she is nervous for the horse, she plans to enjoy herself at the race.

Exercise 13.4

Fill in the blanks with the needed words to form parallel units in the following paragraph.

Stan decided to purchase season tickets for the Titans this year. Since he lives near Nashville, he decided to show his support for the professional football team. He finds both attending the game _____ loving the sport to be a great way to spend a weekend. He would rather attend ball games _____ attend concerts. He believes that it is money well spent. Stan is not only a football fan _____ a hockey fan. However, he had to decide between buying football tickets or hockey tickets. It was either football _____ hockey. Stan loves to be outdoors, so he decided to buy football tickets. He hopes that next year he will have the money to support both the Titans _____ the Predators. For now, he plans to enjoy all of the Titans' games. Stan's wife is also excited about the opportunity to attend the ball games with her husband. Football season is not only a wonderful time of year _____ a fun time of the season as cooler temperatures linger. Stan believes that supporting the team is his responsibility to help the franchise.

Exercise 13.5

Several phrases or clauses in the following paragraph have items that do not match the others in parallel form. Underline the incorrect phrases and clauses and rewrite the paragraph below on the spaces provided.

Billy and Kellie married last Saturday night. After their lavish wedding, they left for Puerto Rico for their honeymoon. Kellie planned their honeymoon trip and books several fun activities. On Tuesday, they will water ski, power biking, and rock climb. Kellie planned for the couple to have several days of unplanned activities. She hopes they can swim, walk, and relaxing. Towards the end of their trip, Kellie has planned to see a concert and viewing a movie. To prepare for their trip, Kellie packed sunscreen, scheduled tours, and planning events. Billy appreciated the hard work that Kellie put forth to make their trip a dream vacation. They hope to travel every year for their anniversary. Next year they might travel to the Bahamas. If they decide to travel to the Bahamas next June, Kellie will begin planning events, calling travel agents, and book tours. Kellie doesn't mind spending time planning vacations because she wants to make sure that Billy has a relaxing vacation and that their money is well spent.

Rewrite of Exercise 13.5

_____

_____

_____

_____

_____

_____

_____

_____

_____

_____

_____

There are certain rules to follow in capitalizing words or phrases. Below are rules to remember about capitalization.

Beginning Words

- Capitalize the first word in a sentence.

Example: *Pumpkins are for sale at the corner market.*

- Capitalize the first word in lines of poetry.

Example: *The world is too much with us; late and soon,*
Getting and spending, we lay waste our powers:
Little we see in Nature that is ours;
We have given our hearts away, a sordid boon!
(From William Wordsworth "The World is Too Much With Us" from Adventures in the
Human Spirit, Fourth Edition by Philip E. Bishop, page 338)

- Capitalize the first word of items in an outline.

Example: *A. Insurance coverage*
1. Auto insurance
2. Life insurance
3. Property insurance

Proper nouns and adjectives

- Capitalize the names of persons, places, and unique things. Note: Adjectives derived from proper nouns are also capitalized.

Example: *I live in the Green Hills area of Nashville, Tennessee.*

The concert was held at Starwood Amphitheater.

Dolly Parton's theme park, known as Dollywood, brings thousands of visitors a year to Pigeon Forge.

Cool Springs Galleria is my favorite place to shop.

The store is owned by Sara Williams.

- Capitalize brand and trade names of products.

Example: *We own a Maytag dishwasher.* (Tip: dishwasher is not capitalized because it is not considered part of the trade name.)

She owns a Compaq computer and printer.

Tip: Usually the first word following a colon is not capitalized. However, the first word following a colon should be capitalized if the word is a proper noun, consists of two or more sentences, presents a formal rule, begins a list, or requires special emphasis.

Exercise 14.1

Circle each capitalization error in the following paragraph.

Sabrina is currently remodeling her kitchen. she decided to contact an interior designer at holden house designs for help. Joan, the interior designer at holden house, suggested that Sabrina decide on a theme for her kitchen. Since her appliances were the original ones from when the home was built in the 1950s, sabrina decided to update all of the kitchen appliances. Joan went with sabrina to home depot to shop for new appliances. Sabrina chose a maytag refrigerator, a general electric stove, and an amana dishwasher. She decided on new lighting fixtures as well. She plans to paint her kitchen walls blue and accent the walls with yellow fixtures and dishes. joan believes that contrasting colors make a beautiful kitchen. After they have the new appliances installed by the home depot technician, they will shop for accessories at green hills mall. In green hills mall there are several stores that feature wonderful kitchen décor. One store that features unique dishes and linens is pottery barn. Another popular kitchen and home décor store in green hills mall is restoration hardware. Sabrina plans to shop both of these stores to find the best deals for her newly painted kitchen.

Exercise 14.2

Rewrite the following paragraph below on the spaces provided correcting all of the capitalization errors in the following paragraph.

Construction recently began in nashville, tennessee, on the parthenon building. The building is a replica of the ancient building from athens, greece. Located in the west end district of the city, the parthenon has become a tourist site that many people visit each year. Located around the building is centennial park. The park features playground areas, picnic areas, and walking trails. There are many unique restaurants near the park. A restaurant called chu's is one popular asian restaurant that many people frequent. Since vanderbilt university is close to the park, many college students study near the parthenon, and many eat at restaurants such as chu's and jack russell's. Construction is set to be completed by august 2005. While construction is underway, certain sections of the park will be closed. However, city officials agree that different parts of the park will remain open unless construction forces the area to be closed. After the parthenon construction, many more events will be held in the park for students and families.

Rewrite of Exercise 14.2

_____

_____

_____

_____

_____

_____

_____

_____

_____

_____

_____

_____

Acronyms and Abbreviations

- Acronyms are always capitalized.

Example: *DON* (director of nursing)

CPA (certified public accountant)

- Capitalize abbreviations only if the words they represent are normally capitalized.

Tip: An exception in capitalizing abbreviations occurs with the abbreviations of academic degrees. Not all of the letters in abbreviations of academic degrees are capitalized.

Example: *Holly Hunt, Ph.D.*

Lettered and Numbered Items

- Nouns that are followed by numbers or letters are capitalized. Exceptions occur in the case of page, line, size, verse, or paragraph numbers.

Example: *The answer is on page 4, section B.*

The number on the back of the television is Model 22345.

Personal and Professional Titles

- Capitalize titles that represent someone's profession, position, rank, or office when it comes directly before a person's name. However, if a person's title is used in place of his or her name, then the title is usually not capitalized.

Example: *The class will be taught by Dr. Julie Lumpkins.*

The new professor is Colonel Jackson.

The election was won by Senator Bill Miller of Alabama.

I was raised by my Aunt Deborah until I was nine years old.

Our new neighbor is Mrs. Jones.

Economics will be taught by Professor Milligan next semester.

Note: the words *ex, elect, late,* and *former* are not capitalized when combined with a title.

Example: *The former President of the United States is Bill Clinton.*

The late President Ronald Reagan was once a Hollywood actor.

Literary Works

- Titles of published works are almost always capitalized. The main words in the titles of albums, magazines, newspapers, books, films, television shows, and works of art are capitalized. Most of the time, the following parts of speech are not capitalized in a published work title: articles, prepositions, and conjunctions.

Example: *The <u>Daily Journal</u> is the local newspaper in our town.*

The final episode of <u>Friends</u> recently aired.

William Faulkner's novel <u>The Sound and the Fury</u> features the stream of consciousness writing technique.

James Taylor's <u>Copperline</u> was a top selling album in the late 1990s.

I have a subscription to <u>Southern Living</u>.

Exercise 14.3

Circle each capitalization error in the following paragraph.

Abby has begun her christmas shopping early this year. Since she is known for waiting until the last minute, her family was surprised that she was preparing for the holidays in advance. Abby decided to buy her brother a book since he loves to read. She went to barnes and noble booksellers and purchased ernest hemingway's novel *for whom the bell tolls.* Abby's younger sister loves to listen to music, so Abby bought her the latest tim mcgraw album called *set this circus down.* She found the album on sale at tower music. Abby's mother hinted that she wanted a magazine subscription to *better homes and gardens*. Abby already has a subscription to that magazine for herself, and her mother borrows her copies on a regular basis. Abby ordered the *better homes and gardens* subscription on the Internet for her mother. Abby's father, who is the most difficult person to buy for because he doesn't need or want anything, hinted that he wanted a movie collection on tape. Since her father loves all of the *godfather* movies, she decided to buy him the entire *godfather* collection. Abby hopes that her family will enjoy the gifts as much as she enjoyed picking them out.

Exercise 14.4

Circle each capitalization error in the following paragraph.

A new business recently opened in madison, tennessee. mr. and mrs. fuller opened a bookstore right off of the town square. They decided to open a bookstore because they both enjoy reading so much. The bookstore is called clara's treasures, named after mr. and mrs. fuller's granddaughter clara ann. In their store, they sell used and new books. Some of the new books that they include are classics like *brave new world* by aldous huxley and newer books by danielle steele and john grisham. mr. fuller was once an english professor so he knows lots of different book titles. They also offer used books that are still in excellent shape. They purchase used books and sometimes trade used books with their customers. They currently have edgar allen poe's short story collection and william shakespeare's comedy and tragedy collections. They hope to expand their store in the future. They currently have a seating area where a coffee bar could go. For now, they are content with having a beautiful bookstore where people can come to read and relax.

Academic Courses and Degrees

- The names of specific courses are capitalized. When referring to academic subject areas, only the proper nouns are capitalized.

Example: *English 1010*

African-American Literature is offered on Tuesdays this semester.

Leigh took a geology class this semester.

Kellie was the smartest student in her French class.

- The names of academic degrees are usually not capitalized. Sometimes when abbreviated and used with a specific proper noun, the names of academic degrees are capitalized.

Example: *Steven graduated with a bachelor of arts degree from the University of Tennessee.*

George Della, Ph.D. will be the guest lecturer today.

Dates, Specific Places, and Organizations

- Main words in an organization's name are capitalized. Official names of departments and offices in business organizations are capitalized. When a department is referred to by its function because the specific name is not given, then the department name should not be capitalized. The names of bureaus and government agencies and offices are capitalized.

Example: *Drew is a member of the Nashville Toastmasters Club that meets on Fridays.*

The oldest professor in the sociology department is Matt Brantley.

Is Jim still a professor in the Humanities Division?

You need to obtain a new card from the Social Security Office.

The road repairs were forwarded to the Office of Road Superintendent.

Exercise 14.5

Rewrite the following paragraph below on the provided lines correcting all of the capitalization errors in the following paragraph.

Tonia recently joined the nashville chapter of the american red cross. The club meets every other monday to help with blood drives in the area. Tonia became interested in the organization after she had an accident two years ago. After a terrifying car accident, Tonia was in need of a rare blood type. Thanks to friends and family who donated blood, Tonia survived her accident. She decided that joining the nashville chapter of the american red cross would be an excellent way to help other people in dire need of blood, like she was two short years ago. michael givens, m.d., helped tonia during surgery and also introduced her to shana young, the director of the american red cross. Tonia hopes after receiving her degree in biology that she will go to medical school someday. She dreams of helping other people. Perhaps the best part of joining the Club is that she has met many Nurses and Doctors that have given her good advice about attending medical school. She hopes to attend the national american red cross convention in austin, texas, next month.

Rewrite of Exercise 14.5

_____

_____

_____

_____

_____

_____

Geographical Locations

- Traditional names of places are capitalized. These places include: countries, continents, cities, states, towns, streets, roads, seas, rivers, lakes, canals, mountains, valleys, and parks. Nicknames of geographical locations are capitalized.

Tip: Words that indicate direction are not capitalized.

Tip: Celestial bodies are capitalized. However, the words *sun, moon,* and *earth* are not capitalized when unless they are used as specific terms in the solar system. Examples include: *Milky Way, the Big Dipper.*

Example: *We canoed the Duck River yesterday.*

Spring Stone Park is located near our house.

Hannah lives at 2020 Winston Road.

The Panama Canal is an important area for trade.

The Smoky Mountains are a beautiful place to visit in the fall.

Time, Time Periods, Dates, and Specific Events

- The days of the week, months of the year, special events, holidays, and historical time periods are capitalized. Typically, seasons are not capitalized unless combined with a year.

Tip: Centuries and decades are not capitalized.

Example: *On Tuesday, the conference will begin.*

We invite the neighbors over every Halloween for a chili dinner.

Martha, who is carrying twins, is due in October.

Religious and Ethnic References

- References to religion, race, language, and culture are usually capitalized.

Example: *Ebony magazine is designed for an African-American audience.*

Our Romanian neighbor is such a nice person.

We are studying the history of Catholicism in our class.

Exercise 14.6

Rewrite the following paragraph below on the spaces provided correcting all of the capitalization errors in the following paragraph.

Since the expected high temperature today was under 80 degrees, we went to winnington park near our home. Located on hasleberg street, winnington park offers a variety of activities for families to enjoy. The tennessee river runs along the backside of winnington park, and many families enjoy boating. One special feature of the park is tiger lagoon, a man-made lagoon that offers additional activities for families to enjoy. Last march, a saint patrick's day celebration was held at tiger lagoon. Many people came to help celebrate. In spring 2004, the park became a popular place to visit. A children's festival was held. The festival, called the children's playground, featured live concerts, face painting, and magicians. The festival was very well received, and plans for a future festival are underway. The event planners hope to hold the festival at winnington park again in spring 2005.

Rewrite of Exercise 14.6

_____

_____

Chapter 15: Number Usage

There are rules that govern how numerals are used in writing. The most common areas where numerals are used include:
- weights and measures
- decimals, percentages, and fractions
- related numbers
- money
- dates
- clock time and periods of time
- age and anniversaries
- addresses

There are a few general rules about using numbers.

- Numbers zero through nine are written in words, and numbers 10 and above are denoted in figures instead of words.

Example: *We expect 11 people, but we only have enough food for eight.*

- Numbers that begin a sentence must be written in words. Typically, if the number cannot be written in one or two words, then the sentence needs to be revised to eliminate having the number come at the beginning of the sentence.

Example: *Nine people were absent from work today.*

- Numbers with four digits may be written with or without a comma. Tip: Page numbers do not require a comma.

Example: *There were 2,000 butterflies in the museum.*

There were 2000 butterflies in the museum. (Either sentence is correct)

- Longer numbers (over four digits) always take a comma to separate each group of three digits. Tip: When using metric measurements, a space is used in place of a comma.

Example: *The current population is 235,898 people.*

- Most code numbers are written in figures (serial, model numbers).

Example: *The serial number of the television that was stolen was A4385948843.*

- Telephone numbers, social security numbers, and zip codes have traditional numerical formats.

Example: *My telephone number is (224) 765-9849.*

- Rounded numbers in the millions and billions are expressed using both figures and words. If used as an approximate figure, then one million is usually written in words.

Example: *He sold over $7.4 million in real estate last year.*

Movie sales topped one million over the weekend.

- To make a numerical figure plural, the letter *s* should be added with no comma.

Example: *We decorated the gym to resemble the 1950s.*

- If numbers are used in the same context in a given sentence, then all of the numbers should be consistent in how they are written.

Example: *The real estate agent has sold 17 houses, rented 12 apartments, and has leased 2 businesses in the past year.*

Exercise 15.1

Underline the number errors in the following paragraph and then above each error write the correction.

Around 3 years ago, Tom decided to open a golf discount store in his hometown. Before opening the business, Tom had to do some research about the town to determine if the business would do well in a town with a population of 343232 people. A golf course was built in the town in the 1970s, and since that time no golf discount store has been available. Tom discovered that one hundred and twenty-four people are members at Oakland Country Club. He developed a survey for the golf members to discover what their golf needs were. Out of one hundred and twenty-four surveys that were distributed, he received one hundred and four completed surveys. The surveys helped Tom realize that a golf discount store was needed in the town. Tom's next step was to talk with potential investors. Tom talked to 4 different investors to see if any of them had an interest in working on a new project. 2 of the investors showed definite interest in Tom's project. After he found financial backing, Tom searched for the perfect location for the store. He had a choice of 5 different places, but he ultimately decided on the location closest to the golf course. Since he has been in business for 3 years, Tom has experienced great success with his business.

Exercise 15.2

Underline the number errors in the following paragraph and then above each error write the correction.

Mayfield, Kentucky, citizens recently celebrated the town's anniversary. Founded in the 1920s, Mayfield was a booming industrial town. In the 1920s, the town population was 4234 people and today the population has risen to 52392 people. 200 people on average move to the town every year. Michael West, the town mayor, began the 3 day celebration with a morning parade. Many of the citizens were excited to see such a great start to the 3 day celebration. The last time Mayfield, Kentucky had a town festival was in the 1950s. Several town citizens had T-shirts printed to celebrate the festival. The T-shirts were white and featured "Mayfield Festival 2004" on the front of the shirt. Over 10000 shirts were printed for people to buy. Many of the local businesses plan to keep their shops open well past their normal closing time. There are at least fifty-five family-owned businesses in the town of Mayfield. Many stores are also offering special sales to honor the town's celebration. The organizers of the event are thrilled to see that so many people in the town are eager to participate.

Measures and Weights

- Measures and weights are expressed using numerical figures. Tip: Single measurements expressed in two or more units are denoted without commas. (7 feet 10 inches)

Example: *The fish tank holds 7 gallons of water.*

She drives 15 ½ miles to work everyday.

- Page numbers are always written using digits.

Example: *We will begin on page 27 on Monday.*

- When numbers act as an adjective and modify the same noun, digits are normally used. Shorter numbers may be written in words, but a comma should not be used to divide the numbers. (Tip: If two digits are consecutive in the same sentence, a comma may be used to separate the digits to avoid confusion. Example: *In 2000, 24 students graduated with honors.*)

Example: *The portrait needs to be framed in an 11-by-13 frame.*

Dollar Amounts

- Money amounts are always expressed using digits. If a dollar amount is an even, whole-dollar amount, the decimals and zeros are omitted.

Example: *Her new backpack cost $25.75.*

She spent $5 on lunch today.

- Typically the word *cents* is spelled out for amount under $1, unless they appear in a combination with other dollar amounts.

Example: *She spent 46 cents on postage.*

The bill included three charges of $7, $4.25, and $ .54.

- Money amounts that are in the millions or higher are usually rounded with a dollar sign before the digit.

Example: *The hospital renovations were estimated to cost $14.5 million.*

Percentages and Decimals

- Percentages are written in digits followed by the word *percentage*. The percent symbol (%) may be used in tables or when using statistical information.

Example: *She paid 20 percent down on the house she currently owns.*

Student enrollment has increased 12.4 percent in one semester.

- Decimals are usually expressed in figures.

Example: *He received 4.2 points for every correct answer.*

Fractions

- Shorter fractions may be expressed in written words. Make sure to hyphenate between the two written words.

Example: *Two thirds of the kindergarten class was out today because of the flu.*

- Longer awkward fractions or fractions used for technical purposes may be expressed in digits.

Example: *The marathon requires a 5 ¼ mile run.*

Exercise 15.3

Underline the number errors in the following paragraph and then above each error write the correction.

The Obion County Fair began last Thursday night. The current fair admission price is $5.00 for children and $7.00 for adults. This year's fair will feature a different activity every evening during the week. On Monday, a weight and height contest will be featured. Contestants have 2 chances to guess the weight and height of the town's mayor. Last year, people were given an opportunity to guess the school principal's weight and height. My friend Susie paid two dollars to guess the principal's weight. She guessed that he weighed one hundred and twenty pounds and that he was six feet three inches tall. Everyone laughed because the principal weighed nearly double that amount, and he stands at six feet nine inches tall. On Tuesday, a cake walk will be held. Most cakes will be priced at four dollars, and some pies will sell for $2.50. Last year, over ninety-five cakes were delivered to the school gymnasium for the cake walk. This year they hope to double the amount of baked goods. On Wednesday night of the fair, a ring toss contest will be held. Participants will have the opportunity to toss rings around empty 0.5 liter bottles. On Thursday, a beauty pageant will be held to crown Miss Obion County Fair.

At least 1/3 of the town's young ladies enter the pageant. Finally, a concert will be held on Friday night after the two-and-a half-mile marathon is held. They hope to have a lot of visitors attend this year as well.

Exercise 15.4

Underline the number errors in the following paragraph, and then above each error write the correction.

Kara recently decided to get out of debt. Over the past 5 years, she has accrued more than seven hundred and fifty dollars in credit card debt. She recently decided to work hard at paying off her debt because she hopes to buy a home someday instead of continuing to rent an apartment. When looking over her finances, Kara realized that 1/3 of her weekly paycheck goes to debt payment. She was upset when she realized that she pays 19% interest every month for each credit card. When she calculated the math, she discovered that she barely makes the minimum payment of $10.00 per month. At this rate, it will take Kara over 7 years to be completely out of debt. She decided to meet with a financial counselor who suggested that she work on a process called debt snowballing. This means that each month Kara will work on paying off her smallest to largest debt. Her current smallest debt is two hundred dollars and her largest debt is around five hundred and fifty dollars. Her financial counselor estimates that it will take Kara eighteen months to be completely out of debt.

Dates

- Use cardinal numbers when a month and day appear together. (Example: *March 14, 2005*) Use ordinal numbers when expressing days without a month. (Example: *the 17th of every month*)

Tip: Ordinal numbers (first, second, third) may be written in one or two words.

Example: *They will be married on October 10, 2005.*

Her car insurance is automatically withdrawn on the 15th of every month.

Time (Clock)

- Clock time is expressed in digits when used with a.m., p.m., noon, or midnight. If the clock time is an even time, omit the zeros and colon. Noon and midnight may be used with the digit 12.

Example: *The flight arrived at 11:47 a.m.*

The key must be returned by noon on Wednesday.

- Words or digits may be used with the word *o'clock*. Either way is acceptable.

Example: *The train leaves at 2 o'clock* (correct)

The train leaves at two o'clock. (correct)

Time (Periods)

- One or two word periods of time are usually expressed in written word. Digits are used with hours, minutes, and seconds when the number is 10 and above. Written numbers are used with hours, minutes, and seconds when the number is 9 or below.

Example: *Sara's book proposal is due in five days.*

The airplane will arrive at the terminal in 14 minutes.

- When referring to time periods in the business industry, digits are normally used.

Example: *The Wilkins qualified for a 30-year mortgage at 7.25 percent.*

Exercise 15.5

Underline the number errors in the following paragraph and then above each error write the correction.

Kevin will travel the entire month of July for Textel Industries. His traveling itinerary

begins on July second, 2005. On the 2nd, he will travel to Hong Kong to meet with

potential investors. The purpose of the meeting is to talk with Rimco Industry officials

about a possible merger. His flight to Hong Kong is scheduled for nine a.m. and is scheduled to arrive in Los Angeles for a brief layover at two p.m. At four o'clock, he will board another plane for a direct flight to Hong Kong. He should arrive in Hong Kong shortly before midnight. His second flight will take him from Hong Kong to Seoul, Korea. His flight will leave Hong Kong on July five. He is scheduled to arrive in Seoul before noon the following day. Kevin has worked for Textel Industries for eleven years and has been promoted 3 times. He is one of the smartest employees at Textel and hopes to become the company's president someday. After Kevin travels for thirty days, he will have a 2 week vacation. He plans to travel to England on his vacation with his wife, Susan. He hopes to continue traveling for Textel Industries, but he plans to minimize his travel to 1 time a year.

Anniversaries and Ages

- References to anniversaries and ages are usually expressed in written form if they are one to two words. If referring to more than two words, anniversaries and ages are written in numerical digits. If a number is used after a person's name (as an appositive) then it should be written as a numerical digit.

Example: *Deborah turns thirty-six in March.*

The college recently celebrated its 30ᵗʰ anniversary.

The teacher, 25, is the youngest to teach in our department.

Addresses

- References to house numbers are expressed in digits.

Example: *Samantha lives at 1275 East Madison Avenue.*

David's office is located at One Elm Street.

- Street names that are nine or below are expressed in written words. Street names that are 10 and above are written in digits. Ordinal addresses are expressed in numerical digits.

Example: *The grocery store is located on the corner of Third Avenue.*

Cam and his brother live at 2400 22nd Avenue.

- Apartment, box, suite, and route numbers should be expressed in digits.

Example: *We traveled Route 47.*

The medical clinic is located in the Carson Center, Suite 12.

Exercise 15.6

Underline the number errors in the following paragraph and then above each error write the correction.

Penny recently turned 22 in September. Her sister, twenty-four, gave her a surprise birthday party to celebrate. Penny was surprised by all of her friends who came out to see her. Penny's party was held at the country club at 1 Sycamore Drive. The guests were escorted in through the back door, and their cars were parked in a back lot to prevent Penny from being suspicious when she arrived. 28 people attended the party, and Penny saw many friends and family that she had not seen in a long time. Perhaps the best part of the party was the band that Penny's sister hired. The band likes to play music from the 1950s. They have a studio on Twenty-Fourth Avenue. Penny's sister learned about the talented band from her friend Sara, who lives at Thirty-Four Oakhill Drive. Sara hired the band to play at her parents' thirtieth anniversary. Penny's sister was surprised at the relatively low cost that the band charged. Because Sara knows the lead singer of the band, she was able to get Penny's sister a discount. Sara, twenty-two, has a cousin that plays in the band. Penny promises to pay her sister back with a surprise party in a few years. Penny will surprise her sister in 6 years with a surprise 30th birthday party.

Exercise 15.7

Rewrite the following paragraph correcting any number errors on the spaces provided below.

Emma decided to purchase a fish tank to put in the living room of her home. The fish tank she wants to purchase holds four gallons of water. She has wanted a fish tank in her home after visiting her cousin who has a fish tank in her den. Her cousin, who lives at Two Thousand Circle Drive, works at a pet supply store. The store, located on the corner of Twenty-Third Avenue, carries a wide variety to exotic fish. Emma plans to arrive at the store at 10 o'clock in the morning to see about setting up an aquarium. She plans to set the aquarium up by twelve noon. She has also inquired about taking an aquarium class at the local pet store. The purpose of the class is to teach people how to take appropriate care of an aquarium. The next class is scheduled for May Fourteen, Two Thousand and Four. When people buy an aquarium, a manual is given to explain the procedure for cleaning and filling the tank. The manual explains on page twelve how to clean an aquarium. However, Emma still feels like the aquarium class will be helpful for her to take. She wants to make sure that she gives her fish the best possible care.

Rewrite of Exercise 15.7

_____

_____

_____

_____

_____

_____

_____

_____

_____

_____

_____

Exercise 15.8

Rewrite the following paragraph correcting any number errors on the spaces provided below.

A new frame shop recently opened at Fourteen Commerce Drive. Since Joan has worked in the framing business for 5 years, she felt ready to open her own business. She hopes to draw customers in by offering weekly specials. For the 1st week, she plans to offer a special on pre-made frames measuring twenty-four-by-thirty-six inches. She plans to hold an open house on October fourteenth, two thousand and four. At her open house, she plans to offer some door prizes and store giveaways to help promote business. Joan will also offer to frame any size portrait for 1 day only for twenty dollars. She wants to entice people to enter her store. Hopefully, once Joan has earned a customer's business, the customer will continue to do business with her. Joan's husband is very supportive of her business. His law office is located nearby at Twenty Commerce Drive. He has promised to help Joan in any possible way. She is thankful that he is so supportive of her dream to open a new business. Hopefully, Joan will celebrate her thirtieth anniversary of being in business someday.

Rewrite of Exercise 15.8

When should abbreviations be used?

Abbreviations are typically used with personal and professional titles, units of measurements, dates and times, organization names, and addresses.

Personal and Professional Titles

- Personal titles are abbreviated and capitalized.

Tip: After a person's name, *Jr.* and *Sr.* are not set off by commas.

Example: *William Hunter Jr. is an attorney.*

Professional Titles and Academic Degrees

- Professional titles and academic titles that follow a person's name are abbreviated and capitalized.

Tip: Abbreviations of academic degrees require periods. Some professional abbreviations are treated as acronyms and do not require the use of periods. (Examples: certified public accountant = CPA, director of nursing = DON, certified professional secretary = CPS)

Example: *Nick Martin, Ph.D., became our new chancellor.*

Units of Measurements

- Common American units of measurement (distance, length, temperature, weight, and volume) are usually spelled out. Metric units are usually abbreviated. Abbreviations may be used on business forms where there is limited space. If abbreviations are used on business forms, then periods are used after the abbreviations. However, metric units do not require the use of periods.

Example: *My SUV gets 35 mpg on the highway.*

The baby weighed 15 pounds at his last checkup.

The label on the box reads "Net wt. 20.2 oz."

Dates and Times

- The days of the week and months of the year should only be abbreviated on tables, charts, or similar illustrations. Typically, days and months are not abbreviated in everyday writing.

Example: *Her dental appointment is on Tuesday, May 16, 2004.*

- Ante meridiem and post meridiem are abbreviated when used with clock times. They should be written in lower case letters followed by periods without spaces.

Example: *One bus leaves at 9 a.m. and the other leaves at 2 p.m.*

Tip: Note that only one period is used after the *m* at the end of the sentence. Two periods are not needed if the abbreviation ends a sentence.

- American time zones are usually abbreviated.

ST = standard time	DT = daylight-savings time
E = Eastern	C = Central
M = Mountain	P = Pacific

Notice how Eastern becomes Eastern standard time when the abbreviation ST is added to E = EST.

Example: *The plane arrives at 10 o'clock EST.*

Organization Names

- Most business, governmental, military, education, professional, civic, and philanthropic names are abbreviated as acronyms.

Tip: Words such as corporation and incorporated are usually not abbreviated unless part of an official organization's name.

Example: *The FBI has produced a top-ten most wanted criminal list.*

I attended college at MTSU.

Addresses

- Most location designations such as *Avenue, Boulevard, Court, Lane, Place, Road,* and *Street* are usually not abbreviated when referring to addresses. Sometimes a location designation may be abbreviated to save space on a mailing label, for example.

Example: *Donna Kates*
1234 Logan Place
Trenton, KY 49509

Kyle McGregor
4672 Hampton Blvd.
Rochester, NY 08736

- Most state names are abbreviated using two-letter state abbreviations.

Tip: A period is sometimes placed after a state name with two words unless the state name is an official postal service abbreviation.

Example: *Hamington, N.D.*

When mailing a letter to Hamington, the address would not include periods.

1234 Winchester Court
Hamington, ND 46573

- If an address has a word that indicates direction that precedes a street name, then the word is spelled out. If the word that indicates direction follows a street name, then an abbreviation is used.

Exercise 16.1

Circle all of the abbreviation errors that occur in the following paragraph.

Michelle Linton recently added C.P.A. after her name when she passed her certified public accountant examination. Her professor of marketing, Edward Smith, EdD., helped her to prepare for the difficult examination. Since Dr Smith worked as a C.P.A for I.B.M., he knew how to properly prepare for the exam. The exam was held in Tennessee, at 2 o'clock C.S.T. and lasted for more than two days. The exam was given on Apr. 10, 2005, in the Ellingston Building on the campus at T.S.U. Michelle's father, Tom Linton Jr is also an accountant. He earned his C.P.A. in 1985 and has been a top accountant with T.W.A. since 1987. He was proud of his daughter for earning her C.P.A and encouraged her to apply for top accounting jobs. Michelle has decided to apply at several accounting firms in Tennessee. She hopes to work for one particular firm located in Nashville on Waverly Rd. She currently works at a firm on London St., but she wants to work for a larger firm to gain more experience. Many of the country music stars in Nashville, TN, do business with the firm located on Waverly Rd. Michelle hopes to have the

opportunity to work with many of these stars in the future.

Exercise 16.2

Rewrite the paragraph from exercise 16.1 correcting any abbreviation errors.

_____

_____

_____

_____

_____

_____

_____

_____

_____

_____

_____

Exercise 16.3

Circle all of the abbreviation errors that occur in the following paragraph.

Ronald Peters Jr recently announced that two major corporations would merge together in

Jun., 2004. The G.M. Company and Chevrolet have decided to merge in the creation of a

new vehicle. Ronald Peters Jr serves as a manager for product line development. He earned a PhD from U.C.L.A. and has served as a manager for over 17 years. Dr Peter's favorite part of his job is developing exciting new vehicles that will be safe and fun to drive. The new merger promises to be a good one as G.M. and Chevrolet want to create a sporty convertible sedan. Hoping to target both an older and younger clientele, Dr Peters and other managers created the new sedan for people who wanted a convertible but didn't want to sacrifice leg and driving room. The new vehicle should be at automobile dealerships by Aug., 2005. The car will hopefully get around 40 m.p.g on the highway and 35 m.p.g. on city and town roads. Perhaps the best part of the vehicle's sporty new look is that it will include a variety of hot new colors for consumers to choose from. Colors range from indigo blue to pumpkin-spice orange. The car will hopefully become G.M's best selling vehicle in the future.

Exercise 16.4

Rewrite the paragraph from exercise 16.3 correcting any abbreviation errors.

_____

_____

_____

_____

_____

_____

_____

_____

_____

_____

_____

_____

_____

Exercise 16.5

Circle all of the abbreviation errors that occur in the following letter.

                                        Sarah Brown
                                        1200 Oak Rd. Northwest
Aug. 10, 2004   Austin, T.X. 46573

Kyle Hart
372 Armstrong Ln.
Lyle, T.X. 46522

Dear Dr Hart:

It has been brought to our attention that you have inquired about an upcoming seminar to be held in Richmond, Virginia. The seminar will be begin on Sept. 30 and will end on Oct. 4, 2004 on the campus of U.V.A. The seminar will begin promptly every morning at 8 am and will end everyday at 4 pm. Many guest speakers have been invited to the seminar. Some of the invited speakers include Kelly Neelson, EdD, and Patricia Hassleman, PhD.

Dr Neelson will be available to answer questions and will serve as a panel moderator for the entire conference. However, Dr Hassleman will only be able to attend for two days since she must attend another conference in M.E. by the end of the week. Please let me know if you need additional information about the registration process. I will be glad to answer any additional questions you may have. Thank you for your inquiry.

Sincerely,

Sarah Brown, EdD

Program Coordinator

Exercise 16.6

Rewrite the letter from exercise 16.5 correcting any abbreviation errors.

_____

_____

_____

_____

_____

_____

_____

_____

_____

_____

_____

_____

_____

_____

_____

_____

What does troubled word usage mean?

One of the most difficult writing challenges to overcome is distinguishing between words and their usages that have similar phonetic sounds or spellings. Below is a list of some of the most commonly misused and confused words in the English language.

- **accept**

The word *accept* means to receive.

I will accept an apology.

- **advise**

The word *advise* means to give advice. *Advise* is used as a verb.

Carl will advise the students today.

- **affect**

The word *affect* means to change. *Affect* is used as a verb.

The weather will affect our plans.

- **are**

The word *are* is a form of the verb be.

We are planning to attend the concert.

- **buy**

The word *buy* means to purchase.

He will buy a new car today.

- **farther**

The word *farther* means distance.

He works farther from the house than me.

except

The word *except* means to exclude.

Everyone felt sick except Timmy.

advice

The word *advice* means a recommendation. *Advice* is used as a noun.

Carl gave me really good advice today.

effect

The word *effect* means a result of a cause. *Effect* is used as a noun.
Tip: *Effect* may sometimes be used as a verb when it means to bring about.
She had a positive effect on her brother.

our

The word *our* is a pronoun.

Our home was damaged in the storm.

by

The word *by* means before or past.

She works by the lake shore property.

further

The word *further* means in addition.

I will look into the allegations further today.

- **it's**

The word *it's* is a contraction for it is.

It's unlike Cameron to be late for work.

its

The word *its* is a word that shows ownership

The dog hurt its paw climbing the steps.

- **knew**

The word *knew* is the past tense of *know*.

He knew better than to be late.

new

The word *new* means recent.

The new carpet is beautiful.

- **know**

The word *know* means to understand.

We know how the story goes.

no

The word *no* is a negative meaning not acceptable.
He is no longer a member of the team.

- **lose**

The word *lose* means to misplace.
Lose is a verb.

They will lose money if they don't invest.

loose

The word *loose* means not tightly fitting.
Loose is an adjective.

Her dress is too loose since she lost weight.

- **passed**

The word *passed* is a form of the verb *pass*.

He passed his medical entrance exam.

past

The word *past* refers to what has already happened.

In the past, we have always had lunch before the service.

- **principal**

The word *principal* means high in rank.

The principal of our school is Mr. Lee.

principle

The word *principle* means an accepted rule or idea.

Christmas is based on the principle of giving.

- **quiet**

The word *quiet* means silence.

quite

The word *quite* means very.

175

You must be quiet in the library.

- **should, could, would have**

It is correct to use should have, could have, or would have.

We should have arrived earlier.

- **suppose**

The word *suppose* means to guess.

I suppose the chicken will be acceptable.

- **than**

The word *than* is used in comparisons.

He is taller than his brother.

- **their/there**

The word *their* shows possession.

The word *there* means a direction or can begin a thought.

Their car is dirty.
We were there to find new shoes.

- **though**

The word *though* shows a contrast.

Though she is a difficult teacher, we must do our best to pass Algebra.

- **to/too**

The word *to* begins an infinitive and also shows movement.

She was quite friendly with my family.

should, could, would of

People often mistake the terms should of, could of, or would of in place of should have, could have, or would have.

We could have avoided the traffic jam.

supposed to

The phrase *supposed to* means ought to.

He is supposed to wash my car today.

then

The word *then* means afterward or at the time.

She was much heavier then.

they're

The word *they're* is a contraction for *they are.*

They're expecting twins in the fall.

through

The word *through* means finished, in one direction and out the other direction, and by means of.

We will run through the park today.

two

The word *two* refers to the number 2.

176

The word *too* means also.

He walked to the store.
It's too cold in the theater.

Hannah just turned two years old.

- **use**

The word *use* (as a noun) means a practical job. The word *use* (as a verb) means to make use of.

I can't get any use out of this.
May I use your orange highlighter?

used to

The phrase *used to* (as a verb) means to do something in the past. The words *used to* (as an adjective) mean accustomed to.

He used to travel alone.
I got used to being called the baby.

- **weather**

The word *weather* refers to outdoor forecasting.

The weather in Arizona is unusually cold for this time of year.

whether

The word *whether* means an unresolved idea or thought.

Whether or not he gets the job, we will still move to Dallas.

- **were/we're**

The word *were* is the past tense of the verb *are*.

The word *we're* is the contraction of *we are*.

We were traveling to the city when we had a flat tire.

We're going on vacation to Hawaii.

where

The word *where* refers to a location.

Where is the golf course located?

who's	**whose**
The word *who's* is the contraction for who is.	The word *whose* implies possession.
Who's going to the ice cream shop?	*Whose gloves are these?*
your	**you're**
The word *your* implies possession. *Your mother called today.*	The word *you're* is the contraction for *you are.*
	You're going to make a fine doctor someday.

Exercise 17.1

Underline all of the troublesome word errors in the following paragraph.

The seventeenth century in Western civilization was quiet an age defined buy contradictions. The art and music of the seventeenth century we're characterized by a style called the baroque. Through the baroque style took different forms in Europe's nations and colonies, it was shaped by two decisive forces, the Catholic Counter-Reformation and the rise of absolutist monarchy. The resurgent Catholic Church in Spain sponsored a knew type of art of mystical spirituality, while Spanish monarchs patronized the affects of major building projects and talented knew artists. The most important painter of the knew Catholic emotionalism was El Greco who's art technique was influenced by Renaissance techniques. El Greco trained as a painter in Venice and while he was their, he absorbed the lessons of the Titian and the Italian mannerists. Around 1570, he resettled in Toledo, Spain's most religious city, and they're he spent his career painting portraits and religious subjects for Toledo's church. El Greco will be remembered though his art for his invention of a distinctively individual baroque style.

(Adventures in the Human Spirit, Fourth Edition by Philip E. Bishop, page 257.)

Exercise 17.2

Underline all of the troublesome word errors in the following paragraph.

All of the students in Mrs. Knox's class we're nervous about receiving there graded social studies exam. Even through the students studied, they felt as if they didn't no much of the information that Mrs. Knox had on the examination. She gave her class some advise about what to study, but several of the students felt as if they studied the wrong information. Mrs. Knox, buy no means, intended to give a hard examination. She would of prepared her students a little better had she known that her students would not do well. Only nine students past the exam, and Mrs. Knox was so alarmed that she made an appointment to speak with the school principle. He suggested that she give the students another opportunity to be tested on the material. Mrs. Knox agreed and told the principle that she would rather retest the students then to have students unclear about the information. After she past out the exams to the students, she announced that she would hold an optional study session on Friday. A different test would be given on Monday and students would be able to combine there first test scores with they're second. The students were relieved that they were given another opportunity to do well on Mrs. Knox's exam.

Exercise 17.3

Underline all of the troublesome word errors in the following paragraph.

I recently borrowed my husband's car since my car was in the shop. I was surprised buy the mess in his console. He had lots of lose change on the floor and several empty cups and food wrappers. I no he doesn't mean to have such a junky car, but the mess was so

179

disgusting I had trouble driving though all of the clutter. It is quiet a shame to see his brand knew car so littered on the inside. When I came home, I asked him about his filthy car. He apologized and said he should of cleaned the front seat. I told him that I would help him clean the car and wash the outside, to. He appreciated the offer but said he would take the car though a car wash and then have the inside of the car detailed. He is suppose to keep his car clean, but he travels so much for his job that he often has too eat his lunch in the car. Even through he drives a filthy car, I still appreciated the fact that he let me borrow his vehicle. However, next time my car is in the shop, I will rent a car for too or more days.

Exercise 17.4

Underline all of the troublesome word errors in the following paragraph.

Are recent vacation to Florida was ruined due to bad whether. Were excited about traveling to the sunshine state since it is the one state that always has beautiful whether. Unfortunately, we planned our trip for May, a month known for unstable whether in Florida. We should of planned our vacation for the month of July, but we would of missed out on receiving a reduced travel rate. Its difficult to plan a trip so many months in advance. Are travel agent helped us with are plans, but he failed to mention the affects of bad whether. Since it rained during are entire trip, we spent most of are days indoors reading and watching television. We where able to relax and sleep late most days. On several nights, we even cooked dinner in our condo and watched old movies. The best part of the trip was that we where together. Than we discovered that we could shop indoors during the day, so we were able to do some early Christmas shopping. Even through our trip was not what we planned, we were happy to experience so much quite time together. My husband still wishes he could have a partial refund from the travel agent. He says it is the principal of the whole thing, but I just laugh and tell him that weather he believes it or not, it was the best vacation of my life.

Exercise 17.5

Underline all of the troublesome word errors in the following paragraph.

Lee Ann will leave for college in too days. She is nervous about leaving home for the first time. Many of her friends gave her lots of advise about how to survive in college during the first year. Lee Ann excepted her friends' advise and thanked them for helping her to build courage. Lee Ann is buy no means afraid of going to class. She is more afraid of living with a complete stranger. She would of roomed with someone she new, but no one from her high school is attending the same college as she is. Its difficult for Lee Ann to leave her mother because they have been such close friends since Lee Ann was a little girl. Her mother realizes that Lee Ann needs to farther her career goals. Her mother would of liked for Lee Ann to attend a school closer to home, but realizes that the school she chose offers Lee Ann a lot of possibilities in her field of study. The day before she left for school, her high school principle called to wish her good luck and to offer some last minute advise. He told her not to loose sight of her dreams and to work hard to reach her goals. She thanked the principle for calling and felt better about leaving home to begin the next phase of her life.

Chapter 18: Misspelled Words

Common spelling errors occur from time-to-time in academic and professional writing. However, spelling errors may be easily eliminated from writing by following a few simple rules:

- Review lists of commonly misspelled words and study the list often.
- Use a computer spell-checker, but don't rely solely on a spell-checker to eliminate all of your spelling errors. While a spell-checker is helpful, it cannot determine mistypes of one word for another (example: accept for except).
- Circle words that you believe are misspelled in your writing and then look these words up in a dictionary to insure that you don't make the same spelling error again.
- Become familiar with a dictionary. It only takes a few minutes to look a word up in the dictionary and words that are looked up in a dictionary for correct spelling are less likely to be forgotten in the future.
- Try to phonetically sound out words. Recognize the differences between vowel and consonant sounds.

Major Spelling Rules to Remember:

- The letter *i* usually comes before the letter *e*, except after the letter *c*. There are a few exceptions to this rule.
  Example: *deceit*
- When adding an ending to a word that ends in *y*, change the *y* to *i*.
  Example: *lucky, luckier*
- If a word ends with a vowel (*a, e, i, o, u*) and then the letter *y*, the *y* remains constant.
  Example: *payment*
- Words ending with the letter *y* remain constant when adding *ing* to the ending.
  Example: *portraying*
- Suffixes that begin with a vowel (*able, ing, ence, ance*) are added to words by dropping the letter *e* from the root word. Suffixes that begin with a consonant (*ly, ment, less, ness*) are added to words by not dropping the letter *e* from the root word. There are exceptions to this rule. If dropping the letter *e* changes the pronunciation of the word, then the letter *e* must remain.
  Example: *definable, excitement*
- When adding a suffix that begins with a vowel (*ed, ing, er, est*) to a word that has one syllable, double the final consonant if the last three letters of the word has the following pattern: vowel, consonant, vowel.
  Example: *wrap, wrapping*
- When adding a suffix that begins with a vowel (*ed, ing, er, est*) to a word that has more than one syllable, double the final consonant if the last three letters of the word has the following pattern: consonant, vowel, consonant (and the syllabic stress is on the last syllable).

Below is a list of the most commonly misspelled words in the English language.

absence	daughter	intelligence	persistent	shriek
accept	deceit	interest	physically	siege
ache	definite	interfere	picnic	similar
achieve	deposit	interrupt	plausible	sincerely
acknowledge	disastrous	irresistible	pleasant	sophomore
advice	disease	jukebox	possible	succeed
advise	distance	kindergarten	precede	suppress
aisle	doubt	leisure	prefer	telephone
alright	efficient	library	preference	tenant
amateur	eighth	lighting	prejudice	tendency
anxious	emphasis	lightning	prescription	tenth
appearance	emphasize	likely	probably	than
appetite	entrance	livelihood	psychology	then
attempt	environment	loneliness	pursue	theater
attendance	exaggerate	loose	quantity	theatre
autumn	examine	lose	quarter	though
awful	existence	lost	quiet	thousand
bachelor	familiar	magazine	quite	through
beautiful	fascinate	maintain	quit	tomorrow
believe	February	marriage	raise	tournament
beneficial	financial	mathematics	recede	toward
breathe	foreign	medicine	receive	transferred
breath	four	mortgage	recognize	trousers
brilliant	forty	muscle	recommend	truly
bureau	furniture	naturally	relieve	twelfth
business	government	necessary	relief	unanimous
cafeteria	grammar	neither	representative	unusual
candidate	grieve	nickel	resistance	usage
category	guidance	niece	restaurant	vacuum
ceiling	handkerchief	obedience	rhythm	vegetable
cement	harass	obstacle	ridiculous	vengeance
cemetery	height	occasion	safety	view
chief	hospital	occurrence	salary	villain
choose	hundred	omission	scarcely	visitor
chose	hundredth	opinion	scholastic	voice
citizen	husband	optimism	science	weather
column	imitation	ounce	scissors	whether
committed	incredible	outrageous	secretary	Wednesday
conceit	independent	pageant	seize	weight
conscience	instant	pamphlet	separate	weird
conscious	instead	people	sergeant	welcome
cruelty	intelligent	perform	severely	yolk

Exercise 18.1

Underline the misspelled words in the following paragraph and write the correct spelling above each misspelled word.

When Pierre Omidyar had the idea to create a marketplace for the sale of goods for individuals, little did he know the idea would become eBay. Pierre recieved help from cofounder Jeff Skoll and business tycoon Meg Whitman. Whitman came from a bussiness background and brought expereince from companies such as Hasbro. The three had a strong vison for eBay to become a company known for conecting people, not simply as an auction house. eBay has become the most popular form of online person-to-person trading and selling on the Internet. eBay has revoltionized the idea of garage sale selling. Buyers bid on items of intrest from an itemized list of goods that are catagorized by topics. Browsing and bidding for items is free of charge, but sellers have nominal fees to list and promote items for sale. What began as an idea in Pierre Omidyar's living room in 1995 has now grown to a millon dollar business, proving that small dreams can become a large, lucrative reality.

Exercise 18.2

Underline the misspelled words in the following paragraph and write the correct spelling above each misspelled word.

When the alarm clock rang, Katelyn Shaw jumped out of bed. Today would be the first day of kindergarden for Katelyn who turned five last Febuary. Katelyn's mother has probaly been dreading this day for the past five years. As she watched Katelyn put her cloths on and tie her shoes, she felt the urge to cry. Watching her daugter begin her first day of kindergarden was difficult for Mrs. Shaw because it meant Katelyn was growing up. Her husband thought that crying was ridculuous, but he comforted his wife anyway.

He knew this day would be dificult for her. Sevral of Mrs. Shaw's friends were also sad because their daugters were begining their first day of school as well. Katelyn didn't even begin to show signs of saddness. Instead, she ran down the stairs of her house and cheered with excitment. Mrs. Shaw got her camera out to take a picture of Katelyn's first day and her father watched as the school bus pulled up in front of their house. Katelyn's parents walked her to the bus and anxiusly watched her board the bus and wave from the window. Mr. Shaw looked at his wife and said, "Our daugter is growing up." Mrs. Shaw watched as Katelyn waved from the window and she blew a kiss to her daugter.

Exercise 18.3

Underline the misspelled words in the following paragraph and write the correct spelling above each misspelled word.

Linda has decided to purseue a graduate degree after she finishes her bachelor of arts from the University of Tennessee. She is considering the field of pyschology and would like to possibly become a conselor. Linda enjoies talking with peple and helping them to sort though their problems. She is persitent in wanting to further her education. One of her college professors gave her some advise about what graduate programs to purseue. She prefurs to stay in the state of Tennessee, so she has applied at several different state institutions. She has taken a few graduate hours during her last semester at the university, and she hopes that the classes will transfur if she choses to attend another school. She wants to attend a school that will emfasize the importance of counseling. She has received guidence from several different people, but she is also searching for finaical guidence. She would like to apply for several graduate teaching assistence positions. Hopefully, she will be able to make a decicion about where to attend soon.

Exercise 18.4

Underline the misspelled words in the following paragraph and write the correct spelling above each misspelled word.

In ancient Rome, family ties were the bassis of social idenity. The male head of the family, known as the paterfamilias, controled the family's membership and its fortunes. A newborn infant was not legaly a family member until the paterfamilias had reconized the infant and given him or her a name. Unreconized children were sometimes given up for adoption to other families. More comonly, newborns (especially girls) were "exposed," that is, left in the forum to die or be adopted as foundlings. Bearing a family name through adoption was no disadvanage: the young Octavian became Rome's first emperor after he had been adopted by Julius Caesar. Married women enjoyied relative freedoms but still suffered confined socail roles. Roman women accompanied their husbands in public, often to banqets and other public ocasions. As in Greece, they supervised the household, but in Rome, women might also hold and inherit property. Women could divorce their husbands and be divorced, often though a simple public declaration. If her husband died or was sent into exile, a wife would inherit her husband's household and weath. She could entertain suitors, take a lover, or cloister herself in morning, sheltered from the world's hypocrisy. (*Adventures in the Human Spirit, Fourth Edition by Philip E. Bishop, pages 83-84*)

Exercise 18.5

Underline the misspelled words in the following paragraph and write the correct spelling above each misspelled word.

The elements of romantic art and literature arose in response to diferent socail and historical circumstances. Romantic-era poets protested the socail injustices of early industrial soceity, while Mary Wollstonecraft demanded equal rights for women. In

Spain, the painter Goya biterly and pasionately depicted the cruely of war. In England

and North America, romantic authors such as Wordsworth and Emerson saw nature as a

miror of the human imagination. They often imputed special nobility to peple who

seemed unspoled by civilization. The painters Constable and Turner, and members of the

Hudson River School, used new affects of color and light to render the natural

landscape's elusive beaty. Still other romantics sought escape in the past, fostering a

taste for picturesque medieval architecture. As industrail life became more dull and

mechenical, the lure of exotic lands spured the imaginations of architects such as Nash

and painters such as Delacroix and Ingres.

Exercise 18.6

Add *ing* suffixes to the words followed by a blank in the following paragraph. Mark out
any unnecessary letters. Make sure to review the rules of adding suffixes to words that
end in consonant, vowel, consonant.

Cameron will be answer _____ phones for this father today at the law office. Since

Cameron is commit _____ to help his father, he will have a busy day. He is

experience _____ what it is like to work in a law firm, since he is consider

_____ a job in the field of law. He is offer _____ to help his father throughout

the entire summer. Cameron is pretend _____ to be a lawyer so he can get an idea of

what the job entails. His father agrees that observe _____ a lawyer practice is the best

way to learn about the job on a daily basis. Cameron will be take _____ the LSAT

exam to see if he will be accepted at a nearby law school. He has been study _____ for

the exam for over six months now. He is worry _____ about pass _____ the exam, but

his father has been help _____ him prepare almost every night. Cameron will be attempt _____ the exam in October and will be receive _____ his test results in

November. He hates wait_____ for his scores but looks forward to the day when he can

actually stop pretend _____ to be a lawyer and actually be one.

Exercise 18.7

Add *ed* suffixes to the words followed by a blank in the following paragraph. Mark out
or add any additional letters as needed. Make sure to review the rules of adding suffixes
to words that end in consonant, vowel, consonant.

When Jake decide ___ to join the high school baseball team, his parents were very

supportive. Jake always like___ playing little league ball, so he thought he would give

baseball a chance. When he first start___ playing, he bat____ exceptionally well, and his

coach notice___ that he truly had talent. When he finally start ___ to play high school

baseball, it became apparent that Jake had keen skill. Several recruiters from colleges

began to notice his game and travel ___ to watch many of his games. Jake decide ____

to attend a college in Wisconsin on a full pay____ scholarship. His parents hope _____

that he would go to school closer to home, but they understood his decision to achieve his

dreams. Jake is not sure if he will continue to play baseball after college, but he has

enjoy _____ the sport so much he can't imagine his life without playing. For now, he has

decide ____ to concentrate on studying since he plans to attend graduate school.

Exercise 18.8

Underline the misspelled words in the following paragraph.

In Febuary, Jessica will begin an internship at the local hopital. Jessica is intersted in

learning more about the feild of nursing. Since her mother is a nurse, Jessica has always

thoght about becomming a nurse. This internship marks an ocassion for Jessica to learn

more about what a nurse does on a daley basis. She is xcited about having the oportunity to see what many heath care proffesionals do day in and day out. She has also thoght about becomming a pharmcist, so she plans to shadow a pharmcist for a few weeks as well. While she knows she wants to work in the heath care proffesion, she is still unsure of what feild of study to enter. Her mother has been very supportative, offering Jessica some advise about many different options that are avalable to her. One consideration for Jessica is the salry she will make at many of the jobs. Wheter or not she decides to become a nurse, pharmcist, or doctor, her mother will support her in whatever decsion she makes.

How can students/writers learn more about the meaning and use of words?

A good dictionary still serves as the best resource for discovering the meaning and use of words. Dictionaries provide word definitions, pronunciations, spelling and syllabication information, and explain the word's part of speech. Purchasing and becoming familiar with a good dictionary is an important skill not only for academic writing, but all writing that occurs on a daily basis.

What are exact words?

The term *exact words* refers to a writer's choice of words and how those words impact the clarity and meaning of writing.

Specific words refer to individual items in a group.
Example: *Chevrolet, Ford*

General words refer to an overall group.
Example: *car, minivan*

Concrete words identify items or people that can be perceived through the senses.
Example: *red brick house*

Abstract words identify concepts, qualities, and ideas.
Example: *work, attendance*

Writers should use specific and concrete words and details to illustrate points more vividly. General and abstract words are equally important in writing. A good variety of all types of words should be used to make writing stronger and more precise.

What is appropriate language?

Appropriate language means that a writer is using word choices that best suit the needs of the targeted audience. When using appropriate language, a writer should consider the age, gender, geographic location, socioeconomic level, experience level, and ethnicity of the audience.

Tip: While using slang in everyday conversation is not bad, slang should be avoided in academic writing.

What is a cliché?

A cliché is an overused expression. Clichés, while once clever, often become old because of overuse. Try to avoid using clichés in academic writing.

Example: *The math test was easy as pie, but the history test was too hard.* (incorrect)

The math test was easier than the history test. (correct)

The math test was easy, but the history test was too hard. (correct)

Chapter 20: Gender-Neutral Language

What is gender-neutral language?

Gender-neutral language refers to choosing words that do not identify if a person is masculine or feminine. Gender-neutral language is different from the term *sexist language* in the fact that *sexist language* assigns characteristics to people because of their gender.
Example: Sexist language

- Assuming that all doctors are male.
- Assuming that all nurses are female.

How can sexist language be avoided?

Tip: To avoid sexist language, use gender-neutral words instead.

Sexist:	Appropriate:
mankind	*humans*
policemen	*police officer*
saleswoman	*sales person*

Avoiding Sexist Language	
Rules	**Example**
Use a pair of pronouns when writing	*A nurse must complete his or her CPR training.*
Use a plural pronoun when writing.	*Nurses must complete their CPR training.*
Omit gender-specific pronouns.	*Everyone wants his dog to be walked.* *Everyone wants dogs to be walked.*
Avoid gender stereotypes.	*businessperson instead of businessman*

Tip: When writing a letter or addressing a couple, if you use the first name of one person use the first name of the other person as well.

Example: *Mr. Smith and his wife, Samantha, live on Elm Street.* (incorrect)

John and Samantha Smith live on Elm Street. (correct)

Answer Key

Exercise 1.1

     P   **P**   **T**   **PL**
Anthropologists are individuals who travel to little-known corners of the world to study
     P   **PL**   **T**   **T**
exotic peoples or who dig deep into the earth to uncover the fossil remains or the tools
  T   **P**   **T**   **T**
and pots of people who lived long ago. These views indicate how anthropology differs
          T   **P**   **T**   **T**
from other disciplines concerned with humans. Anthropology is broader in scope, both
                      T   **T**   **P**
geographically and historically. Anthropology is concerned with all varieties of people
          PL   **P**   **P**
throughout the world. Anthropologists are also concerned with people who have lived in
  T   **P**
all periods. An anthropologist has not always been global and comprehensive.
                  P   **T**
Traditionally, anthropologists have concentrated on non-Western cultures and left the
 T   **T**   **T**   **T**
study of Western civilization and similar complex societies to other disciplines. In recent
 T   **T**   **T**   **T**
years, this division of labor among the disciplines has begun to disappear. Now
     P   **T**
anthropologists work in other complex societies.

Exercise 1.2

       P   **P**   **C**   **C**
Ludwig van Beethoven was born in 1770 into a family of musicians. Both his
   C   **C**   **C**   **C**   **P**
grandfather and his father were professional musicians in the German town of Bonn.
          C   **C**
Beethoven's grandfather was highly respected, but his father became something of a
 C   **C**   **C**   **C**   **P**
problem at the court because he was an alcoholic. As a teenager, Beethoven was put in
 C   **C**   **C**   **C**   **P**   **C**
charge of the family finances and started a job at the court. In 1790, an important visitor
           P   **P**   **P**
passed through Bonn. Joseph Haydn met the young Beethoven and agreed to mentor him
          P   **P**   **P**   **P**   **P**
when he returned from London to Vienna. In 1792, Beethoven moved to Vienna to study
      C   **P**   **P**   **P**
with the great master. He was much younger than Haydn . In 1802, Beethoven
                      C   **C**   **C**

discovered the tragic <u>truth</u> that was to haunt him. He was going <u>deaf</u>. His <u>disease</u>
                  C   **C**

progressed gradually. It took some <u>years</u> for him to become totally <u>deaf</u>, and there were
C   **C**   **P**   **P**

<u>periods</u> when normal <u>hearing</u> returned. But by <u>1817</u>, <u>Beethoven</u> could not hear a single
C   **C**   **C**   **C**   **C**

<u>note</u>, and his <u>conversations</u> were carried on by <u>means</u> of an ear <u>trumpet</u> and a <u>notebook</u>
           C   **P**   **C**   **C**

slung around his <u>neck</u>. <u>Beethoven</u> could still hear <u>music</u> inside his <u>head</u>.

Exercise 1.3
Answers will vary.

Exercise 1.4
Answers will vary.

Exercise 1.5
                A
My <u>mother</u> always said that "<u>honesty</u> is the best <u>policy</u>." As a <u>child</u>, I remember a few

<u>occasions</u> when I lied to my <u>teacher</u> or to my <u>parents</u>, but I quickly learned that

<u>dishonesty</u> is not so easily forgotten. One <u>day</u>, when I was a <u>teenager</u>, I lied to my

<u>parents</u> about attending a <u>party</u>. I told my <u>mother</u> that I was studying at a friend's <u>house</u>,

but actually I was at a <u>party</u> on the other <u>side</u> of <u>town</u>. On the <u>way</u> to the <u>party</u>, I

accidentally rear-ended a <u>vehicle</u> in front of me. I had to call my <u>father</u> to explain what

had happened. It was the first <u>time</u> I lied to my <u>parents</u> and I was caught. While my
        A   **A**
<u>parents</u> felt <u>sadness</u> and <u>disappointment</u>, they respected me for eventually telling the
                                            A   **A**
<u>truth</u>. Now that I have <u>children</u> of my own, I tell them that "<u>honesty</u> requires <u>integrity</u>."
                A
I will always remember that "<u>honesty</u> is the best <u>policy</u>."

Exercise 1.6
         P   **S**   **S**   **P**
Should <u>teachers</u> go on <u>strike</u>? This <u>question</u> often leads to heated <u>exchanges</u> between
P   **P**   **P**   **P**   **P**   **P**
<u>supporters</u> and <u>opponents</u> of <u>strikes</u>. <u>Strikes</u> may undermine teachers' <u>images</u>. <u>Strikes</u>
                                    P
may alienate middle and upper-class <u>citizens</u> who traditionally have been among public
                P   **P**

education's strongest <u>supporters</u>. Becoming disgusted with <u>strikes</u> could lead these
   P   S   P   P   P
<u>citizens</u> to oppose needed <u>funding</u> for the <u>schools</u>. <u>Supporters</u> of <u>strikes</u> might include
   P   P   P   P   P   P
<u>teachers</u>, <u>politicians</u>, <u>governors-elect</u>, <u>citizens</u> and community <u>leaders</u>. <u>Supporters</u> point
         P   P   P
to <u>obligations</u> many state <u>legislatures</u> have placed on <u>teachers</u> to raise learners'
     P   S   P   P
achievement <u>levels</u> in the <u>absence</u> of new <u>commitments</u> of state <u>revenues</u> to help them get
     S   P   P   P   S
the <u>job</u> done. <u>Proponents</u> of <u>strikes</u> contend that <u>people</u> may talk a good <u>line</u> about the
     S   P   S   S
<u>need</u> to improve <u>schools</u>, but little real <u>action</u> is likely without <u>pressure</u> that can be
                          S
exerted by a <u>strike</u>.

Exercise 1.7

When (student, <u>students</u>) create an oral presentation, they often think first about how they

feel nervous. Preparing a (<u>speech</u>, speeches) takes lots of time and patience, not to

mention confidence. Public speaking is the number one fear of most top (executive,

<u>executives</u>) in the work force. Most company (president, <u>presidents</u>) are more fearful of

public speaking than of heights or even death. Most college speech (professor,

<u>professors</u>) would agree that public speaking is one of the most valuable (class, <u>classes</u>)

that (student, <u>students</u>) take during their college experience. In most public speaking

(course, <u>courses</u>) students present at least four (speech, <u>speeches</u>) per semester.

Sometimes visual aids may help a speaker feel more confident in front of a large

audience. Visual aids may include the use of computer generated slides, (poster board,

<u>poster boards</u>), or flip charts to name a few. Most students who practice making speeches

by using visual aids find that public speaking is easier to successfully accomplish after

they graduate.

Exercise 1.8

Studies have shown that (child/children) who study dance at an early age have better coordination as (adult/adults). A (dancer/dancers) who studies dance or gymnastic strengthens lower muscles in the body. Dancing and gymnastics also help (parent/parents) teach responsibility and discipline. Perhaps the most beneficial part of early dance study is the opportunity for families to interact with one another. A dance (class/classes) allows parents to meet and form friendships. Most (class/classes) are relatively inexpensive for a (child/children). Dance (costume/costumes) are additional items that are not included in most dance instruction fees. An average (costume/costumes) ranges from $30 to $50 depending on material. However, most dance (instructor/instructors) have their (student/students) wear dance outfits at least several times for different performances. Overall, money for dance classes is well spent.

Exercise 1.9

Many people are now aware of industrial pollution. The dumping of industrial wastes into the ground or into rivers, and the spewing of chemicals into the air through smokestacks are examples of pollution. People don't often realize how much humans have altered the environment by the ways they collect and produce food. Irrigation is one consideration. Water can be channeled from rivers. Rainwater can be caught in terraces carved out of hillsides. Ancient water can be pumped up from vast underground reservoirs called aquifers. Much of the water evaporates, leaving behind minerals and salts. The ground becomes salty with more irrigation. Eventually, the soil becomes too salty to grow crops effectively. Too many people raising too many animals can also have serious effects on the environment. People can easily imagine how the possibility of profit might inspire people to try to raise more animals than the land will support. For example, 300 years ago the Great America <u>Desert</u> was a vast grassland. The <u>grassland</u> supported large herds of buffalo, which became exterminated by overhunting. However, not all environmental <u>problems</u> are associated with food production. Food <u>production</u> has been greatly reduced by mankind.

Exercise 1.10

<u>Texan-style line dancing</u> became popular across the United States in the early 1990s. While line dancing has been around for several decades before the 90s, a <u>new salsa style</u> of dancing has since evolved. This <u>quaint new dancing style</u> originates from a mixture of pop and country music. The <u>fancy footwork</u> is just as challenging as traditional country line dancing, but <u>the steps</u> have been freshened up a bit to resemble more of a Latin feel. The <u>growing popularity</u> of this dancing style is due in large part to the fresh new sounds of Latino artists, such as Marc Anthony, Jennifer Lopez, and Enrique Iglesias. Many <u>night clubs</u> and <u>karaoke stages</u> now feature the Latino, top pop sound. <u>Growing interest</u> in Latino music and dancing has not only revolutionized dancing, but has shed some much needed attention to diverse, ethnic performers.

Exercise 2.1

Sociologists are men and women who are endlessly fascinated by human social life and who actively strive to understand why people behave as <u>they</u> do. The topics <u>they</u> study vary from the routines of everyday life to the great transformations that remake <u>our</u> world. Some disciplines are best defined by <u>their</u> subject matter: botanists study plants; political scientists study governments. But sociology is quite different. <u>It</u> is the study of human relationships. The sociological perspective does not focus on individuals in isolation, but focuses on the impact of social forces on human behavior. The sociological

perspective—the way <u>they</u> view social life—has several important qualities: <u>it</u> employs

the scientific method; <u>it</u> encourages people to debunk or be skeptical of many

conventional explanations of social life; <u>it</u> directs <u>our</u> attention to social diversity with a

special emphasis on race and gender, and <u>it</u> displays a strong global orientation.

Exercise 2.2

        P   **P**
When <u>we</u> awoke today, <u>we</u> learned that school was closed because eight inches of snow
       S   **P**   **S**
had fallen. <u>My</u> mother told <u>us</u> that more snow was on the way. <u>My</u> sister was glad that
          S   **S**   **S**
school was cancelled since <u>she</u> had a scheduled math exam. <u>It</u> was difficult for <u>her</u> to
                S   **S**   **S**
prepare for the exam since math is not <u>her</u> best subject. <u>You</u> should see <u>my</u> father trying
   S   **P**   **S**
to tutor <u>her</u> in math. <u>They</u> work on math problems together for hours. <u>My</u> mother said
                                 S
that school would probably be closed for the rest of the week. <u>You</u> should have seen how
   S   **S**   **S**
excited <u>my</u> sister was to hear the news. <u>She</u> jumped up and down and <u>my</u> father started
        S   **P**
to laugh. <u>My</u> mom and dad decided to take the day off from work. <u>They</u> both agreed that
S   **P**   **P**
<u>it</u> was the perfect day to play in the snow. After breakfast, <u>we</u> bundled up in <u>our</u> warmest

clothes and played outside for several hours.

Exercise 2.3

The Tim McGraw concert **<u>that</u>** <u>I</u> attended last night was exciting. <u>I</u> received free tickets

from <u>my</u> sister **<u>who</u>** works for a talent scout. When <u>my</u> sister called to tell <u>me</u> about the

tickets, <u>I</u> couldn't believe <u>it</u>. Since <u>I</u> am a country music fan, <u>I</u> have seen Tim McGraw

perform several times. The song **<u>that</u>** <u>I</u> love most is from his recent album. <u>He</u> sang <u>my</u>

favorite song for <u>his</u> encore performance. The album **<u>that</u>** <u>I</u> think will be <u>his</u> best is due

in stores in a few months. The performer <u>who</u> <u>I</u> believe is one of the hottest country acts today is also very kind. I met <u>him</u> backstage before the show, and <u>he</u> gave <u>me</u> an

autograph. The autograph, **<u>which</u>** <u>I</u> carry in <u>my</u> purse, will be something <u>I</u> will treasure

for many years. The person **<u>who</u>** <u>I</u> appreciate most is <u>my</u> sister for giving <u>me</u> the free

ticket.

Exercise 2.4

<u>My</u> brother and <u>I</u> recently visited the zoo. <u>It</u> was the first time <u>we</u> had spent the entire

                      D

day at any zoo. When <u>we</u> arrived <u>he</u> exclaimed, "look at <u>that</u>!" When <u>I</u> looked, <u>my</u>

                               D

brother was pointing to a group of elephants near the zoo's entrance. <u>Those </u>were

                             D

some of the biggest elephants <u>I</u> had ever seen in <u>my</u> life. <u>These</u> were special elephants

donated from the South African area. The smallest elephant, a four foot tall baby, already

            D

weighed over 150 pounds. <u>This</u> was the smallest, but the cutest animal out of the group.

                               D

<u>We</u> were able to see a live bird show as well. The parrots were <u>my</u> favorite. <u>This</u> is a

                    D

worthwhile show to view. The trainer told <u>us</u> <u>these</u> were the most colorful animals in the

zoo. <u>I</u> plan to visit the zoo again next year.

Exercise 2.5

<u>Who</u> was considered one of the greatest English Baroque poets? Perhaps John Donne

(1572-1631) was just as important to the seventeenth century as William Shakespeare

was to the sixteenth century. <u>What </u>are some of Donne's greatest poetic achievements?

His most famous poem *Death, Be Not Proud*, is an affirmation of the triumph that

salvation wins over death. To <u>whom</u> were his poems addressed? For the most part,

Donne wrote love poems to a woman some speculate was the niece of his most famous

patron. <u>What </u>poems were most popular? His metaphysical poems, poems that are

characterized by jarring associations and comparisons, are his most popular. Later in his writing career, he wrote a series of religious, devotional sonnets that are still widely read and studied in many religions today. <u>What</u> will John Donne always be remembered most for accomplishing? Perhaps his largest writing contribution was that he applied his complex imagery to both sacred and secular themes.

Exercise 2.6

Stan and Jeff recently celebrated the first anniversary of their company's success. They should be proud of <u>themselves</u>. Their computer web design company has become the largest business in the northeastern part of the United States. Stan <u>himself</u> was never a firm believer that the company would be so successful, but Jeff knew the company would be a hit. The computer business <u>itself</u> is a large, growing industry. Stan and Jeff <u>themselves</u> were once college roommates that both majored in computers. They <u>themselves</u> saw a need for a web enhanced design company to handle major corporations' internet advertisement needs. Stan <u>himself</u> admits that a large part of his success is due to Jeff. Jeff even said in a recent magazine interview, "I <u>myself</u> am grateful for the opportunity to work with Stan. You should never doubt <u>yourself</u> if you have a dream." Stan and Jeff's dream has proven to be not only worthwhile, but lucrative as well.

Exercise 2.7

<u>My</u> grandparents recently celebrated <u>their</u> fiftieth wedding anniversary. <u>They</u> love and
    R   **I**
respect <u>each other</u>. <u>Everyone</u> is always saying <u>my</u> grandparents make a wonderful
                                                                 R
couple. <u>My</u> grandfather says the secret to a good relationship is to always love <u>one</u>
R   **I**
<u>another</u>. <u>He</u> credits the longevity of <u>their</u> relationship to good communication. <u>Anyone</u> would agree that <u>my</u> grandparents have good communication between <u>them</u>. <u>They</u> listen

　　　　R　　　　　　　　　　**R**

to one another and support each other in their hopes and dreams. At their fiftieth

　　　　　　　　　　　　　　　　　　　　I

anniversary party, they danced to their song. Everyone agreed that the party was a

　　　　　　　　　　　　　　　　　　　　　　　R

wonderful event. It gave our family the opportunity to visit with one another.

Exercise 2.8

By 1799, ten years after revolution erupted, the French found *their* republic of virtue

inhabited by citizens full of greed and prejudice. Having beheaded a king, the French

were now ready to entrust *their* hard-won liberties to the military hero Napoleon

Bonaparte. Napoleon personified *his* principles of revolution. Napoleon satisfied *his*

middle-class supporters by revising France's legal system and modernizing *its*

government, thus erasing the vestiges of absolute monarchy and aristocratic privilege.

He satisfied *his* own dreams of a French empire by crowning *himself* emperor in 1804

and embarking on a military campaign that devoured virtually all of Western Europe.

With each conquest, Napoleon proclaimed *his* revolutionary values of liberty and

republicanism, infecting Europe with liberal ideas. Napoleon proved a skillful

propagandist for *his* own reign, disguising *his* power and cleverly manipulating the

symbolism of the Revolution.

Exercise 2.9

Numerous museums have fine collections of period and contemporary garments,

particularly the Metropolitan Museum in New York, the Smithsonian Institution in

Washington, D.C., and the Los Angeles County Museum of Art. Also, many (maintain,

maintains) excellent libraries of fashion books and periodicals. Both garments and

sketches (is, are) available for viewing by special request. Everybody (believe, believes)

the Musee des Arts de la Mode in Paris is most impressive. Museums are important for up and coming designers to visit. Many (<u>exhibit</u>, exhibits) vast collections of costumes and periodicals. Some (<u>feature</u>, features) a permanent show for visitors to see. No one (know, <u>knows</u>) the importance of fashion on the world of architecture, history, and interior design. Many (is, <u>are</u>) directly related to the fashion industry. Few in the fashion industry (<u>determine</u>, determines) the fashion designs year to year. These designers are the top in the industry.

Exercise 2.10

<u>One</u> of my nephews has <u>his</u> own car. He received the car as a prize on a game show last week. <u>Each</u> of the game show winners accepted <u>his</u> prize before leaving California. My cousins also attended the taping of the show. <u>Neither</u> of them was present when <u>his</u> name was called. They were eating lunch nearby. <u>One</u> of the audience members had <u>his</u> lunch inside the building to ensure he would hear his name called. <u>Each</u> of the contestants wanted <u>his</u> turn at winning the grand prize. Luckily, my nephew was the winner. Everyone at the game show was excited for my nephew. He chose the car he wanted to drive home. <u>Each</u> of the cars had <u>its</u> special features. However, my nephew had always wanted a Ford, so he chose a Mustang convertible.

Exercise 2.11

When (<u>I</u>, me) was younger, my family and (<u>I</u>, me) always watched the Olympic games on television. My father believed that Olympic winners were true heroes to be admired. (<u>We</u>, Us) watched the games, and we ranked the winners on notebook paper. My mother made popcorn for (we, <u>us</u>). My sister and (<u>I</u>, me) were allowed to stay up later than usual to watch all of the nighttime events. My favorite was the swim competition, but my sister's favorite was the gymnastics competition. My parents loved all of the games. We watched (they, <u>them</u>) discuss the importance of good sportsmanship and the commonality

between the different nations. My parents disagreed on the outcome of the medals. Mom

laughed at Dad, and she claimed that (<u>he</u>, him) was too easy of a judge. Dad always said

that Mom would be too difficult if (<u>she</u>, her) was to actually judge. Looking back, some

of my favorite memories of watching television were seeing the Olympics every four

years.

Exercise 2.12

My first day of college was not what <u>I</u> imagined it would be. When <u>I</u> went

to register for classes, all of <u>them</u> were full. I asked my advisor about other classes I

could take. <u>He</u> told <u>me</u> to join a class waiting list in case other students did

not attend the first day. Many students will not attend the first day and professors then

allow <u>their</u> spots to be filled. I was placed on a class waiting list and then <u>I</u>

showed up on the first day. My professors allowed <u>me</u> to add <u>their</u> classes, so

my advisor's advice worked. <u>I</u> was lucky to get the classes needed to graduate. Not

all students that try to add classes late are as lucky as <u>me</u>.

Exercise 2.13

What exactly does a designer do? No two designers will answer this question in the same

way because <u>they</u> do so many different jobs. As a rule, <u>they</u> work for a wholesale apparel

house or manufacturer. <u>You</u> might not realize, but a designer works well over 40 hours a

week. The head of the company, or chief operating office, directs the overall operations

that allow the company to function. <u>She</u> supervises the sales personnel as well as the

functions considered to be the business side of the operation. In addition, depending on

the size of the company, <u>they</u> may work closely with the designer in choosing fabrics and finalizing the styles selected for the line. Steve Maddox, a famous designer, has worked in the industry for many years. <u>His</u> clothing line has been popular for several decades. Many that have worked with <u>him</u>, believe <u>he</u> is truly today's hottest designer.

Exercise 2.14

Recently, four downtown business owners were rewarded for their financial support to the local humane association. Joseph Smith is the one (<u>who</u>, whom) is responsible for donating the most time and money. Raising over $15,000, Mr. Smith credited his office assistant. She helped in raising money and making phone calls to solicit volunteer help. Mr. Smith's employees held an interoffice contest in which a silent auction was held. (<u>Whoever</u>, Whomever) was the highest bidder received the auctioned items. The auction raised over $5,000 total. Mr. Smith felt his business associate, Mr. Thompson, was a big help as well. Mr. Thompson was the person (<u>who</u>, whom) organized volunteer help in the community. (<u>Whoever</u>, Whomever) could help after work hours was encouraged to join the animal humane cause. When Mr. Smith received his award, he exclaimed, "This award will also go to (whoever, <u>whomever</u>) helped along the way." The event was such a success.

Exercise 2.15

Miss Tennessee was the contestant (who, <u>whom</u>) the judges selected as the new Miss America. When her name was called, she cried tears of joy. The new Miss America thanked (<u>whoever</u>, whomever) had chosen her for this important role. To (who, <u>whom</u>) will she grant her first interview as the new Miss America? She will speak on the *Today Show* to (whoever, <u>whomever</u>) will fill in for the vacationing Katie Couric. This Miss America will make history as the youngest contestant to wear the crown. (<u>Who</u>/Whom) was the youngest contestant to date to wear the crown? Miss Alabama, who became Miss America in 1957, was the youngest to wear the crown at age 19. The new Miss America becomes the youngest to earn the crown as she just turned 19 two days ago. She credits her grandmother for her success.

Exercise 3.1

Richard Wagner (1813-1883) <u>was</u> a flamboyant, artistic egoist whose life had enough passion, betrayal, triumph and failure to be an opera itself. He <u>blamed</u> his initial musical failures on opera's commercialism and finally <u>convinced</u> a mad Bavarian king to finance his operas at the lavish Festival House at Bayreuth. Throughout his career, he <u>engaged</u> in titanic love affairs with the wives of patrons and musical colleagues. Wagner's musical ideas <u>exceeded</u> even the extravagance of his life. He <u>envisioned</u> opera as the synthesis of all the arts—myth, music, poetry, drama, and pictorial design. Wagner <u>believed</u> that he <u>had</u> to control everything about his operas: the text, music, design, and production. He <u>rejected</u> the trivial plots of conventional opera and <u>turned</u> instead to Germanic myth and legend.

Exercise 3.2
Answers will vary.

Exercise 3.3

Recently, there **has been** a growing popularity with reality television shows. Reality shows **seem** to air on every major network. In the 1970s, television family sitcoms **were** popular. Shows like *All in the Family* and *The Jeffersons* **were** favorites in many American households. In the 1980s, television dramas **were** the new favorites among avid television viewers. *Dallas* and *Dynasty* <u>received</u> the highest ratings week after week. Viewers <u>tuned</u> in to discover what shady, but powerful characters like J.R. Ewing or Alexis Colby <u>were doing</u> in their plush homes and high-rise offices. While television dramas <u>remained</u> popular throughout the decade, the 1990s <u>brought</u> about a new revolution in television. The coined phrase "water cooler show" <u>described</u> hits like *Seinfeld* and *Friends*. These sitcoms **seemed** to generate talk around every office water cooler in the nation. Finally in 2000, the overabundance of reality shows <u>hit</u> the scene. Shows like *The Bachelor* and *Survivor* <u>have become</u> the newest reality sensation.

Exercise 3.4

Today the topic of film and literature <u>is</u> more lively than ever before, both inside and outside of classrooms. There <u>are</u> many reasons: From the cultural questioning of artistic hierarchies and canons to the increased mixing of different media in both literary and film practices, film and literature clash against and invigorate each other in more and more complicated fashions. Film and literature <u>are</u> two disciplines that work well with one another. One of the consequences of this renewed interest <u>is</u> that the intersections of film and literature need to be viewed from an unprecedented variety of angles. Novels, dramatic literature, short stories, and poetry <u>are</u> all intertwined with film. It <u>seems</u> that film is directly connected with any form of literature. Film <u>was</u> once only thought of as a mere form of entertainment. Today, film <u>seems</u> to encompass more than entertainment. Film <u>is</u> an important part of American lifestyle.

Exercise 3.5

In the 1880s and 90s, several important artists intensified the impressionists' break with tradition. These artists <u>will</u> always remain known as post-impressionists because their works extended impressionist techniques in different directions. The most important post-impressionists, Georges Seurat, Paul Cezanne, Paul Gauguin, and Vincent van

Gogh, <u>shall</u> never lose their popularity. Georges Seurat <u>was</u> the closest in technique to Monet's pure impressionism, depicting scenes of urban life and applying unmixed colors directly to the canvas. Seurat's most famous picture, *Sunday Afternoon on the Island of LaGrande Jatte*, <u>may</u> serve as the best example of the pointillist style. The scene <u>should be</u> seen as a typical scene of Parisian modernity. <u>Had</u> an impressionist painted this scene, we <u>might</u> <u>have</u> expected the casual manner of Renoir. Instead, Seurat creates a subtle pattern of parallel lines and interlocking shapes. The pattern <u>is</u> created in the repeated shapes of the umbrellas, the ladies' bustles and bodices, and the gentlemen's hats and canes. Each figure <u>should be</u> treated with scientific dispassion and precision, flattened and contained by Seurat's formulas.

Exercise 3.6

I <u>will</u> always remember my years in college. It <u>may have</u> been the most exciting time of my life. I was fortunate to attend a smaller university. I became involved in many student activities, and I met many friends. I never thought I <u>would</u> enjoy college. Actually, I <u>was</u> determined not to give university life a chance. I remember being angry at my parents for sending me to school, forcing me to leave my high school friends behind. I <u>have</u> never regretted attending college. I hate to admit that my parents were correct. Some of my closest friends I met while I attended college. The key to making new friends in a new area <u>is</u> to become involved. I still try to make friends any time I move to a new community. Perhaps my favorite part of college is the memories. I <u>will</u> always remember the friendships and the opportunities give to me. I appreciate my parents' support while I attended college. I hope to help my children in the same way someday when they attend a university or college of their choice.

Exercise 3.7

   I   **I**   **T**

We <u>swam</u>. Since it <u>was</u> over 95 degrees, we <u>stayed</u> all day. We <u>applied</u>

                                   I

sunscreen on our faces several times. Even though the sky <u>appeared</u> overcast, we <u>were</u>

                             I   **I**

afraid of becoming sunburned. After lunch, we <u>relaxed</u>. We <u>floated</u>.

                                 T

Since it <u>was</u> so hot outside, the wave pool <u>was</u> crowded. We <u>visited</u> the putt-putt golf

                            I   **T**

course at the entrance of the water park. We <u>played</u>. I <u>won</u> two games and my brother

  T   **I**   **I**

<u>won</u> one. We also <u>rode</u> on an inner tube down the lazy river. I <u>floated</u>. My brother

  I   **T**

<u>swam</u>. Our parents just <u>relaxed</u> by the poolside. Perhaps the highlight of the entire day

                              T

<u>was</u> the late evening fireworks show. We <u>watched</u> fireworks for about an hour. The

fireworks <u>were</u> beautiful and the show <u>was</u> choreographed to music. On the ride home,

we <u>were</u> so exhausted from the day's events that there <u>was</u> complete silence in the car.

                   I

My brother and I <u>slept</u>.

Exercise 3.8

Michael (enjoy, <u>enjoyed</u>) the concert last night. His favorite band (perform, <u>performed</u>)

for three hours. The press has (call, <u>called</u>) the show an exciting performance for all

ages. Michael and Christy (receive, <u>received</u>) free tickets from a radio contest. They

correctly (answer, <u>answered</u>) a trivia question about the band. After the concert, they

(introduce, <u>introduced</u>) themselves to the lead singer backstage. The band (ask, <u>asked</u>)

Michael and Christy to join them for an autograph session. Christy (call, <u>called</u>) her

mother to tell her the exciting news. Michael and Christy (vow, <u>vowed</u>) to remain

members of the band's fan club for life. The band (agree, <u>agreed</u>) that Michael and

Christy were devoted fans. Michael's friends were (amaze, <u>amazed</u>) at how lucky he was

to spend time with the hottest band on the charts. Michael and Christy (contact, contacted) the radio station to thank them for the free tickets. They (explain, <u>explained</u>) to the station manager that the concert had been the highlight of their entire summer.

Exercise 3.9

The senior class president was (chose, <u>chosen</u>) last Friday. Elections were held for one week and over two hundred classmates voted. The presidential winner (send, <u>sent</u>) each classmate a thank you note and his running mate publicly thanked everyone that had voted for him. Jack will be (swore, <u>sworn</u>) in as the new class president on Monday. He had (got, <u>gotten</u>) the idea to run for office from his brother, a former senior class president. They (spend, <u>spent</u>) many hours making campaign signs together. Jack (know, <u>knew</u>) that becoming class president would not be easy since his running mate was the class valedictorian. However, Jack (feel, <u>felt</u>) that running for office was important whether he (win, <u>won</u>) or not. During the final debate before final voting, Jack (<u>went</u>, gone) to the podium and (freeze, <u>froze</u>) in front of everyone. He was nervous. After a few minutes, he laughed and said he needed to start over. The crowd cheered because he was honest about his nervousness. Since finding out that he is the new class president, Jack has already (began, <u>begun</u>) to make significant changes.

Exercise 3.10

We (was, <u>were</u>) traveling to Georgia last summer when we took a detour. We (<u>had</u>, has) been to Georgia before, but we (<u>had</u>, has) never taken back roads. We (does, <u>did</u>) get lost a few times, but luckily we stopped to ask for directions. When we travel, we (<u>do</u>, does) read maps, but on this trip a map (<u>was</u>, were) no help. On our detour, we traveled to a flea market where we (was, <u>were</u>) able to purchase souvenirs. The flea market (<u>is</u>, were) an ideal place to shop since most vendors will let patrons bargain shop. We (has, <u>had</u>)

shopped for three hours when we became hungry. Some local townspeople told us about a restaurant. We (do, <u>did</u>) go to the restaurant and discovered wonderful cuisine. We hope to visit next year. It was amazing how a simple detour allowed us to explore new territory.

Exercise 4.1

    S   **S**

S
<u>Sculpture</u> is the shaping of material into a three-dimensional <u>work</u> of art. Like painting,

S   **S**
it <u>is</u> one of the most ancient arts. Sculpture can take virtually any <u>shape</u> and can be

                   S   **S**
crafted in virtually any <u>material</u>. This art form <u>ranges</u> from the exquisitely proportioned

                                        P
stone of ancient Greek statuary to the playfully modern <u>combinations</u> of Alexander

                                      S
Calder. A full-round sculpture is shaped so that the work <u>stands</u> freely and can be seen

               P
from all sides. Full-round <u>statues</u> of human figures may be on any scale, from small

P
<u>figurines</u> to colossal statues. Relief sculpture is attached to a wall or panel and is

                         S   **P**
commonly used to decorate a <u>building</u>, as in the reliefs on Lorenzo Ghiberti's <u>panels</u> for

                                      S
the east doors on the Florence Baptistery and the sculptural <u>decoration</u> on the Gothic cathedral at Chartres, France.

Exercise 4.2

<u>Sara</u> (enjoy, <u>enjoys</u>) cooking classes at the local community center. <u>She</u> (take, <u>takes</u>) the class every Saturday with her mother. In the class, <u>they</u> (<u>learn</u>, learns) to make muffins, knead dough, and sauté vegetables. <u>They</u> (<u>cook</u>, cooks) desserts together as well. For part of their weekly assignments, <u>Sara</u> and her <u>mother</u> (<u>create</u>, creates) new gourmet dishes. Last week, the duo created a fresh baked apple cobbler. Sometimes Sara and her mother (make, makes) appetizers. Sara (plan, plans) the appetizer and her mother actually (create, creates) the dish.. <u>Sara</u> and her <u>mother</u> (<u>enjoy</u>, enjoys) spending time

together planning and creating their culinary masterpieces. <u>Sara</u> (love, <u>loves</u>) the

opportunity to learn cooking tips from her mother. Her <u>mother</u> (appreciate, <u>appreciates</u>)

the time <u>she</u> (spend, <u>spends</u>) with her daughter in the kitchen.

Exercise 4.3

<u>Nashville</u> and <u>Memphis</u> (is, <u>are</u>) two fun cities to visit. <u>Logan</u> and <u>Michael</u> (<u>travel</u>,

travels) to Nashville every fall and to Memphis every summer. <u>Logan</u> or <u>Michael</u> (<u>has</u>,

have) visited more than three times in the past two years. <u>Either</u> Logan or Michael

(drive, <u>drives</u>) each year. <u>Nashville</u> and <u>Memphis</u> (<u>offer</u>, offers) visitors a lot to do.

<u>Neither</u> Logan nor Michael (feel, <u>feels</u>) like there is enough time while visiting. Last

year, <u>Cynthia</u> and her <u>brother</u> (was, <u>were</u>) traveling with Logan and Michael. The <u>zoo</u>

and the <u>museum</u> (was, <u>were</u>) two places they all visited. <u>Cynthia</u> and her <u>brother</u> (has,

<u>have</u>) only traveled to Memphis once, and they have never been to Nashville. Many

<u>restaurants</u> and <u>museums</u> in Nashville and Memphis (<u>offer</u>, offers) discount coupons

during the summer for all visitors. <u>Logan</u> and <u>Michael</u> (<u>participate</u>, participates) in the

coupon program every year. Perhaps this is why their annual trip is so inexpensive.

Exercise 4.4

"(Is, <u>Are</u>) there any questions in regards to the information covered in chapter four?"

asked our teacher. "(Is, <u>Are</u>) we being tested on just the first four chapters or over all of

the chapters in section one?" asked Katie. "There (is, <u>are</u>) four sections that students will

be responsible for knowing," our teacher exclaimed. "(Do, <u>Does</u>) everyone have a copy

of the study questions?" remarked Miss Stephens. The study guide and the chapters

(<u>contain</u>, contains) lots of important information for the exam. "(<u>Has</u>, Have) everyone

received all of the class lecture notes?" Miss Stephens asked. The class notes and chapter supplements (<u>make</u>, makes) a difference in the success of passing the exam. "Finally, (do, <u>does</u>) anyone have questions in regards to the test?" asked Miss Stephens. There (was, <u>were</u>) no questions, so Miss Stephens dismissed class early.

Exercise 4.5

The <u>class</u> of 2004 recently celebrated their graduation ceremony. The high school <u>faculty</u> was present to help with the celebration. When the ceremony first began, the <u>audience</u> was sitting quietly while the graduates entered the gymnasium. The <u>audience</u> saw the graduates; cheers were heard from all over the gymnasium. The <u>crowd</u> waved to the graduates while taking photos. The high school <u>orchestra</u> set the mood by playing three classical selections. The <u>faculty</u> commented on how lovely the ceremony was overall. The class of 2004 has made plans. The class president is attending a local college. Other classmates are entering the military. The local <u>college</u> has accepted many of the graduates for the fall semester. Overall, the <u>group</u> of graduates was one of the brightest to attend high school in quite some time. The <u>faculty</u> said they would be sad to see so many bright faces leave. The <u>class</u> agreed that leaving their friends behind would be difficult.

Exercise 4.6

Yesterday was Sarah's birthday. She (*give*) <u>was given</u> the day off from work. She (*celebrate*) <u>was celebrating</u> with her family at a restaurant when she realized her keys were locked in her car. She (*expect*) <u>was expecting</u> the locksmith to come to the restaurant parking lot within minutes, but it took over two hours for him to come. She (*wait*) <u>was waiting</u> on the locksmith while her friends ate birthday cake without her. She (*angry*) <u>was angry</u> at herself for forgetting her keys in the first place. She (*wear*) <u>was</u>

worn to a frazzle in the parking lot knowing her keys were locked in the car. When the locksmith arrived, the door (*open*) was opened immediately and Sarah entered the restaurant once again. Even though she felt angry, she (*enjoy*) was enjoying her company. They (*laugh*) were laughing at Sarah for locking her keys in the car. They (*agree*) were agreeing that locking the keys in the car is an easy thing to do. Next year, Sarah vowed not to drive to her own party and she, too, (*laugh*) was laughing at herself before the night was over.

Exercise 4.7

Jill rises early in the morning since her job begins at 8:00. . She has risen late out of bed several times. Usually, her boss is very understanding about her occasional tardiness. Every night before bed, Jill and her sister set their alarm clock for 6:00 to allow extra time. Jill has lain in bed after her alarm has rung hoping to sleep a little later. Her sister makes sure that Jill rises out of bed in enough time to eat breakfast and catch the bus. Once Jill gets on the bus, she sits in the front since her stop is one of the first on the route. Doug, the bus driver, lets Jill set her briefcase and lunch in the aisle of the bus since there is not much room for storage. As a thank you gesture, Jill sets a fresh danish on the dashboard of the bus every morning for Doug. Doug sets the danish in his lunch box and enjoys the pastry on his morning break.

Exercise 4.8

    S   **O**

Eating a balanced diet is important for people of all ages. Parents need to practice eating

                                                S

healthy foods. Since children learn from their parents or guardians, eating healthy foods

                                                   O

should be an important part of a child's routine. Children enjoy watching their parents

           S

create healthy habits. Establishing good habits requires patience and repetition.

> **S**
>
> Avoiding junk food after school and at night is one way to practice healthy habits.
>
> **O**
>
> Children need to be involved in establishing a good exercise routine and a good eating
>
> **S**   **S**
>
> regime. Involving children in good health requires time. Exercising can be a fun activity
>
> that parents and their children share. The hardest decision for parents to make is deciding
>
>   **S**
>
> how to channel their child's energy into a productive activity. Creating new fun
>
>   **S**
>
> memories is most important. Exercising should be an activity that the family may enjoy
>
>   **S**
>
> year round. Establishing an activity that works well with the entire family may take some
>
> time, but will be well worth the effort.

Exercise 4.9

Impressed by the recent theater performance, Katelyn bought season passes for the

performance series. Katelyn attended the most recent performance, having heard the

show was a Broadway success. The series, interesting to most of the season ticket

holders, promises to be the best yet. Katelyn has seen many Broadway musicals, having

been involved in college theater productions. The most recent production that Katelyn

saw was *Oklahoma*. Impressed by the musical talent of the actors, Katelyn has decided

to try out for the next local production in her town. Having heard the musicians perform

has inspired Katelyn to pursue singing as a hobby. The inspiration, coming when it did,

has helped Katelyn to have more confidence. Singing as she works, Katelyn dreams of

her big day on stage.

Exercise 4.10

Tara loves to play croquette, a game that requires players to hit a wooden ball with a

mallet through a type of obstacle course. The primary objective of croquette is to

entertain. To build a player's skills is one of the biggest challenges of the game. Most croquette players agree that the purpose of practicing is <u>to play a stronger game</u>. Tara loves <u>to play the game</u> with her family. When she was eleven, she started playing at the amateur level. Finally at age 13, she played the game <u>to win</u>. <u>To gain self-confidence</u> is a great feeling, and Tara practices five times a week <u>to gain confidence</u> in her skills. The person <u>to beat</u> is the person who is able <u>to play</u> with control and with grace. When she first started playing, Tara's biggest mistake was <u>to play the game</u> without mental preparation. <u>To maintain skill</u> is Tara's main responsibility. Tara's family supports her desire <u>to play competitively</u>.

Exercise 5.1

The invention of <u>modern </u>dance—the <u>expressive</u> and often <u>spontaneous dance</u> form based
P
on a rejection of <u>ballet's classical</u> rules—is often credited to <u>American</u> Isadora Duncan. Duncan earned her <u>first dancing</u> job after she exclaimed, "I have discovered the art of which has been lost for <u>two thousand</u> years." She was known for her "<u>free</u> dances," in a <u>flowing white</u> costume, moving lyrically on her scandalously <u>bare</u> feet to the strains of
P
Beethoven and Wagner. The <u>American </u>scene also fostered a <u>budding</u> genius in
P
<u>symphonic</u> music. <u>Composer</u> Charles Ives captured the <u>aural</u> flavor of <u>American</u> popular life. Ives's <u>musical</u> techniques had none of the <u>abstract</u> rigor of composer <u>Schoenberg's</u> methods, but did explore <u>broad</u> dissonances. The <u>creative</u> architecture of Frank Lloyd
P
Wright fit into the <u>same</u> flavor of <u>American popular</u> life. Influenced by his <u>boyhood</u>
P
summers on a <u>Wisconsin</u> farm, Wright believed that a building should reflect its <u>natural</u> surroundings and mediate between its occupants and their <u>natural</u> environment. Wright's <u>organic</u> sense of form is best expressed in his houses.

Exercise 5.2
Answers will vary.

Exercise 5.3

Answers will vary.

Exercise 5.4

Rachel is **taller** than her sister Catherine. Since Rachel is the **youngest** of three daughters, the fact that she is the **tallest** one of the group is amazing. Rachel's sisters are excellent racquetball players. Out of the three, Rachel is the **worst** racquetball player. Catherine and Hillary have more time to practice than their sister. Catherine has the **least** crowded schedule out of all three girls. Hillary is **faster** than Catherine on the court, but Catherine is the **kindest** out of the group. While Rachel may be the **slowest** of her sisters, she is **more** gracious than Hillary and is **smarter** than Catherine. Rachel says she doesn't mind being the **worst** racquetball player since she is the **most** articulate out of her sisters. One day Rachel hopes to be the **best** racquetball player out of her two sisters. She hopes to be the **fastest** one of the three.

Exercise 5.5

In the small town of Smithville, a beauty pageant is held every year to name the (pretty) prettiest girl in town. The pageant officials also decide on the contestant who is the (gracious) most gracious. The (soon) sooner the pageant gets started, the more people that attend. When the pageant begins, the high school gymnasium is the (crowded) least crowded. However, as it gets closer to time, the gymnasium fills up quickly. Most Smithville residents find the pageant to be (good) better and more entertaining than the county fair. Local merchants offer prizes for the winners. The (good) best prize offered is a trip to the mountains for the winner and her family. Perhaps the (big) biggest prize offered is a television set from the local appliance store. Next year's pageant might be held outdoors since the park is (crowded) <u>more crowded</u> than the gymnasium.

Exercise 5.6

Glenn and Bobby recently went on a fishing trip to Lake Ontario. They arrived at
DR   **IR**
10:00 a.m., at *which* time the fishing lure store was busy. Bobby decided *which* lures to
        IR
buy for his fishing expedition. Glenn asked him, "*What* lure should I buy?" Bobby said,
D   **IR**
"*That* lure in front of you is the best." "*Whatever* bait you buy should be fine," suggested
              D
the store clerk. Glenn also purchased a homemade fried pie, the *very* dessert the bait
            I
store was famous for making. Bobby decided *which* fried pie to buy and Glenn asked,
 I   **DR**
"*Which* flavor is the best?" "Was the pie *which* was on the top of the counter the best?,"
           I
wondered Glenn. The store clerk said, "*Whichever* flavor you choose will be a good

choice." After biting into a peach fried pie, Glenn agreed that no other pie would ever
     D   **P**
top it. "*Those* pies are wonderful," exclaimed Glenn. "*Your* place is terrific too,"

remarked Bobby. Every year, Glenn and Bobby return to the tackle and lure snack shop
  DR
whose employees offer good food and service.

Exercise 5.7
Answers will vary.

Exercise 5.8
Answers will vary.

Exercise 5.9

Marsha recently bought a <u>new red</u> car. She had trouble deciding between a <u>blue economy</u>

sedan and the <u>red</u> convertible that she always wanted. Since Marsha is a <u>young energetic</u>

woman, she felt the <u>sporty red</u> car best fit her personality. The <u>new car</u> dealer felt she

made the <u>right</u> choice. While Marsha knows her <u>car</u> insurance will be higher driving the red car, she can afford the payment since she paid for over half the car before driving it off of the crowded lot. Marsha works at the ice cream parlor to help make her monthly car payments. She asked her tall manager if she could work extra hours to help with her monthly payments. He agreed to offer her at least five more hours on the weekend. Marsha thanked her kind manager for allowing her to work longer shifts. Marsha figures that if she works at least two extra days each week, she will have plenty of money to afford her car payment. Marsha's parents have agreed to help her with her car insurance.

Exercise 5.10

Dance is so closely allied with music that musical styles are often named for the dance they accompany. From the waltz to hip-hop, interpretative dance and beautiful music have evolved. The dance form of the minuet, which originated in France, was preserved in the eighteenth century symphonies of Mozart. In the 1970s, disco music fueled a popular dance revival among young people dissatisfied with rock-and-roll's informal dance styles. In the same way, the improvisational style of jazz has fostered the equally inventive form of jazz dance. A dance's form, much like the form of music or theater, is the artful combination of dancing gestures and movements. In a dance performance, a dancer's movements create a changing combination of line, motion, pattern, tension, and rhythm. More so than with any other art, the form of dance is perceptible only in performance. The three-dimensional energy and complexity of a dance performance cannot be fully captured by a system of notation or even by film, although filmed dance has been revived by the popularity of music video.

218

Exercise 6.1

Since we had <u>only</u> four days to create a prom in our gymnasium, we <u>anxiously</u> started hanging paper on the walls. The junior class is responsible for skillfully crafting a prom set out of some lumber and paper supplies. The deadline is one week and is <u>often</u> missed because there is <u>so</u> much work to be done. Several members of the junior class <u>enthusiastically</u> accept the challenge of building a major set in such a short period of time. Class members <u>never</u> feel confident that their work is good enough, despite how <u>aggressively</u> they work all week. When the last day of building occurs, the class <u>nervously</u> awaits as the senior class president gets a sneak peek of the prom. Once the senior class president gives his or her stamp of approval, the junior class <u>silently</u> feels a sense of relief. Working <u>so</u> <u>diligently</u> to complete the project, the junior class members <u>often</u> become closer to one another. Many members of the class have an opportunity to meet other classmates for the first time. The class members <u>politely</u> work with one another to achieve their one goal, a perfect prom.

Exercise 6.2
Answers will vary.

Exercise 6.3

One **contemporary** revival grew <u>directly</u> out of **pop** art. Superrealism in painting <u>faithfully</u> reproduced in paint the qualities of the **photographic** image. Chuck Close was <u>quite</u> **explicit** in his aim to transfer **photographic** information to paint, <u>often</u> painting **oversized** portraits <u>directly</u> from photographs. **Sculptor** Duane Hanson sculpted **mannequin-like** figures <u>faultlessly</u> crafted of polymers to resemble **breathing** humans. Placed in airports or banks, **Hanson's** figures were <u>often</u> mistaken for **real** people. **Another** trend in art was to move outside the studio and find a **new** relation to nature and the **social** world. An outgrowth of **minimalist** sculpture, called **earth** art or **land** art, merged sculpture with the environment. **Earth** art was constructed of materials <u>virtually</u> **identical** to the **surrounding natural** site, often **primeval** landscapes in the desert or prairie. The **best-known** work of **earth** art was **Robert Smithson's** *Spiral Jetty*, a **spiral** form built from **black** basalt, **limestone** rocks, and earth in the Great Salt Lake of Utah.

Exercise 6.4

Kara talks **faster** than her brother, Ken. Sometimes when Kara is talking, her mother tells her to talk **slower**. Often, it is difficult to understand Kara on the telephone because she talks the **fastest** on the phone. When talking to Kara in person, it is easier to understand her even though she talks the **fastest**. She has a tendency to talk **faster** to her friends than when she is talking in school. When the teacher calls on Kara, she answers **more** rapidly than her friend Heather. Heather talks **more slowly** than Kara, but Heather does not talk the **slowest** in the class. Ben usually answers **slowest** in the entire class. Ben, however, smiles happily because his answers are usually correct. He answers **better** than Kara and feels **bad** if he gets an answer incorrect. Kara volunteers less than her classmates to answer questions. Kara works best when she is not under the pressure of answering a question in front of her classmates.

Exercise 6.5

Dina and Sara always walk (quick, <u>quickly</u>) into their aerobic class. However, Sara usually arrives (soon, <u>sooner</u>) than Dina. As a result, the aerobic instructor believes that Sara is a (real, <u>really</u>) punctual person. When Dina arrives at the workout club, she (quiet, <u>quietly</u>) gets prepared to do aerobics. She stretches and warms-up (good, <u>well</u>) whereas Sara just starts to exercise (rapid, <u>rapidly</u>). Since Sara doesn't warm-up properly, she has seen (<u>poor</u>, poorly) results. Dina, however, has experienced (<u>good</u>, well) results after working out for only several weeks. Dina watches (anxious, <u>anxiously</u>) as her aerobic classmates advance in workout skill. She hopes to join the advanced class someday (<u>soon</u>, sooner). Dina can see (<u>more</u>, most) results since she has worked out with a professional trainer. Her trainer (positive, <u>positively</u>) encourages her to maintain a healthy and happy lifestyle.

Exercise 6.6

                      ADJ
Steve and Mike decided to take an *adventurous* vacation before returning to school in the
                                           ADJ
fall. After looking on a map, the two decided to drive to the *sunny* shores of California.
                                        ADV
Since Mike had been to California several times in the past, he *reluctantly* agreed to go.
                                     ADV
Steve and Mike enjoy playing golf, so they *anxiously* called several golf courses in the
                                     ADJ
California area. They decided to play golf at several *upscale* courses. Mike reminded
      ADJ   **ADV**
Steve to pack his *golf* clubs and shoes because he *notoriously* forgets something when he
                       ADJ   **ADV**
plays golf. Steve believes that a *good* golfer always plays *patiently*. Mike just likes to
                       ADJ   **ADJ**
have fun when he plays the *challenging* game. When Steve and Mike arrived at the *first*
                       ADV
course in California, Mike hit the ball *aimlessly* and Steve laughed at his efforts. Then
                       ADV   **ADJ**
when Steve hit the ball, he hit the ball *well*. Mike realizes that Steve is a *better* golfer,
                       ADJ
but Mike still enjoys playing *different* courses. Steve has played golf since he was a

teenager, so he has experience putting and chipping. When Steve putts, he hits the ball
  ADV   **ADV**   **ADJ**
slowly and *smoothly*. He believes that having *enough* patience is the key to succeeding in
                       ADV   **ADV**
golf. Perhaps this is why Steve plays *tremendously well*.

Exercise 6.7
Answers will vary.

Exercise 6.8
Answers will vary.

Exercise 6.9

Cam never sees a movie because he works the night shift at the local pizza parlor. He only has one night off every week. Cam usually gets off work at 11:00 p.m., and the last movie begins at 10:00 p.m., so he rents movies from the local video store. He doesn't know how to tell his boss that he would like at least one weekend night off every month. Cam doesn't say anything to his boss because he worries about his boss becoming angry. Cam's boss doesn't have any employee to fill in when Cam is off. His boss only has two people working, and his other employee can only work part-time. While the pizza parlor is busy most nights, Cam doesn't make much money in tips. However, Cam likes his job because he gets to meet different people every day. He has worked at the pizza parlor for two years, and he hasn't asked for a raise, but his boss has offered to pay him more because Cam has been such a valuable employee.

Exercise 6.10

When Hannah awoke this morning, she could hear the birds <u>merrily chirping</u> and the sun was <u>brightly shining</u> through her window. Hannah <u>got up hurriedly</u> and made her bed <u>quickly</u>. She was in a hurry to get dressed because today was her birthday. She had been <u>anxiously waiting</u> for this day to come for weeks. After she chose her outfit, she <u>rapidly ran</u> down the stairs to eat breakfast. When her parents saw Hannah at the breakfast table, they <u>laughed hysterically</u> because Hannah, in all of the excitement, had put her dress on <u>backwards</u>. Hannah was in such a hurry to <u>frantically get dressed</u> that she did <u>not even</u> notice the mistake. She was <u>deeply embarrassed,</u> but she too laughed at her obvious mistake. After breakfast, Hannah's parents set the table and began to hang party decorations. The colorful balloons <u>floated aimlessly</u> in the kitchen. The decorations filled the room and Hannah <u>anxiously watched</u> the clock until it was time for the party. When the guests <u>slowly started</u> to <u>arrive</u>, Hannah became <u>very</u> excited. Many of her friends <u>graciously attended</u> her party and she <u>fortunately received</u> many wonderful gifts. The day was perfect and Hannah <u>exhaustedly slept well</u> that night while dreaming about her perfect birthday.

Exercise 7.1

Charles and his family recently purchased a cottage <u>by the lake</u>. Since Charles and his sons love to fish, they decided that driving a couple <u>of hours to a lake home</u> would be money well spent. Charles began to fish <u>in the lake</u> when he was just a little boy. His grandfather would take him on fishing expeditions <u>instead of baseball games</u>. <u>Aside from never wanting</u> to leave, the two suddenly realized that fishing would become their favorite hobby. <u>In addition to the lake home</u>, Charles also purchased a small pontoon boat <u>for his children</u> to ride <u>at the lake</u>. <u>Despite the occasional months of hot weather</u>, the lake home is the perfect retreat <u>from the everyday hassles of city life</u>. <u>Until six months ago</u>, Charles never realized how much he needed the rest and relaxation. <u>In addition</u> to stress, Charles felt as if he never made time <u>for his family</u>. <u>With this new home</u>, Charles is excited <u>about having</u> an opportunity to reconnect <u>with his family</u>. <u>In front of his wife</u>, Charles told his children that he would make every Sunday a family day. Sundays would become the days to spend time <u>together as a family</u>. <u>With the exception of Charles' youngest daughter</u> who likes to spend Sundays riding her bike, the family was ecstatic <u>about spending much needed quality time together</u>.

Exercise 7.2

<u>In</u> 1509, Pope Julius II followed his architect's advice and commissioned a young painter to decorate his apartment chambers. The artist, known as Raphael, was already famed <u>for</u> a series <u>of</u> graceful Madonnas painted <u>in</u> Florence. Working <u>under</u> the Pope's patronage, Raffaello Sanzio became Renaissance Rome's busiest and most beloved artist. <u>Besides</u> painting, Raphael used his talents <u>on</u> projects <u>for</u> the Pope, such <u>as</u> the excavation <u>of</u> Roman ruins and the construction <u>of</u> the new St. Peter's Basilica. <u>In</u> a city <u>of</u> intrigues and jealousies, Raphael was loved <u>for</u> his good humor and modesty. When he died <u>at</u> thirty-seven, he was the most popular artist <u>of</u> the Renaissance. <u>As</u> a painter, Raphael was known for the clarity and spiritual harmony <u>of</u> his works, which eloquently embodied the High Renaissance style. His most famous work, the *School <u>of</u> Athens*, is a virtual textbook <u>of</u> Renaissance technique. The painting depicts a gathering <u>of</u> the great pagan philosophers. The two central figures are Plato, who points <u>to</u> the world <u>of</u> ideal forms above, and Aristotle, reaching <u>for</u> the natural world below. <u>On</u> either side, figures representing ancient philosophy are arranged <u>in</u> lively symmetry, balanced <u>between</u> the abstract and the practical. The painting's overall effect is <u>of</u> learning, tolerance, perfect harmony, and balance.

Exercise 7.3

     CP   **SP**
<u>According to</u> recent research, studies show that the facial patterns <u>of</u> some emotional
               SP
expressions, <u>such as</u> fear and joy, are similar cross-culturally. But because nonverbal
                       SP
communication is learned largely <u>through</u> socialization, only an observer who knows the
                   SP   **SP**
culture very well can detect leakage <u>of</u> other hidden emotions. <u>If</u> deception can be
                     SP
uncovered, then impression management may fail. <u>Among</u> many Asian cultures,
                      SP   **SP**

including Korea, Japan, and Thailand, displays <u>of</u> emotion <u>such as</u> broad grins or angry
                CP   **SP**

outbursts are considered impolite. <u>In addition</u>, it is also rude to show disagreement <u>with</u>
                  SP

another person's behavior <u>in</u> these cultures. Middle Eastern and Latin cultures expect
           SP   **SP**   **SP**

such displays <u>as</u> signs <u>of</u> interpersonal closeness. <u>In</u> the United States smiling is
      SP   **SP**

associated <u>with</u> friendliness and happiness, but not necessarily so <u>in</u> Korea. Smiling is a
      SP   **SP**   **SP**   **SP**

taken-for-granted cultural norm <u>in</u> most parts <u>of</u> the United States, especially <u>by</u> a
                                SP   **SP**

shopkeeper hoping to make a sale. Some consequences <u>of</u> breaking norms <u>of</u> nonverbal
                                      CP

behavior are even more unsettling. People who do not show emotions—referred to <u>as</u> flat
      CP   **SP**

affect <u>by</u> psychologists—<u>in</u> situations that call for emotional expression may be
                                    SP

considered mentally ill because they violate taken-for-granted culture rules <u>of</u> nonverbal

communication.

Exercise 7.4
      CP   **SP**   **SP**
<u>According to</u> symbolic interactionists, society <u>as</u> a whole is constructed <u>through</u> the
                            SP

subjective meanings brought <u>to</u> all social interactions. They assert that we are not born
SP   **SP**   **CP**
<u>with</u> the social statuses <u>of</u> gender, race, social class, and the like. <u>In addition</u>, social
                        SP   **SP**

interactionists emphasize that choices <u>of</u> behavior <u>in</u> social interaction are optional, but

since race and gender cannot be disguised, people invariably use these categories to help

structure their interaction. Class is less obvious and can be disguised or eliminated in a
      SP   **SP**
variety <u>of</u> ways, <u>such as</u> learning appropriate class-based behavior. Eliza Doolittle, a
      SP   **SP**
character <u>from</u> the Broadway play *My Fair Lady*, was elevated <u>to</u> a much higher social
      SP
class <u>by</u> changing her language, clothing, and "lower class" behavior. Professor Higgins
                                  SP
may agree she is no longer the pitiful flower girl he found <u>on</u> the street, but she will
                                    SP
always be a woman and relegated to the less-privileged category designated <u>by</u> the social
      SP   **CP**   **SP**

construction <u>of</u> her gender. <u>In regard to</u> the play, the last line <u>of</u> *My Fair*
SP   SP
Lady illustrates the class-gender distinction <u>in</u> terms <u>of</u> privilege when Professor Higgins

calls out imperiously, "Eliza, bring me my slippers."

Exercise 7.5

Socrates is one (<u>of</u>, for) the greatest philosophers belonging (<u>to</u>, from) the Western

rational tradition. (In place of, <u>In addition to</u>) being a great philosopher, he has been a

model and source (at, <u>of</u>) inspiration (off, <u>for</u>) many philosophers (unto, <u>throughout</u>) the

centuries, including the stoics and the cynics who came before. Socrates actually wrote

no philosophy himself, though Plato, one (<u>of</u>, for) his students, did incorporate many

Socratic ideas (<u>into</u>, like) his writings. As many commentators point out, it is sometimes

difficult to clearly distinguish (<u>between</u>, beside) Plato's original thought and what he

borrowed (to, <u>from</u>) Socrates. Alfred North Whitehead, a famous twentieth-century

philosopher, once suggested that all (<u>of</u>, at) philosophy is but a series of footnotes (<u>to</u>,

upon) Plato. (From, <u>To</u>) an extent this is true, and insofar as Plato was strongly

influenced by Socrates, perhaps Western rational philosophy should extend its series (to,

<u>of</u>) footnotes a little further back (upon, <u>to</u>) Plato's mentor. Socrates had a reputation (to,

<u>for</u>) being indifferent (of, <u>to</u>) fashion and what we sometimes call today the "creature

comforts" (<u>of</u>, for) life. He believed in minimizing wants and needs (in, <u>for</u>) self-

mastery.

Exercise 7.6

(<u>In regard to</u>, In spite of) fashion, street fashion has tremendous influence (underneath,

<u>over</u>) fashion trends. Most designers travel a great deal, pursuing information (<u>on</u>,

outside) the latest trends, new color stories, and textile innovations. Inevitably, constant exposure (for, <u>to</u>) different cultures and the way people interpret fashions around the world influences fashion trends. Fashion (<u>from</u>, till) the street usually evolves (for, <u>from</u>) the ways young people experiment (for, <u>with</u>) existing garments, often recycling period pieces or customizing basics (near, <u>like</u>) denim garments and wearing them in new ways. Adding accessories typical (<u>of</u>, from) native costumes, wearing oversized garments, distressing clothes, and recycling vintage clothes are inexpensive ways to individualize fashion. The "grunge look" popular (for, <u>with</u>) today's youth has profoundly influenced high fashion. Creative people (in, <u>from</u>) the world (in, <u>of</u>) advertising, photography, and publishing are constantly (<u>on</u>, in) the lookout (<u>for</u>, in) the latest popular trends. They quickly document and integrate new looks (over, <u>into</u>) the international language (off, <u>of</u>) advertising and photography. Designers pick up on street trends firsthand or (outside, <u>through</u>) media images, and the look filters (over, <u>into</u>) the fashion cycle, particularly (of, <u>in</u>) the junior market, though high-fashion designers are also influenced (<u>by</u>, of) street fashions.

Exercise 7.7

Carley and Timmy recently purchased their first home (of, <u>in</u>) the town of Greenville. They were excited to move (by, <u>into</u>) their home because they had saved (in, <u>for</u>) two years to make the down payment. (<u>According to</u>, In spite of) Timmy, the home purchase went well. Carley and Timmy began searching (in, <u>for</u>) a home last fall. They contacted a local realtor and expressed their interest in searching (to, <u>for</u>) the perfect A-frame house. (Except for, <u>Due to</u>) low home interest rates, Timmy qualified (<u>for</u>, over) a first-time buyers' home loan. (Around, <u>Among</u>) the many houses they viewed, Carley and Timmy knew (in, <u>at</u>) first sight that the home they had purchased was perfect (over, <u>for</u>)

them. (<u>Outside</u>, Inside) the home, trees cover a beautiful shady lot. (Outside, <u>Inside</u>) the home, faux painting adorns the walls and hardwood floors can be found (without, <u>throughout</u>) the home. (<u>Because of</u>, With the exception of) their hardworking realtor, Carley and Timmy's first offer to the seller was accepted. The day that Carley and Timmy found out that their offer had been accepted, they jumped up and down. Carley immediately called her family and shared the good news (for, <u>with</u>) her parents. Before they moved in their furniture, Carley's father painted one room and her mother helped clean the kitchen and bathrooms. (Upon, <u>Since</u>) moving (<u>into</u>, before) their new home, Carley and Timmy have discovered that they not only have a beautiful home, but they have friendly neighbors as well.

Exercise 7.8

The elements of a man's business suit were established <u>at</u> the beginning <u>of</u> the twentieth century, and the evolution <u>of</u> fit and detailing <u>throughout</u> the century have formed the basis <u>for</u> restyling the business suit. The 1920s were notable <u>for</u> the introduction <u>of</u> the Ivy League look and the natural-shoulder suit. <u>During</u> the 1930s, the English drape suit, characterized by padded shoulders, a fitted waistline, and wide lapels, was popular. The 1940s contributed a modified padded-shoulder business suite silhouette and introduced many military-style garments <u>for</u> civilian use. <u>During</u> the 1950s, the natural-shoulder suite and Ivy League details returned <u>to</u> popularity. The 1960s were a decade <u>of</u> experimentation <u>for</u> the young generation, contrasted <u>with</u> conservative, Ivy League business suits <u>for</u> the establishment. Men began to wear active sportswear <u>for</u> leisure activities <u>during</u> the 1970s. Business suits were either conservative, natural-shoulder silhouettes or the fitted and padded continental look; this trend continued <u>into</u> the last decades of the twentieth century. Lifestyle changes have occurred rapidly during the last 25 years, and men's clothing reflects the casual, comfortable, sports-and-fitness orientation that continues to influence modern life.

Exercise 7.9

Ray and Stan recently traveled to Augusta, Georgia, to see the professional Master's golf tournament. Since Ray has played golf since he was a boy, he always dreamed of attending a professional golf tournament. Stan agreed to travel with Ray since he loves to watch Tiger Woods play golf on television. Ray invited Stan by winning tickets from a radio station contest. Ray answered the question, "What golfer has won the most major tournaments in his career?" Ray was the first correct caller who answered, "Jack Nicholas." Ray was given an all expense paid trip to Georgia as the grand prize winner. When Ray and Stan arrived at the Master's tournament, they met several professional golfers. Ray stood in front of Tiger Woods, and Stan shook hands with Phil Mickelson. After the tournament, Ray and Stan had the opportunity to tour the Augusta area. They spent three days playing golf and two extra days touring the sights of the beautiful town. Stan was thankful to Ray for taking him on the trip of a lifetime.

Exercise 7.10

In regards to the fashion industry, coordinates are typically described as a closely developed group of garments, carefully linked by color or detailing. These garments are designed in an interrelated group to encourage the customer to complete an outfit by buying several pieces. A typical coordinated group usually consists of jackets, with a few accessory sweaters, blouses, pull-over sweaters, and T-shirts. Basic and novelty pants and skirts, accessories, and sometimes dresses complete the mix. The group can be rounded out <u>by</u> adding shorts, halters, and bandeaus <u>during</u> the summer, and pantsuits, long skirts, vests and tunics <u>in</u> the fall. Current hot items will be adapted <u>for</u> the coordinated group. To buy this complete package, the buyer will select many components so that the customer will have several possible outfits <u>from</u> which to choose. Each component will be bought <u>in</u> several colors and <u>in</u> a range <u>of</u> sizes. This will be an expensive purchase that will consume much <u>of</u> the "open to buy." The buyer usually purchases coordinated groups <u>from</u> large manufacturers who can ensure delivery and can provide cooperate merchandising programs. One problem <u>with</u> purchasing coordinates is that some odd pieces are left unsold. After most components <u>of</u> a group have been sold, the remainder must be marked down.

Exercise 8.1

Christa <u>and</u> Breana celebrated their fifth birthday last Saturday. Neither Christa <u>nor</u> Breana have ever had a birthday party apart because the two girls are twins. Christa is taller than Breana, <u>yet</u> Breana was born twenty minutes earlier than her sister. The two girls share everything, <u>but</u> they don't look like one another. In fact, Christa has brown hair <u>and</u> Breana has blonde hair. They do have similar eyes, <u>so</u> people can usually tell they are twins. Every year for their birthday, they invite ten of their closest friends. Christa <u>and</u> Breana's mother bakes two separate cakes, <u>for</u> she wants the girls to each have an opportunity to blow out candles on the cakes. Christa likes chocolate cake, <u>so</u> her mother makes her a chocolate cake with fudge frosting. Breana likes white cake, <u>so</u> her mother makes her a white cake with cream cheese frosting. Both cakes are delicious, <u>for</u> they are homemade. During their most recent birthday party, Christa opened her gifts first, <u>so</u> Breana watched <u>and</u> helped her sister. Then Breana opened her gifts <u>and</u> Christa anxiously watched. Christa <u>and</u> Breana's father loaded up the gifts in the car. Neither Christa <u>nor</u> Breana left the party until the gifts were loaded <u>and </u>the decorations were taken down. The girls feel fortunate to have parents that create such wonderful parties in their honor.

Exercise 8.2

In 1900, Sigmund Freud published his study *The Interpretation of Dreams*, a work that revolutionized psychology much as Picasso transformed art. According to Freud, the mind was not the center of reason <u>and </u>self-mastery, <u>but</u> a battleground between unconscious desires <u>and</u> the oppressive demands of society. The family was not a sanctuary of innocent love, <u>but</u> a cauldron of incestuous attachments <u>and</u> murderous wishes. Freud applied his scientific analysis to subjects that were normally taboo, <u>so</u> many ideas have been created by Freud. His writings have given people a new vocabulary for understanding human thought, including now-familiar terms such as "unconscious," "ego," <u>and</u> "Oedipus complex." Every domain of the humanities, from surrealist art to philosophy <u>and</u> religion, has been affected by Freud's theories. Freud was the inventor of psychoanalysis, a method of treating mental illness by analyzing unconscious desires. One psychoanalytical method required a patient to talk freely about his <u>or</u> her thoughts <u>and</u> feelings. This "free association" of ideas revealed the unconscious thoughts behind the mental symptom <u>and </u>exposed the patient's thoughts to interpretation.

Exercise 8.3

A job opening became available last week at the local bank. Over twenty people applied for the position, <u>but</u> only two applicants were called back for a second interview. Mr.

Smith and Mr. Jones were the two favored applicants. Both applicants had exceptional work experience and creative ideas to bring to the bank. Neither Mr. Smith nor Mr. Jones had ever worked in the banking field. Mr. Smith worked at an insurance agency, yet had some experience in handling money and loans. Mr. Jones had experience working in retail sales, but his father and grandfather were bankers. The decision was a tough one, so the bank president asked for the loan officer and the bank manager to attend the second interview. The bank president asked if the job should be given to the applicant with the most money experience and the most education. The loan officer and the bank manager agreed that neither experience nor education would make that big of a difference. During the second interview, the bank president learned that another bank branch had a job opening as well, so he was able to hire both Mr. Smith and Mr. Jones for the same job, but at two different locations.

Exercise 8.4

Glenn decided to run for president of his senior class. It is rumored that he will receive many votes, for Glenn has the highest grade point average in his class. He is honest and hardworking, but he is unsure about winning since Bobby is also running for the position. Bobby is the quarterback of the football team and the center of the basketball team. He is involved in many activities in school, yet his grade point average is not as high as Glenn's. Neither Glenn nor Bobby would be a bad choice for president, but a problem does exist since the two are best friends. Glenn and Bobby have known each other for years and their parents are friends as well. Glenn would like to win the position, but he feels Bobby would do an excellent job if elected. Bobby, while campaigning, has said that Glenn is an excellent candidate and is his best friend. Either Glenn or Bobby would be a positive influence on the senior class. Perhaps the best part of this campaign has been the fact that both candidates are supportive of one another, _for_ regardless of who wins, a wonderful president will be elected.

Exercise 8.5

Jana _and_ Neal recently bought a car. It was the first time Jana had ever purchased a new car, _so_ she felt uncomfortable talking at car dealerships. Her first stop was the BMW dealership, _for_ a BMW had always been Jana's dream car. She test drove several vehicles on the lot _but_ didn't immediately feel comfortable in any one car. Neal agreed that he didn't see one particular vehicle that he felt comfortable driving, _yet_ the two went to another dealership. Jana was interested in test driving a sports utility vehicle, _so_ Neal suggested that they look at Ford Explorers. Jana drove a silver Ford Explorer _but_ wasn't convinced that she could drive a vehicle that size. Neither Jana _nor_ Neal felt comfortable in a sports utility vehicle, _yet_ they liked driving a Ford. They decided to test drive a Ford car, _but_ after driving through town in a sedan, Jana decided that she truly liked the BMW X3. She felt the X3 was the perfect size vehicle, _so_ they returned to the BMW dealership and test drove several different styles of the X3. Jana found a light blue X3 that she felt was the perfect vehicle for her, _and_ Neal agreed it was the perfect car for Jana. After test driving vehicles all day, they purchased their first BMW.

Exercise 8.6

Whenever Jim is around, people seem to always have fun. Jim is the kind of guy that doesn't know a stranger. In fact, he may be the friendliest person I know. As long as people are willing to listen, he tells the funniest stories. Provided that he isn't busy with his job or other hobbies, Jim enjoys spending leisure time visiting with friends. He usually spends his Saturdays, <u>if time permits</u>, playing basketball with his four best friends. The four men have played basketball every Saturday <u>since they were in high school</u>. <u>Because they have such a good time on Saturday mornings</u>, they often play football on Sunday afternoons. <u>Even though they all live several miles away from the gym</u>, they make it a point to play sports every week. <u>Whenever he can</u>, Jim tries to invite his friends and their wives to his house for outdoor cookouts. Jim loves to grill outside <u>provided that the weather is nice</u>. Altogether, Jim is a well-rounded, likeable guy and his friends think he is truly a supportive, kind friend.

Exercise 8.7

Before Whitney starts her new job, she has to spend several days in orientation. <u>Because her job requires meeting new people on a continuous basis</u>, proper training is a must. Her job, which begins next Monday, will require some travel. Whitney will be reimbursed for her travel <u>provided that she completes the proper travel reimbursement forms</u>. <u>Even though her job will require travel</u>, she will not travel every week. Some of her travel will require flying <u>unless she can drive the distance in one day</u>. Perhaps the best part of Whitney's new job will be the locations that she will be required to visit. Her company has branches in Hawaii, London, and Miami. <u>Even though Whitney loves to travel</u>, she is afraid that traveling will be difficult at times. <u>Since Whitney has children</u>, she is afraid that she will miss her husband and children when she has to travel overnight. <u>As long as her husband and children pay their own travel expenses</u>, Whitney is allowed to have them travel with her on an occasional business trip. Her children are looking forward to going to Hawaii <u>provided that they will travel with her to the beautiful island.</u>

Exercise 8.8
Answers will vary.

Exercise 8.9

Coffee shops have become popular all over America. *Although* not everyone likes to drink coffee, coffee shops have become the coolest places in town to hang out. Coffee drinks are delicious cold *as long as* the outside temperature is hot. *Since* coffee houses serve tea, people who don't drink coffee also stop by from time to time. Poetry readings and books for sale in coffee shops have also made them popular places. *Although* coffee shops specialize in coffee, most also serve hot sandwiches and snacks. *Because* coffee is served, people enjoy reading. Several businesses have opened coffee shops in the middle of their bookstores. Most people like to read in coffee shops *except when* occasionally the coffee shop gets busy and then noisy. This can make it difficult to read *while* people receive their coffee. *Because* of the recent popularity of coffee shops, book clubs and reading lists have once again become popular. Coffee and reading seem to mix well together. *Since* socializing over coffee has become the cool thing to do, hopefully reading will also remain a cool activity.

Exercise 8.10

Mary was looking forward to leaving for college, *but* she was also afraid. *Since* this
                                             C   S

would be the first time she ever lived alone, Mary was nervous about leaving her small
town. *Even though* her parents will only live two hours away, Mary still worries that she
     S

will have no friends and that she will have a hard time living on her own. Leigh *and*
                                                      C

Regina are also going to the same college. The three girls went to high school together,
 C   S

but they don't really know each other very well. *Since* they will be attending the same
                                                             S

college, they have called each other several times over the summer. Mary, *provided that* her roommate still attends, will room with a girl from another state. Mary is excited about the possibility of meeting new friends. *Because* she is from a small town, Mary

chose a college that has a small student body. The college is in a town that is similar to

the town where Mary was raised. Mary's mother has promised to visit whenever

possible. Mary's mom *and* dad are excited about the new possibilities college has to

offer.

Exercise 9.1

Our next-door neighbor, Mrs. Golden, recently traveled to Europe. She had always

planned to travel to Europe in August 2004, but she had to cancel because of work.

Finally, she was able to fly to Europe with her daughter in November, 2004. Their first

stop was a fun, exciting country. They began their trip in France where they shopped,

toured sights, and dined at outdoor cafes. Since Paris, France, is a popular tourist

attraction, the hotel where Mrs. Golden stayed was busy. After a trip to the Eiffel Tower,

Mrs. Golden and her daughter traveled by train to Germany. While in Germany, they

toured several museums, attended several music festivals, and ate at many unique

restaurants. Heidelberg, Germany, was by far their favorite city to visit. While in

Heidelberg, Mrs. Golden met a famous European actor. The highlight of their trip was

touring the Tate Gallery in London, England. At the Tate Gallery, many nineteenth-

century paintings were on exhibit. The art gallery director, Mr. Redding, suggested that

many paintings in the gallery are worth more than a million dollars. Hopefully, Mrs.

Golden and her daughter will make their trip an annual event.

Exercise 9.2

On May 25, 2004, Christina graduated from college with a degree in business. Her

parents, grandparents, and brothers attended the ceremony. Her favorite professor,

William Sneed, also attended the event. William Sneed, Ph.D., is the chair of the business department. When Professor Sneed saw Christina at graduation he said, "I am so proud of you." Christina felt that Professor Sneed was the most helpful instructor at the college. After graduation, Christina approached Professor Sneed and said, "Thank you for always encouraging me to finish my degree." Christina now hopes to attend graduate school in the fall. If she does attend graduate school, she will be the first person in her family to ever complete a graduate degree. After the graduation ceremony, Christina's family hosted a party in her honor. She received a clock, a briefcase, and a collection of several books as graduation gifts. The day was perfect, and Christina was thankful to her family for helping her celebrate.

Exercise 9.3

Leigh discovered this summer that she has a love for reading. At the beginning of the summer, she decided to form a book club; she invited many of her friends to join. Forming a book club requires the following: at least three members, a variety of novels, and a meeting place, such as a coffee house or library. Leigh started by calling her closest friends. She called Bella and said, "Please join our book club"; Bella never hesitated. Bella helped Leigh build the group, and the club held their first meeting a week ago. When the group met, they decided to let Leigh choose the first novel. She had trouble deciding, so she asked for the group to buy the following: *Wuthering Heights, The Pearl,* and *Mother Night.* The group agreed to begin with *Wuthering Heights*; Leigh was responsible for leading the first discussion. Since beginning the book club, Leigh has read many wonderful books; she is glad that the group was able to come together, and she hopes to continue meeting monthly for many years to come.

Exercise 9.4

Science impacts our everyday world. Late in 2002, a Canadian chemist created quite a stir at a press conference; she announced that her company had cloned a human being. Now, set aside for the moment the fact that no evidence was ever offered for this claim; just consider the announcement. Average citizens may not have understood exactly how the company carried off its supposed feat, but they had a rough idea of what the company was claiming: that it had produced one human being who was a genetic copy of another. Moreover, they understood that this person was conceived not through sex but through genetic manipulation in the laboratory. Though this announcement may have been surprising, it was not startling; for the first time, it caused people to have some context in which to place cloning. The remarkable thing is how far the concept of cloning had to come to reach this common-knowledge status. Here at the start of the twenty-first century, scientific innovations are moving with breathtaking speed; people will now hear more about cloning on a daily basis.

Exercise 9.5

Tommy's sister-in-law recently accepted a new job in Nashville. The committee decided to award her the job after taking a vote. Over two-thirds of the committee agreed that Karen was the right person for the job. Karen was thrilled when she received the news. She called her in-laws to share the news. Thirty minutes later—at the insistence of her family—she went out to eat to celebrate. Karen made sure to thank the committee for their decision—especially the president-elect who helped Karen with her resume. Perhaps the best part of her new job is that she will receive a pay raise of around thirty-five percent. With her new job, she will be able to travel two or three times a year.

When Karen starts her new job, she will be working in the second-, third-, and fourth-floor courtrooms with Judge Wheeler. Karen is glad that her brother-in-law, who is a lawyer, encouraged her to attend paralegal school.

Exercise 9.6

Jack and Jana's house is a beautifully restored Victorian home. They purchased the home at an estate auction last October. Since the house needs some work, they won't move in until summer. Jana's dream has always been to own a Victorian home. When Jana was growing up, she lived in a Victorian home in a small town in Kentucky. She loved her parents' house and vowed to own a similar type of home someday. In most Victorian homes the bedrooms are smaller than in a standard house, but Jana and Jack's home is a little different. Their children's bedrooms are just as large as the master bedroom. Also, the house features large closets. Overall, they don't have a lot of work to do on the home before moving, so they'll move during the month of May. Many of Jana's neighbors have come by to welcome the new family to the subdivision. Martha and Bob Jones, Jack and Jana's next-door neighbors, have already been over to welcome the family. The Jones' house is similar to Jack and Jana's. They are both southern Victorian homes with beautiful wraparound porches in the front. Jack and Jana know they will enjoy their new home.

Exercise 9.7

Carolyn is going to her first job interview tomorrow morning. Since she just graduated from college, she is nervous about interviewing. Dr. Cantrell, her biology professor, told her about the job possibility. Dr. Cantrell's advice was to prepare a strong resume, which wasn't difficult for Carolyn to do since she received help from Mr. Richards in the career department. Carolyn graduated with all A's with a degree in biology. She hopes to follow in her father's footsteps and teach high school biology. Carolyn's father has tried to advise her in the biology field, but he agrees that the field has changed a lot in the past thirty years. Carolyn's mother offered to practice interviewing with her, but Carolyn didn't think that practicing was necessary. She believes that she won't feel too nervous once the interview begins. Carolyn's attitude about interviewing has been positive overall. She believes that the right job will come along for her. She hopes that a teaching position will make her happy.

Exercise 9.8

Mary recently had a dinner party to celebrate Tom's birthday. Several people from her office attended. Since it was a surprise party, Tom was shocked when he opened the front door and saw his friends. His friends shouted, "Surprise!" Tom laughed and responded, "You got me!" He was truly surprised. After the guests entered, they began to sing "Happy Birthday." Tom's face turned bright red from embarrassment. "I am thankful," he said, "to have so many wonderful friends who care about me." Tom's friends wanted to make sure that Mary received the credit for putting the whole party together, so his friends began to cheer, "Mary, Mary." Mary smiled and said, "It was my pleasure to organize this party for Tom since he is such a terrific guy." After the speeches were made, the band played the slow song "You Look Wonderful Tonight," and Mary and Tom began to dance. Tom thanked Mary for her hard work and said, "I am so proud to have you for my best friend. No one on earth," Tom said, "knows me as well as you." Mary blushed, for she has strong feelings for Tom. As the song was coming to an end, Tom lightly kissed Mary's cheek and Mary said, "Wow!"

Exercise 9.9

Jena wanted to make homemade cinnamon rolls for her husband's birthday breakfast. She called her grandmother for the recipe. Jena's grandmother told her that the secret of making wonderful cinnamon rolls is to let the dough rise (also known as dough growing) to have fluffy results. Jena made sure to follow the recipe exactly as written because last time she attempted to make them she only used 1/4 cup of yeast instead of 1/2 cup. This time she followed the recipe exactly, but she was nervous about rolling out the dough. Her grandmother told her that once the dough had risen she would need to punch the dough (also known as pushing the dough down) in order to get the right texture. Jena divided the dough and took 1/3 of the dough to knead. Jena kneaded the dough (also referred to as working the dough) for several minutes before rolling the dough. She then stuffed 1/2 of the dough with brown sugar, nuts, and cinnamon before stuffing the other 1/2 of the dough. After she baked the rolls, she frosted the rolls (also known as icing the rolls) before they cooled. The cinnamon rolls were a huge hit with her family, and her husband said they were the best cinnamon rolls he had ever eaten.

Exercise 9.10

Jon was at work when he received the news. The phone rang, and when he answered, the voice on the other end of the phone said, "Is this Jon, the luckiest man in the world?" Jon then found out that he had won an all expense paid vacation to London. "Wow! I won!" screamed Jon. "Yeah!" cheered Jon. He was so excited that he called his mother. Jon will leave in a few weeks from Dallas, Tex. and will then fly back into New York before driving home to Memphis, Tenn., in a rental car. "How many people entered the contest?" Jon wondered. Out of 2,500 people, Jon won. When the radio station manager brought the plane tickets and the hotel reservations, Jon screamed. "Thank you! Thank you! Thank you!" Jon cheered. Jon's wife is equally as excited. She has dreamed about taking a European vacation for years. When she heard the news, she began researching London on the Internet. She found information about restaurants and tourist attractions. She also learned the average temperature in Europe in the fall is 70.5 degrees. She is looking forward to taking a dream vacation with her husband.

Exercise 10.1

<u>When Betsy decided to become a nurse.</u> She investigated several nearby colleges in her community. <u>Although she already has a degree in finance.</u> Betsy decided a year after graduating from college that she wanted to become a nurse. Betsy fears that nursing school might be too expensive. <u>Even though she has received a partial scholarship.</u>

<u>While Betsy's</u> parents have agreed to help her with expenses. She wants to avoid having to rely on her parents for help. Betsy works part-time at a bank. <u>So that she can earn extra money for books and supplies.</u> Thankfully, her parents still let her live at home. <u>Though she doesn't have to worry about making a house payment.</u> She still tries to give her parents extra money at the end of the month to help with bills. <u>Even though she feels a little guilty for still living at home.</u> Betsy still wants to be a nurse. Her parents are happy to help her in her career choice. <u>Because they know the importance of loving a job.</u> Betsy's father understands her love for nursing. <u>Because he is a nurse.</u> Betsy wants to follow in his footsteps. <u>So that there will be two nurses in the family someday.</u>

Exercise 10.2

<u>Because of the recent addition of several factories.</u> The town of Spring Hill has grown dramatically. The population doubled. <u>Because of the recent opening of a textile plant.</u>

<u>Since the rise in population.</u> The town has recently decided to build another elementary school, doubling the size of the original building. <u>Even though a new middle and high school are also needed.</u> Spring Hill only has enough funding for one new school project this year. The city is also building a brand new city hall building. <u>Unless the funding for this project falls through.</u> <u>Whenever funding is not enough.</u> The townspeople will have to come up with additional ways to fund the project. One recent idea that the city council came up with was to hold a city clean-up auction. The auction will be held on the town square, and any town citizen will be able to auction any goods, with proceeds going to the building fund. <u>Until the idea has passed the city council.</u> The auction is on hold. <u>Although the auction seems to be favored by most Spring Hill citizens.</u> Some townspeople don't believe the money raised will be enough.

Exercise 10.3

Fred recently won money playing in a local golf tournament. Fred began playing golf in high school but really began enjoying the sport in college. <u>Especially his sophomore year.</u> Fred has been a successful golfer since he plays every other day. <u>Except on Saturdays when he spends time with his family.</u> Fred feels that the game of golf helped him to connect with his father. <u>Especially since his father loved the sport as well.</u> Fred and his father would spend many mornings on the golf course and would talk about their lives. <u>Especially about work and school.</u> Fred's father has introduced him to some famous golfers. <u>Including Jack Nickolaus and Arnold Palmer.</u> Since Fred's father worked in sports sales, he was able to take Fred to several golf charity events a year. Fred will always cherish the golf memories with his father. <u>Especially the weekend trips they would take to different golf courses around the nation.</u> Fred hopes to pass his love of golf on to his own children. <u>Especially his son</u>. Because of his love for the sport, Fred will continue to build a relationship with his children and hopefully his grandchildren.

Exercise 10.4

The most celebrated literary work of the Middle Ages is the epic poem *The Divine Comedy* by the Italian poet Dante Alighieri. Born in Florence in 1265, Dante was involved in politics as well as literature. <u>Especially in writing poetry</u>. Dante was exiled from his home city, never to return. <u>Including the place he was born</u>. *The Divine Comedy* was completed in Ravenna shortly before Dante's death. In the poem, Dante makes numerous references to the politics of his day. <u>Especially to the rivalry between the Guelphs and Ghibellines, two opposing Florentine political parties, that left him in exile from this native city</u>. The influence of Dante's *Divine Comedy* can hardly be exaggerated. It was first mentioned in English by Chaucer in the fourteenth century, and in the twentieth century, it has continued to influence poets such as T.S. Eliot. Dante still continues to influence upcoming writers. <u>Especially poets who are in the beginning stages of their writing careers</u>. Dante will always be remembered for writing *The Divine Comedy*. <u>Including his vivid creativity</u>.

Exercise 10.5

Henry called for reservations at the new restaurant called Escape. <u>Hoping to be seated before seven o'clock</u>. The new restaurant recently opened. <u>Featuring fresh seafood</u>. <u>Attempting to broaden his taste for different foods</u>. Henry decided to invite his family to join him. Henry has never been a huge seafood fan, but he felt ready to try this restaurant. <u>Hoping he would find something on the menu to his liking</u>. <u>Not realizing that Escape was already on a three-day wait</u>. Henry was told it would be two weeks before he and his family would be able to dine there. <u>Being disappointed</u>. Henry understood that the wait would be long, so he made the reservation for two weeks later. After Henry hung up the phone, he realized that two weeks would be perfect because his mother's birthday would be around the same time. <u>Confirming the reservations with his family</u>. Henry called his mother and told her that going to Escape would be her birthday celebration. She was excited to hear that Henry had already remembered her birthday. <u>Knowing that last year Henry forgot his mother's birthday</u>. She was delighted that he made the reservation.

Exercise 10.6

In the early 1890s, the Impressionist style of painting was widely accepted. <u>Challenging the mainstream of art</u>. The Post-Impressionists became the next group of talented artists. The term Post-Impressionist is, in fact, an extremely broad one to define. <u>Meaning "to work in isolation."</u> The Post-Impressionist artists did not band together. <u>Not completely rejecting Impressionism.</u> Post-Impressionists considered Impressionism too objective, too impersonal, and lacking control. They did not think that recording a fleeting moment or portraying atmospheric conditions was sufficient. <u>Placing greater emphasis on composition and form, on the "eternal and immutable," what Baudelaire described as the "other half" of art.</u> The Post-Impressionists worked to control reality, to organize, arrange, and formalize. The Post-Impressionist painters wanted more personal interpretation and expression, greater psychological depth. <u>Shaping the art world as we know it today</u>. The Post-Impressionists were responsible for creating an art movement that is still enjoyed, admired, and imitated in today's artistic movements.

Exercise 10.7

Perhaps the most influential architect of the twentieth century was American Frank Lloyd Wright, a student of Louis Sullivan. To study and design with Sullivan. Wright was fortunate to learn from the best. Early in his career, in the first decade of the twentieth century, he designed what he called "prairie houses." To design his prairie house. Wright embodied the idea that the character of a building must be related to its site and blend with the terrain. To imitate the prairie on which it stands. Wright used shapes related to the surrounding landscape. The Robie House is low and flat, stressing the horizontal as it seems to spread out from its walls. To make the house seem part of the surrounding natural environment. Wright used extensive windows and broad reinforced concrete cantilever overhangs to relate interior and exterior. The brick used to build the house is made from sand and clay from a nearby quarry. To demonstrate his love of natural materials. Wright will be remembered for being an organic architecture. Wright considered his building organic, but his critics said his buildings were sometimes too impersonal.

Exercise 10.8

Joan recently received a computer for her birthday from her grandchildren. To help her set up the computer. Her grandson, Michael, agreed to spend a few nights at his grandmother's house. Joan was very reluctant. To have a computer in her house. She has never been the type of person to work well with computers. She decided on having a computer installed at her house. To have the ability to e-mail her family members. Since she will now have a computer at home, she will be able to send and receive pictures of her great-grandchildren. To help his grandmother with simple computer tasks. Michael bought Joan a book about how to use everyday functions on a computer. With Michael's help, Joan hopefully will be able to check e-mail, use the word processor features, and create a budget on her computer. Michael has shown his grandmother how to use the computer. To really know how to use all of the features. Michael told his grandmother that it simply takes lots of time and practice. With the help of Michael, Joan did send her first e-mail. To show the latest picture of her great-granddaughter, Hannah. Joan is excited about having the opportunity to communicate with her family in such a quick and efficient way.

Exercise 10.9

Candace recently became engaged to her boyfriend of four years. She has begun to prepare for the big day. But is nervous about expenses. Candace's parents agreed to help her with expenses. And hope to help with the planning as well. Candace has decided to have an outdoor wedding. Then a reception under outdoor tents. Jim, Candace's fiancé, agrees with Candace's wedding decisions. He is thrilled that she is taking on the headache of planning this major event. Candace decided on having the wedding in her parents' backyard. But worries about the chance of rain. Candace decided to have a rented room in case her outdoor plans fall through. The caterer agreed to set up under a tent at Candace's parents' home. But will charge extra for setting up outdoors. They have agreed to serve some hot and cold foods. And will serve buffet-style to guests. Finally, the photographer agreed to reserve Candace's wedding date. But needed a small deposit. Candace's mother helped her with the deposit. And helped with other costs as well. Candace feels fortunate to have parents who are willing to help so much.

Exercise 10.10

Jennifer had a minor fender bender in the parking lot where she works yesterday. A gentleman hit her front fender. But didn't realize he had hit it. Jennifer got out of her car to see the damage. But didn't see who hit her car. The man who hit Jennifer's car saw Jennifer in his rearview mirror. And decided to stop. It was then that Jennifer told him her car had been hit. The man felt terrible about hitting Jennifer's car. But didn't know what to do. Jennifer suggested that they call the police to fill out an incident report. Jennifer made the call on her cell phone. And waited for the police to arrive. When the police officer arrived, he was relieved to discover that no one was hurt. Jennifer said they were lucky. Everyone was fine. Except for the man who had a little pain in his shoulder. The man apologized over and over again for hitting Jennifer. And causing an accident. Jennifer graciously accepted the man's apology. But realized the damage to her car would be expensive. Luckily both Jennifer and the man have the same insurance agent, so they won't have to meet a deductible.

Exercise 11.1

America's foremost Romantic landscape painter in the first half of the nineteenth century was Thomas Cole. He emigrated from England to the United States at seventeen, and by 1820, he was working as an itinerant portrait painter. On trips around New York City, Cole sketched and painted the landscape, which quickly became his chief interest, and his paintings launched what became known as the Hudson River School. With the help of a patron, Cole traveled in Europe between 1829 and 1832. In England he was impressed by Turner's landscapes, and in Italy, the classical ruins aroused his interest in a subject that also preoccupied Turner: the course of empire. In the mid-1830s, Cole went on a sketching trip that resulted in *The Oxbow*, which he painted for exhibition at the National Academy of Design in New York. Cole considered it one of his "view" paintings, and the painting was monumental. The painting shows the top of Mount Holyoke in western Massachusetts, and a spectacular oxbow-shaped bend in the Connecticut River appears in the background. Cole contrasts a dense, stormy wilderness to a pastoral valley, and the fading storm suggests that the wild will eventually give way to the civilized.

Exercise 11.2

A new law has recently been put into place in the state of Tennessee. All passengers under the age of four are still required to ride in a car seat. All passengers under the age of nine are now required to ride in a child booster seat. This law was passed to ensure the safety of small children over the age of four traveling on Tennessee roads and highways. The new law comes into effect as vehicle standards and lengths of average commutes have changed over the years. Today, more people are commuting longer distances to work. This causes more children to ride in vehicles for longer periods of time than twenty or thirty years ago. Another significant difference in vehicle safety today is the installation of car air bags designed to prevent serious injuries during an automobile accident. Air bags can sometimes harm a child by deploying from a minor fender bender or accidentally. Recent studies have shown that air bags deploying into the faces of small children, especially in the front seat of a vehicle, cause serious harm to children. Now the law states that children under the age of nine must ride in booster seats and in the backseats of vehicles to ensure they are protected from injuries sustained in an accident or by air bags. This law will hopefully help to eliminate the number of injuries and deaths per year caused by accidents and air bags releasing onto children.

Exercise 11.3

In 1848, seven young London artists formed the Pre-Raphaelite Brotherhood in response to what they considered the misguided practices of contemporary British art. Instead of the conventions taught at the Royal Academy, the Pre-Raphaelites advocated a naturalistic approach of early Renaissance masters; they concentrated on the Renaissance masters of northern Europe. The use of naturalism is best represented in one of the leaders of the Pre-Raphaelite movement, William Holman Hunt. A well-known painting by Hunt is *The Hireling Shepherd*; Hunt painted the landscape portions of the composition outdoors, an innovative approach at the time, leaving space for the figures, which he painted in his London studio. The work depicts a farmhand neglecting his duties to flirt with a woman while pretending to discuss a death's-head moth that he holds in his hand; meanwhile, some of his employer's sheep are wandering into an adjacent field, where they become sick or die from eating green corn. Hunt later explained that he meant to satirize pastors who, instead of tending their flock, waste time discussing what he considered irrelevant theological questions; the painting can also be seen as a moral lesson on the perils of temptation. The woman is cast as a latter-day Eve, as she feeds an apple—a reference to humankind's fall from grace—to the lamb on her lap and distracts the shepherd from his duty.

Exercise 11.4
Answers will vary.

Exercise 11.5

Marsha decided to throw a Halloween party for all of her daughter's friends. She invited all of the children in the neighborhood, and she invited the parents to attend as well. Since Marsha loves Halloween, she looks forward to having a party in October every year. This year she has decided to have an apple-bobbing contest, but she also plans to hang a Halloween piñata for the children to hit with a broomstick. Katie, Marsha's little girl, has decided to dress up as a princess, so Marsha will dress to match her daughter. Marsha has also requested that the neighborhood children dress up as their favorite character or person, and she has encouraged their parents to do the same. Marsha also plans to make popcorn balls and caramel apples for all of the children and their parents, and she learned how to make Halloween goodies when she was a little girl from her grandmother and mother. She also plans to give each child a Halloween treat bag to be filled with candy. Marsha loves the fall weather and Halloween, yet she becomes sad when the holiday is over because it means she will have to wait another year to see her beautiful daughter dressed up with her friends once again.

Exercise 11.6

Feminist art emerged in the context of the Women's Liberation movement of the late 1960s and early 1970s. A major aim of feminist artists and their allies was increased recognition for the accomplishment of women artists, both past and present. A 1970 survey revealed that although women constituted half of the nation's practicing artists, only 18 percent of commercial New York galleries carried works by women. Of the 143 artists in the 1969 Whitney Annual, one of the country's most prominent exhibitions of the work of living artists, only eight were women. The next year, the newly formed Ad Hoc Committee of Women Artists, disappointed by the lukewarm response of the Whitney's director to their concerns, staged a protest at the opening of the 1970 Annual. To focus more attention on women in the arts, feminist artists began organizing women's cooperative galleries. While feminist art historians wrote in books and journals about women artists and the issues raised by their work, feminist curators and critics promoted the work of both emerging women artists and long-neglected ones, such as Alice Neel, who had her first major museum retrospective at age seventy-four.

Exercise 11.7

The town of Mayfield recently declared the last day of summer as community clean-up day; this day will be set aside for community members to clean up around the downtown area. One area that will be cleaned and addressed this year will be the planting of new fall flowers. Also, many merchants will plant seasonal flowers in flower boxes outside their stores; many store owners have also agreed to paint the exterior of their building if needed. The mayor of Mayfield has also agreed to fund a new project for new streetlights, replicas of street lights from the 1950s. The most exciting project scheduled during the clean-up day is the installation of a fountain on the square; the fountain will operate year-round as weather permits. The funding for this project will come from donations and fund-raisers that have been held over the past year; the largest amount of funding will come from the water plant in Mayfield. After the town citizens spend all day cleaning and building, they will hold a square dance and carnival on the square. Everyone in town is looking forward to the big day; they can't wait to celebrate at the dance and carnival in the evening.

Exercise 11.8
Answers will vary.

Exercise 11.9
Answers will vary.

Exercise 11.10
Answers will vary.

Exercise 12.1

Jack recently received his second speeding ticket in two months. He was caught driving nine miles over the posted speed limit. <u>While driving quickly, the speed limit sign appeared.</u> Jack tries to be conscious of his speed, but sometimes he gets distracted. <u>Dancing to the music of the radio, the siren loudly blared.</u> When Jack heard the siren, he immediately pulled his car over. <u>After accepting the speeding citation, the car was parked on the side of the road.</u> The officer politely questioned Jack about his careless driving habits. Jack promised to slow down and to attend driving school in lieu of having the citation on his permanent record. <u>While negotiating the hours of driving school, the speeding citation flew out of the window.</u> The police officer grabbed the citation and placed it back in Jack's hands. <u>Immediately after talking to the officer, the car started.</u> Jack shook hands with the officer and thanked him for courtesy. The officer told Jack to slow down and to drive safely. <u>While waving goodbye, the car traveled on the highway.</u> Hopefully, Jack has learned his lesson.

Exercise 12.2
Answers will vary.

Exercise 12.3
Answers will vary.

Exercise 12.4

While vacationing in Las Vegas, Nevada, I saw many tourist sites. <u>Strolling down Las Vegas Boulevard, the architecture of the hotels impressed me</u>. We saw hotels that resembled the Eiffel Tower, the Statue of Liberty, and even a castle. The restaurants in Las Vegas were unique as well. At one restaurant they served homemade dinner rolls by throwing them in the air for all the patrons to catch. <u>Being hungry, the rolls looked</u>

delicious. I ate four rolls before eating my meal. Another fun activity to do in Las Vegas is to attend several shows. The shows often attract more tourists than the casinos located in every hotel. <u>Watching the Celine Dion concert, the chairs were uncomfortable</u>. However, we were tired so we were glad to have the opportunity to sit for awhile. <u>After walking all day, a concert is soothing</u>. The concert was truly spectacular. After the concert, we stopped at a corner café for coffee and dessert. <u>Immediately after eating dessert, the temperature began to drop</u>. On our walk back to the hotel, it began to rain. Since we were tired, we decided to wait until the next day to finish touring Las Vegas.

Exercise 12.5

Miss Thompson recently began teaching the first grade. Teaching has always been Miss Thompson's dream. Miss Thompson has wanted to teach young children since she was in elementary school. Miss Thompson met her class for the first time last Wednesday. <u>She told the children what to expect with a smile</u>. She wanted to teach the children how to read and how to add numbers together. <u>The students gave a welcome card to the principal of the school in a rush</u>. They also gave Miss Thompson flowers on the first day of school. <u>The principal welcomed the students from the main office</u>. <u>The students attended the school early in the morning who wanted breakfast</u>. After breakfast, Miss Thompson read to the students until all the other students arrive. The best part about being in Miss Thompson's class on that day was activity time. <u>She gave out stickers and other prizes wearing a silly hat</u>. <u>Miss Thompson also sang funny songs to the class with a ukulele</u>. <u>She hopes someday that her students will look back at the time spent in her class with fond memories</u>.

Exercise 12.6
Answers will vary.

Exercise 12.7
Answers will vary.

Exercise 12.8

Clara decided to cook a large Italian dinner for Christmas dinner this year. Since Clara is Italian, she wanted to surprise her parents with the special dinner. <u>She served homemade spaghetti to her parents, loaded with mushrooms and peppers.</u> She also decided to surprise her grandparents with manicotti. Since the trick to making manicotti is to boil the noodles for the proper length of time, she was nervous about creating the Italian feast. After boiling the noodles for nine minutes, Clara added garlic to the sauce. She had never stuffed manicotti noodles before. She called her sister for help. Her sister had cooked several Italian dinners before. Clara brought the manicotti to the table<u>.</u> Her father cheered with excitement. <u>Clara's sister brought spaghetti to the table with fresh herbs and mushrooms.</u> Clara's parents appreciated all of her hard work. <u>Clara found some old pictures in the closet of her mother in the kitchen.</u> She, too, made wonderful Italian dinners when she was younger.

Exercise 12.9

<u>Jim and his brother found an old scrapbook in the attic that was dusty.</u> Since they were cleaning the attic, they found lots of boxed pictures and letters. <u>The scrapbook featured pictures of his father that was maroon.</u> The pictures were from holidays, birthday parties, and family vacations. <u>One picture featured a vacation to Yellowstone National Park that was black and white.</u> It was a picture of Jim's father with his parents. He was eight years old in the photo. <u>Jim also found a journal in a box that was handwritten by his grandmother.</u> <u>Jim's grandmother wrote in her journal nearly every day her real life</u>

experiences. <u>One entry discussed a surprise party for his grandmother in the journal.</u> Her many friends were invited to attend. Jim also found his father's tuxedo from his wedding day. <u>The tux fit Jim like a glove from his wedding.</u> Jim and his brother laughed at how out of style the jacket appeared. Jim and his brother had a good time looking through lots of different boxes.

Exercise 12.10

Nicki and her mother organized a recent food drive for their community. <u>Nicki attended organizational meetings to develop the program for about eight months.</u> With the help of her mother, she was able to find over 50 volunteers. The volunteers offered to work whenever possible. <u>Nicki organized the drive wearing a food drive T-shirt.</u> When a local newswoman saw Nicki's shirt, she felt it was important to feature Nicki's group on television. The volunteers raised over 75 cases of food for the homeless. Nicki's mother was proud of her accomplishment. <u>After celebrating the victory, the telephone rang.</u> It was the mayor of St. Louis. He called to thank Nicki and her friends for their hard work and consideration. <u>Trying to thank the mayor, her heart pounded.</u> She was nervous talking to the mayor, and she thanked him for taking the time to call. Nicki felt wonderful about the difference she was able to make in the lives of others. She hopes to continue the food drive in the future.

Exercise 13.1
Answers will vary.

Exercise 13.2
Answers will vary.

Exercise 13.3

Karen, a local horse trainer, recently entered her horse in the Kentucky Derby. Neither her assistant horse trainer <u>nor</u> her assistant veterinarian technician has ever entered a horse in a major contest. They have decided to enter Bread-N-Butter, a beautiful brindle stallion. Bread-N-Butter not only runs quickly <u>but also</u> runs smoothly. Both the trainer <u>and</u> the technician have high hopes for the horse to win. Karen would rather watch from the stands <u>than</u> watch from the ground level. This is not only the most exciting race Karen has ever witnessed <u>but also</u> the most challenging. Karen hopes that Bread-N-Butter will at least finish the race in the top ten. If the horse does finish in the top ten, Karen will still win a substantial amount of prize money. Both courage <u>and</u> strength will help the horse win. Karen is either nervous <u>or</u> scared because as the race gets closer she is acting weird. While she is nervous for the horse, she plans to enjoy herself at the race.

Exercise 13.4

Stan decided to purchase season tickets for the Titans this year. Since he lives near Nashville, he decided to show his support for the professional football team. He finds both attending the game <u>and</u> loving the sport to be a great way to spend a weekend. He would rather attend ballgames <u>than</u> attend concerts. He believes that it is money well spent. Stan is not only a football fan <u>but also</u> a hockey fan. However, he had to decide between buying football tickets or hockey tickets. It was either football <u>or</u> hockey. Stan loves to be outdoors, so he decided to buy football tickets. He hopes that next year he will have the money to support both the Titans <u>and</u> the Predators. For now, he plans to enjoy all of the Titans' games. Stan's wife is also excited about the opportunity to attend the ballgames with her husband. Football season is not only a wonderful time of year <u>but</u>

<u>also</u> a fun time of the season as cooler temperatures linger. Stan believes that supporting the team is his responsibility to help the franchise.

Exercise 13.5

Billy and Kellie married last Saturday night. After their lavish wedding, they left for Puerto Rico for their honeymoon. Kellie planned their honeymoon trip and <u>booked</u> several fun activities. On Tuesday, they will water ski, <u>power bike</u>, and rock climb. Kellie planned for the couple to have several days of unplanned activities. She hopes they can swim, walk, and <u>relax</u>. Towards the end of their trip, Kellie has planned to see a concert and <u>view</u> a movie. To prepare for their trip, Kellie packed sunscreen, scheduled tours, and <u>planned</u> events. Billy appreciated the hard work that Kellie put forth to make their trip a dream vacation. They hope to travel every year for their anniversary. Next year they might travel to the Bahamas. If they decide to travel to the Bahamas next June, Kellie will begin planning events, calling travel agents, and <u>booking</u> tours. Kellie doesn't mind spending time planning vacations because she wants to make sure that Billy has a relaxing vacation and that their money is well spent.

Exercise 14.1

Sabrina is currently remodeling her kitchen. She decided to contact an interior designer at Holden House Designs for help. Joan, the interior designer at Holden House, suggested that Sabrina decide on a theme for her kitchen. Since her appliances were the original ones from when the home was built in the 1950s, Sabrina decided to update all of the kitchen appliances. Joan went with Sabrina to Home Depot to shop for new appliances. Sabrina chose a Maytag refrigerator, a General Electric stove, and an Amana dishwasher. She decided on new lighting fixtures as well. She plans to paint her kitchen walls blue and accent the walls with yellow fixtures and dishes. Joan believes that contrasting colors make a beautiful kitchen. After they have the new appliances installed by the Home Depot technician, they will shop for accessories at Green Hills Mall. In Green Hills Mall there are several stores that feature wonderful kitchen décor. One store that features unique dishes and linens is Pottery Barn. Another popular kitchen and home décor store in Green Hills Mall is Restoration Hardware. Sabrina plans to shop both of these stores to find the best deals for her newly painted kitchen.

Exercise 14.2

Construction recently began in Nashville, Tennessee, on the Parthenon building. The building is a replica of the ancient building from Athens, Greece. Located in the west end district of the city, the Parthenon has become a tourist site that many people visit each year. Located around the building is Centennial Park. The park features playground areas, picnic areas, and walking trails. There are many unique restaurants near the park. A restaurant called Chu's is one popular Asian restaurant that many people frequent. Since Vanderbilt University is close to the park, many college students study near the Parthenon, and many eat at restaurants such as Chu's and Jack Russell's. Construction is set to be completed by August, 2005. While construction is underway, certain sections of the park will be closed. However, city officials agree that different parts of the park will remain open unless construction forces the area to be closed. After the Parthenon construction, many more events will be held in the park for students and families.

Exercise 14.3

Abby has begun her Christmas shopping early this year. Since she is known for waiting until the last minute, her family was surprised that she was preparing for the holidays in advance. Abby decided to buy her brother a book since he loves to read. She went to Barnes and Noble booksellers and purchased Ernest Hemingway's novel *For Whom the Bell Tolls.* Abby's younger sister loves to listen to music, so Abby bought her the latest Tim McGraw album called *Set This Circus Down.* She found the album on sale at Tower Music. Abby's mother hinted that she wanted a magazine subscription to *Better Homes and Gardens.* Abby already has a subscription to that magazine for herself, and her mother borrows her copies on a regular basis. Abby ordered the *Better Homes and Gardens* subscription on the Internet for her mother. Abby's father, who is the most difficult person to buy for because he doesn't need or want anything, hinted that he wanted a movie collection on tape. Since her father loves all of the *Godfather* movies, she decided to buy him the entire *Godfather* collection. Abby hopes that her family will enjoy the gifts as much as she enjoyed picking them out.

Exercise 14.4

A new business recently opened in Madison, Tennessee. Mr. and Mrs. Fuller opened a bookstore right off of the town square. They decided to open a bookstore because they both enjoy reading so much. The bookstore is called Clara's Treasures, named after Mr. and Mrs. Fuller's granddaughter Clara Ann. In their store, they sell used and new books. Some of the new books that they include are classics like *Brave New World* by Aldous Huxley and newer books by Danielle Steele and John Grisham. Mr. Fuller was once an English professor so he knows lots of different book titles. They also offer used books that are still in excellent shape. They purchase used books and sometimes trade used books with their customers. They currently have Edgar Allen Poe's short story collection and William Shakespeare's comedy and tragedy collections. They hope to expand their store in the future. They currently have a seating area where a coffee bar could go. For now, they are content with having a beautiful bookstore where people can come to read and relax.

Exercise 14.5

Tonia recently joined the Nashville chapter of the American Red Cross. The club meets every other Monday to help with blood drives in the area. Tonia became interested in the organization after she had an accident two years ago. After a terrifying car accident, Tonia was in need of a rare blood type. Thanks to friends and family who donated blood, Tonia survived her accident. She decided that joining the Nashville chapter of the American Red Cross would be an excellent way to help other people in dire need of blood, like she was two short years ago. Michael Givens, M.D., helped Tonia during surgery and also introduced her to Shana Young, the director of the American Red Cross. Tonia hopes after receiving her degree in biology that she will go to medical school someday. She dreams of helping other people. Perhaps the best part of joining the club is that she has met many nurses and doctors that have given her good advice about attending medical school. She hopes to attend the National American Red Cross Convention in Austin, Texas, next month.

Exercise 14.6

Since the expected high temperature today was under 80 degrees, we went to Winnington Park near our home. Located on Hasleberg Street, Winnington Park offers a variety of activities for families to enjoy. The Tennessee River runs along the backside of Winnington Park, and many families enjoy boating. One special feature of the park is Tiger Lagoon, a man-made lagoon that offers additional activities for families to enjoy.

Last March, a Saint Patrick's Day celebration was held at Tiger Lagoon. Many people came to help celebrate. In Spring 2004, the park became a popular place to visit. A children's festival was held. The festival, called The Children's Playground, featured live concerts, face painting, and magicians. The festival was very well received, and plans for a future festival are underway. The event planners hope to hold the festival at Winnington Park again in Spring 2005.

Exercise 15.1

Around three years ago, Tom decided to open a golf discount store in his hometown. Before opening the business, Tom had to do some research about the town to determine if the business would do well in a town with a population of 343,232 people. A golf course was built in the town in the 1970s, and since that time no golf discount store has been available. Tom discovered that 124 people are members at Oakland Country Club. He developed a survey for the golf members to discover what their golf needs were. Out of 124 surveys that were distributed, he received 104 completed surveys. The surveys helped Tom realize that a golf discount store was needed in the town. Tom's next step was to talk with potential investors. Tom talked to four different investors to see if any of them had an interest in working on a new project. Two of the investors showed definite interest in Tom's project. After he found financial backing, Tom searched for the perfect location for the store. He had a choice of five different places, but he ultimately decided on the location closest to the golf course. Since he has been in business for three years, Tom has experienced great success with his business.

Exercise 15.2

Mayfield, Kentucky, citizens recently celebrated the town's anniversary. Founded in the

1920s, Mayfield was a booming industrial town. In the 1920s, the town population was

4,234 people and today the population has risen to 52,392 people. Two hundred people

on average move to the town every year. Michael West, the town mayor, began the

three-day celebration with a morning parade. Many of the citizens were excited to see

such a great start to the three-day celebration. The last time Mayfield, Kentucky, had a

town festival was in the 1950s. Several town citizens had T-shirts printed to celebrate the

festival. The T-shirts were white and featured "Mayfield Festival 2004" on the front of

the shirt. Over 10,000 shirts were printed for people to buy. Many of the local

businesses plan to keep their shops open well past their normal closing time. There are at

least 55 family-owned businesses in the town of Mayfield. Many stores are also offering

special sales to honor the town's celebration. The organizers of the event are thrilled to

see that so many people in the town are eager to participate.

Exercise 15.3

The Obion County Fair began last Thursday night. The current fair admission price is $5

for children and $7 for adults. This year's fair will feature a different activity every

evening during the week. On Monday, a weight and height contest will be featured.

Contestants have two chances to guess the weight and height of the town's mayor. Last

year, people were given an opportunity to guess the school principal's weight and height.

My friend Susie paid $2 to guess the principal's weight. She guessed that he weighed

120 pounds and that he was 6 feet 3 inches tall. Everyone laughed because the principal

weighed nearly double that amount, and he stands at 6 feet 9 inches tall. On Tuesday, a cake walk will be held. Most cakes will be priced at $4, and some pies will sell for $2.50. Last year, over 95 cakes were delivered to the school gymnasium for the cake walk. This year they hope to double the amount of baked goods. On Wednesday night of the fair, a ring toss contest will be held. Participants will have the opportunity to toss rings around empty 0.5 liter bottles. On Thursday, a beauty pageant will be held to crown Miss Obion County Fair. At least one-third of the town's young ladies enter the pageant. Finally, a concert will be held on Friday night after the two-and-a-half mile marathon is held. They hope to have a lot of visitors attend this year as well.

Exercise 15.4

Kara recently decided to get out of debt. Over the past 5 years, she has accrued more than $750 in credit card debt. She recently decided to work hard at paying off her debt because she hopes to buy a home someday instead of continuing to rent an apartment. When looking over her finances, Kara realized that one-third of her weekly paycheck goes to debt payment. She was upset when she realized that she pays 19 percent interest every month for each credit card. When she calculated the math, she discovered that she barely makes the minimum payment of $10 per month. At this rate, it will take Kara over 7 years to be completely out of debt. She decided to meet with a financial counselor who suggested that she work on a process called debt snowballing. This means that each month Kara will work on paying off her smallest to largest debt. Her current smallest debt is $200 and her largest debt is around $550. Her financial counselor estimates that it will take Kara 18 months to be completely out of debt.

Exercise 15.5

Kevin will travel the entire month of July for Textel Industries. His traveling itinerary begins on July 2, 2005. On the second, he will travel to Hong Kong to meet with potential investors. The purpose of the meeting is to talk with Rimco Industry officials about a possible merger. His flight to Hong Kong is scheduled for 9:00 a.m. and is scheduled to arrive in Los Angeles for a brief layover at 2:00 p.m. At four o'clock, he will board another plane for a direct flight to Hong Kong. He should arrive in Hong Kong shortly before midnight. His second flight will take him from Hong Kong to Seoul, Korea. His flight will leave Hong Kong on July 5. He is scheduled to arrive in Seoul before noon the following day. Kevin has worked for Textel Industries for 11 years and has been promoted three times. He is one of the smartest employees at Textel and hopes to become the company's president someday. After Kevin travels for 30 days, he will have a two week vacation. He plans to travel to England on his vacation with his wife, Susan. He hopes to continue traveling for Textel Industries, but he plans to minimize his travel to one time a year.

Exercise 15.6

Penny recently turned twenty-two in September. Her sister, 24, gave her a surprise birthday party to celebrate. Penny was surprised by all of her friends who came out to see her. Penny's party was held at the country club at One Sycamore Drive. The guests were escorted in through the back door, and their cars were parked in a back lot to prevent Penny from being suspicious when she arrived. Twenty-eight people attended the party, and Penny saw many friends and family that she had not seen in a long time. Perhaps the best part of the party was the band that Penny's sister hired. The band likes to play music from the 1950s. They have a studio on <u>24</u>th Avenue. Penny's sister learned

about the talented band from her friend Sara, who lives at <u>34</u> Oakhill Drive. Sara hired

the band to play at her parents' <u>thirtieth</u> anniversary. Penny's sister was surprised at the

relatively low cost that the band charged. Because Sara knows the lead singer of the

band, she was able to get Penny's sister a discount. Sara, <u>22</u>, has a cousin that plays in

the band. Penny promises to pay her sister back with a surprise party in a few years.

Penny will surprise her sister in <u>six</u> years with a surprise <u>thirtieth</u> birthday party.

Exercise 15.7

Emma decided to purchase a fish tank to put in the living room of her home. The fish

tank she wants to purchase holds 4 gallons of water. She has wanted a fish tank in her

home after visiting her cousin who has a fish tank in her den. Her cousin, who lives at

2000 Circle Drive, works at a pet supply store. The store, located on the corner of 23rd

Avenue, carries a wide variety to exotic fish. Emma plans to arrive at the store at 10

o'clock in the morning to see about setting up an aquarium. She plans to set the

aquarium up by noon. She has also inquired about taking an aquarium class at the local

pet store. The purpose of the class is to teach people how to take appropriate care of an

aquarium. The next class is scheduled for May 14, 2004. When people buy an aquarium,

a manual is given to explain the procedure for cleaning and filling the tank. The manual

explains on page 12 how to clean an aquarium. However, Emma still feels like the

aquarium class will be helpful for her to take. She wants to make sure that she gives her

fish the best possible care.

Exercise 15.8

A new frame shop recently opened at 14 Commerce Drive. Since Joan has worked in the

framing business for five years, she felt ready to open her own business. She hopes to

draw customers in by offering weekly specials. For the first week, she plans to offer a

special on pre-made frames measuring 24-by-36 inches. She plans to hold an open house

on October 14, 2004. At her open house, she plans to offer some door prizes and store

giveaways to help promote business. Joan will also offer to frame any size portrait for

one day only for $20. She wants to entice people to enter her store. Hopefully, once

Joan has earned a customer's business, the customer will continue to do business with

her. Joan's husband is very supportive of her business. His law office is located nearby

at 20 Commerce Drive. He has promised to help Joan in any possible way. She is

thankful that he is so supportive of her dream to open a new business. Hopefully, Joan

will celebrate her thirtieth anniversary of being in business someday.

Exercises 16.1 and 16.2

Michelle Linton recently added **CPA** after her name when she passed her certified public

accountant examination. Her professor of marketing, Edward Smith, **Ed.D.**, helped her

to prepare for the difficult examination. Since **Dr.** Smith worked as a **CPA** for **IBM**, he

knew how to properly prepare for the exam. The exam was held in Tennessee, at 2

o'clock **CST** and lasted for more than two days. The exam was given on Apr. 10, 2005,

in the Ellingston Building on the campus at **TSU.** Michelle's father, Tom Linton **Jr.** is

also an accountant. He earned his **CPA** in 1985 and has been a top accountant with

TWA since 1987. He was proud of his daughter for earning her **CPA** and encouraged

her to apply for top accounting jobs. Michelle has decided to apply at several accounting firms in Tennessee. She hopes to work for one particular firm located in Nashville on Waverly **Road** She currently works at a firm on London **Street**, but she wants to work for a larger firm to gain more experience. Many of the country music stars in Nashville, **Tennessee**, do business with the firm located on Waverly **Road.** Michelle hopes to have the opportunity to work with many of these stars in the future.

Exercises 16.3 and 16.4

Ronald Peters **Jr.** recently announced that two major corporations would merge together in **June,** 2004. The **GM** Company and Chevrolet have decided to merge in the creation of a new vehicle. Ronald Peters **Jr.** serves as a manager for product line development. He earned a **Ph.D.** from **UCLA** and has served as a manager for over 17 years. **Dr.** Peter's favorite part of his job is developing exciting new vehicles that will be safe and fun to drive. The new merger promises to be a good one as **GM** and Chevrolet want to create a sporty convertible sedan. Hoping to target both an older and younger clientele, Dr. Peters and other managers created the new sedan for people who wanted a convertible but didn't want to sacrifice leg and driving room. The new vehicle should be at automobile dealerships by **August,** 2005. The car will hopefully get around 40 **mpg** on the highway and 35 **mpg** on city and town roads. Perhaps the best part of the vehicle's sporty new look is that it will include a variety of hot new colors for consumers to choose from. Colors range from indigo blue to pumpkin-spice orange. The car will hopefully become **GM's** best selling vehicle in the future.

Exercises 16.5 and 16.6

Sarah Brown

1200 Oak **Road** Northwest

Aug. 10, 2004

Austin, **TX** 46573

Kyle Hart

372 Armstrong **Lane**

Lyle, **TX** 46522

Dear Dr. Hart:

It has been brought to our attention that you have inquired about an upcoming seminar to

be held in Richmond, Virginia. The seminar will be begin on **September** 30 and will end

on **October** 4, 2004 on the campus of **UVA**. The seminar will begin promptly every

morning at 8 **a.m.** and will end everyday at 4 **p.m.** Many guest speakers have been

invited to the seminar. Some of the invited speakers include Kelly Neelson, **Ed.D.,** and

Patricia Hassleman, **Ph.D**. **Dr.** Neelson will be available to answer questions and will

serve as a panel moderator for the entire conference. However, **Dr.** Hassleman will only

be able to attend for two days since she must attend another conference in **Maine** by the

end of the week. Please let me know if you need additional information about the

registration process. I will be glad to answer any additional questions you may have.

Thank you for your inquiry.

Sincerely,

Sarah Brown, **Ed.D.**

Program Coordinator

Exercise 17.1

The seventeenth century in Western civilization was <u>quiet</u> an age defined <u>buy</u>

contradictions. The art and music of the seventeenth century <u>we're</u> characterized by a

style called the baroque. Through the baroque style took different forms in Europe's

nations and colonies, it was shaped by two decisive forces, the Catholic Counter-

Reformation and the rise of absolutist monarchy. The resurgent Catholic Church in Spain

sponsored a <u>knew</u> type of art of mystical spirituality, while Spanish monarchs patronized

the <u>affects</u> of major building projects and talented <u>knew</u> artists. The most important

painter of the <u>knew</u> Catholic emotionalism was El Greco <u>who's</u> art technique was

influenced by Renaissance techniques. El Greco trained as a painter in Venice and while

he was <u>their</u>, he absorbed the lessons of the Titian and the Italian mannerists. Around

1570, he resettled in Toledo, Spain's most religious city, and <u>they're</u> he spent his career

painting portraits and religious subjects for Toledo's church. El Greco will be

remembered <u>though</u> his art for his invention of a distinctively individual baroque style.

Exercise 17.2

All of the students in Mrs. Knox's class <u>we're</u> nervous about receiving <u>there</u> graded

social studies exam. Even through the students studied, they felt as if they didn't <u>no</u>

much of the information that Mrs. Knox had on the examination. She gave her class

some <u>advise</u> about what to study, but several of the students felt as if they studied the

wrong information. Mrs. Knox, <u>buy</u> no means, intended to give a hard examination. She would of prepared her students a little better had she known that her students would not do well. Only nine students past the exam, and Mrs. Knox was so alarmed that she made an appointment to speak with the school principle. He suggested that she give the students another opportunity to be tested on the material. Mrs. Knox agreed and told the principle that she would rather retest the students then to have students unclear about the information. After she past out the exams to the students, she announced that she would hold an optional study session on Friday. A different test would be given on Monday and students would be able to combine there first test scores with they're second. The students were relieved that they were given another opportunity to do well on Mrs. Knox's exam.

Exercise 17.3

I recently borrowed my husband's car since my car was in the shop. I was surprised buy the mess in his console. He had lots of lose change on the floor and several empty cups and food wrappers. I no he doesn't mean to have such a junky car, but the mess was so disgusting I had trouble driving though all of the clutter. It is quiet a shame to see his brand knew car so littered on the inside. When I came home, I asked him about his filthy car. He apologized and said he should of cleaned the front seat. I told him that I would help him clean the car and wash the outside, to. He appreciated the offer but said he would take the car though a car wash and then have the inside of the car detailed. He is suppose to keep his car clean, but he travels so much for his job that he often has too eat his lunch in the car. Even though he drives a filthy car, I still appreciated the fact that he let me borrow his vehicle. However, next time my car is in the shop, I will rent a car for too or more days.

Exercise 17.4

Are recent vacation to Florida was ruined due to bad whether. Were excited about traveling to the sunshine state since it is the one state that always has beautiful whether. Unfortunately, we planned our trip for May, a month known for unstable whether in Florida. We should of planned our vacation for the month of July, but we would of missed out on receiving a reduced travel rate. Its difficult to plan a trip so many months in advance. Are travel agent helped us with are plans, but he failed to mention the affects of bad whether. Since it rained during are entire trip, we spent most of are days indoors reading and watching television. We where able to relax and sleep late most days. On several nights, we even cooked dinner in our condo and watched old movies. The best part of the trip was that we where together. Then we discovered that we could shop indoors during the day, so we were able to do some early Christmas shopping. Even though our trip was not what we planned, we were happy to experience so much quite time together. My husband still wishes he could have a partial refund from the travel agent. He says it is the principal of the whole thing, but I just laugh and tell him that weather he believes it or not, it was the best vacation of my life.

Exercise 17.5

Lee Ann will leave for college in too days. She is nervous about leaving home for the first time. Many of her friends gave her lots of advise about how to survive in college during the first year. Lee Ann excepted her friends' advise and thanked them for helping her to build courage. Lee Ann is buy no means afraid of going to class. She is more afraid of living with a complete stranger. She would of roomed with someone she new, but no one from her high school is attending the same college as she is. Its difficult for

Lee Ann to leave her mother because they have been such close friends since Lee Ann was a little girl. Her mother realizes that Lee Ann needs to <u>farther</u> her career goals. Her mother would <u>of</u> liked for Lee Ann to attend a school closer to home, but realizes that the school she chose offers Lee Ann a lot of possibilities in her field of study. The day before she left for school, her high school <u>principle</u> called to wish her good luck and to offer some last minute <u>advise</u>. He told her not to <u>loose</u> sight of her dreams and to work hard to reach her goals. She thanked the <u>principle</u> for calling and felt better about leaving home to begin the next phase of her life.

Exercise 18.1

When Pierre Omidyar had the idea to create a marketplace for the sale of goods for individuals, little did he know the idea would become eBay. Pierre <u>received</u> help from cofounder Jeff Skoll and business tycoon Meg Whitman. Whitman came from a <u>business</u> background and brought <u>experience</u> from companies such as Hasbro. The three had a strong <u>vision</u> for eBay to become a company known for <u>connecting</u> people, not simply as an auction house. eBay has become the most popular form of online person-to-person trading and selling on the Internet. eBay has <u>revolutionized</u> the idea of garage sale selling. Buyers bid on items of <u>interest</u> from an itemized list of goods that are <u>categorized</u> by topics. Browsing and bidding for items is free of charge, but sellers have nominal fees to list and promote items for sale. What began as an idea in Pierre Omidyar's living room in 1995 has now grown to a <u>million</u> dollar business, proving that small dreams can become a large, lucrative reality.

Exercise 18.2

When the alarm clock rang, Katelyn Shaw jumped out of bed. Today would be the first

day of <u>kindergarten</u> for Katelyn who turned five last <u>February</u>. Katelyn's mother has

<u>probably</u> been dreading this day for the past five years. As she watched Katelyn put her

<u>clothes</u> on and tie her shoes, she felt the urge to cry. Watching her <u>daughter</u> begin her

first day of <u>kindergarten</u> was difficult for Mrs. Shaw because it meant Katelyn was

growing up. Her husband thought that crying was <u>ridiculous</u>, but he comforted his wife

anyway. He knew this day would be <u>difficult</u> for her. <u>Several</u> of Mrs. Shaw's friends

were also sad because their <u>daughters</u> were <u>beginning</u> their first day of school as well.

Katelyn didn't even begin to show signs of <u>sadness</u>. Instead, she ran down the stairs of

her house and cheered with <u>excitement</u>. Mrs. Shaw got her camera out to take a picture

of Katelyn's first day and her father watched as the school bus pulled up in front of their

house. Katelyn's parents walked her to the bus and <u>anxiously</u> watched her board the bus

and wave from the window. Mr. Shaw looked at his wife and said, "Our <u>daughter</u> is

growing up." Mrs. Shaw watched as Katelyn waved from the window and she blew a

kiss to her <u>daughter</u>.

Exercise 18.3

Linda has decided to <u>pursue</u> a graduate degree after she finishes her bachelor of arts from

the University of Tennessee. She is considering the field of <u>psychology</u> and would like to

possibly become a <u>counselor</u>. Linda <u>enjoys</u> talking with <u>people</u> and helping them to sort

<u>through</u> their problems. She is <u>persistent</u> in wanting to further her education. One of her

college professors gave her some <u>advice</u> about what graduate programs to <u>pursue</u>. She

<u>prefers</u> to stay in the state of Tennessee, so she has applied at several different state

institutions. She has taken a few graduate hours during her last semester at the university, and she hopes that the classes will <u>transfer</u> if she <u>chooses</u> to attend another school. She wants to attend a school that will <u>emphasize</u> the importance of counseling. She has received <u>guidance</u> from several different people, but she is also searching for <u>financial</u> guidance. She would like to apply for several graduate teaching <u>assistance</u> positions. Hopefully, she will be able to make a <u>decision</u> about where to attend soon.

Exercise 18.4

In ancient Rome, family ties were the <u>basis</u> of social <u>identity</u>. The male head of the family, known as the paterfamilias, <u>controlled</u> the family's membership and its fortunes. A newborn infant was not <u>legally</u> a family member until the paterfamilias had <u>recognized</u> the infant and given him or her a name. <u>Unrecognized</u> children were sometimes given up for adoption to other families. More <u>commonly</u>, newborns (especially girls) were "exposed," that is, left in the forum to die or be adopted as foundlings. Bearing a family name through adoption was no <u>disadvantage</u>: the young Octavian became Rome's first emperor after he had been adopted by Julius Caesar. Married women <u>enjoyed</u> relative freedoms but still suffered confined <u>social</u> roles. Roman women accompanied their husbands in public, often to <u>banquets</u> and other public <u>occasions</u>. As in Greece, they supervised the household, but in Rome, women might also hold and inherit property. Women could divorce their husbands and be divorced, often through a simple public declaration. If her husband died or was sent into exile, a wife would inherit her husband's household and <u>wealth</u>. She could entertain suitors, take a lover, or cloister herself in mourning, sheltered from the world's hypocrisy.

Exercise 18.5

The elements of romantic art and literature arose in response to <u>different</u> <u>social</u> and historical circumstances. Romantic-era poets protested the <u>social</u> injustices of early industrial <u>society</u>, while Mary Wollstonecraft demanded equal rights for women. In Spain, the painter Goya <u>bitterly</u> and <u>passionately</u> depicted the <u>cruelty</u> of war. In England and North America, romantic authors such as Wordsworth and Emerson saw nature as a <u>mirror</u> of the human imagination. They often imputed special nobility to <u>people</u> who seemed <u>unspoiled</u> by civilization. The painters Constable and Turner, and members of the Hudson River School, used new <u>effects</u> of color and light to render the natural landscape's elusive <u>beauty</u>. Still other romantics sought escape in the past, fostering a taste for picturesque medieval architecture. As <u>industrial</u> life became more dull and <u>mechanical</u>, the lure of exotic lands <u>spurred</u> the imaginations of architects such as Nash and painters such as Delacroix and Ingres.

Exercise 18.6

Cameron will be answering phones for this father today at the law office. Since Cameron is committing to help his father, he will have a busy day. He is experiencing what it is like to work in a law firm, since he is considering a job in the field of law. He is offering to help his father throughout the entire summer. Cameron is pretending to be a lawyer so he can get an idea of what the job entails. His father agrees that observing a lawyer practice is the best way to learn about the job on a daily basis. Cameron will be taking the LSAT exam to see if he will be accepted at a nearby law school. He has been studying for the exam for over six months now. He is worrying about passing the exam, but his father has been helping him prepare almost every night. Cameron will be attempting the exam in October and will be receiving his test results in November. He hates waiting for his scores but looks forward to the day when he can actually stop pretending to be a lawyer and actually be one.

Exercise 18.7

When Jake decided to join the high school baseball team, his parents were very supportive. Jake always liked playing little league ball, so he thought he would give baseball a chance. When he first started playing, he batted exceptionally well, and his coach noticed that he truly had talent. When he finally started to play high school baseball, it became apparent that Jake had keen skill. Several recruiters from colleges began to notice his game and traveled to watch many of his games. Jake decided to attend a college in Wisconsin on a full paid scholarship. His parents hoped that he would go to school closer to home, but they understood his decision to achieve his dreams. Jake is not sure if he will continue to play baseball after college, but he has enjoyed the sport so much he can't imagine his life without playing. For now, he has decided to concentrate on studying since he plans to attend graduate school.

Exercise 18.8

In February, Jessica will begin an internship at the local hospital. Jessica is interested in learning more about the field of nursing. Since her mother is a nurse, Jessica has always thought about becoming a nurse. This internship marks an occasion for Jessica to learn more about what a nurse does on a daily basis. She is excited about having the opportunity to see what many health care professionals do day in and day out. She has also thought about becoming a pharmacist, so she plans to shadow a pharmacist for a few weeks as well. While she knows she wants to work in the health care profession, she is still unsure of what <u>field</u> of study to enter. Her mother has been very <u>supportive</u>, offering

Jessica some <u>advice</u> about many different options that are <u>available</u> to her. One

consideration for Jessica is the <u>salary</u> she will make at many of the jobs. <u>Whether</u> or not

she decides to become a nurse, <u>pharmacist</u>, or doctor, her mother will support her in

whatever <u>decision</u> she makes.